# Culture &
# Comfort

# *Culture &*
# *Comfort*

## PARLOR MAKING AND
## MIDDLE-CLASS IDENTITY, 1850–1930

### *Katherine C. Grier*

SMITHSONIAN INSTITUTION PRESS

Washington and London

The original version of this book was published by The Strong Museum in conjunction with an exhibition entitled "Culture and Comfort: People, Parlors, and Upholstery, 1850–1930," on view from 8 September 1988 to 16 January 1989.

Copy editor: D. Teddy Diggs
Production editor: Duke Johns
Designer: Kathleen Sims

Library of Congress Cataloging-in-Publication Data

Grier, Katherine C., 1953–
    Culture and comfort : parlor making and middle-class identity, 1850–1930 / Katherine C. Grier.
        p.   cm.
    Revised and slightly condensed version of Culture and comfort. Rochester, N.Y. : Strong Museum, c1988.
    Includes bibliographical references and index.
    ISBN 1-56098-715-4 (cloth : alk. paper). — ISBN 1-56098-716-2 (pbk. : alk. paper)
    1. Material culture—United States.   2. Living rooms—United States—History.
3. Upholstery—United States—History.   4. Middle class—United States—History.
5. United States—Social life and customs—19th century.   6. United States—Social life and customs—1865–1918.   7. United States—Social life and customs—1918–1945.
I. Grier, Katherine C., 1953–   Culture & comfort.   II. Title.
E166.G83   1997
392'.36—dc20                                                                              96-43927

British Library Cataloguing-in-Publication Data is available

Manufactured in the United States of America
04  03  02  01  00  99  98  97    5  4  3  2  1

# Contents

# $\mathcal{P}$*reface*

This book is about the waxing and waning of the Victorian parlor, a room whose elaborate decor and accompanying social performances seem, from the perspective of the late twentieth century, emblematic of the artifice, even phoniness, of Victorian culture. It is the story of how tens of thousands of middle-class American families devoted their financial and emotional resources to create rooms that none of them needed, strictly speaking, and that some of them seem rarely to have used. But bare necessity was not the point. Parlor-making families were participants in a rapidly commercializing world in which readily available goods—center tables, window draperies, and sets of matching chairs—could make manifest core cultural ideals that were, supposedly, timeless and beyond the reach of transient consumer tastes. And parlors were settings that allowed Victorian Americans to represent themselves as full participants in their world. The convention-laden contents of parlors, which had roots as much in the gala salon of elite houses as in the old-fashioned "best room" of modest dwellings in the previous century, were constant reminders of what Victorian culture valued highly: the principles of gentility and domesticity, along with the material refinement that inevitably accompanied civilized progress.

Gentility and domesticity were also at odds, however, and the tension was something that middle-class people learned to negotiate in both their consumer choices and their public social performances. The details of many families' negotiations with a contradictory public discourse on middle-class identity are often beyond recovery. However, the general outlines of the debates can be reconstructed through the hectoring voices of several generations of domestic advisers and, more important, through the artifacts themselves—the furnishings, the trade catalogs, the popular prints and illustrations, and the photographs that ordinary people made of their own parlors. Taken together, these material documents reveal the ideals and realities of parlor making in middle-class households as consumers balanced their budgets and dreams to create a representation of their desired public facade in a private room.

The word *culture* always vibrates with more than one meaning, and in this text I use it in two senses. The first, an anthropological conception of a group of people joined by their manipulation of a common system of symbols, underlies my general discussion of Victorianism, the transatlantic culture of the middle classes in the industrializing, commercializing nineteenth century. But the "culture" of this book's title is also my shorthand for gentility, the international standard of personal excellence—indeed an international system of material symbols from wallpaper to tea tables—that first guided the social behavior and consumption habits of Anglo-American elites in the eighteenth century.[1] It is difficult to overstate the power of this ideal, precisely because of its vision of life's possibilities. And gentility continued to shape Victorian culture in profound ways. Its authority even lingered into the twentieth century with the generations who were educated in its standards of manners, deportment, and taste.

Gentility's focus on fashionable consumption and self-presentation was tempered by a second cultural position. A highly self-conscious domestic ideal asserted that middle-class family life lay outside the shallow world of purchasing an identity, and its apologists regarded the fashion-consciousness of gentility with suspicion. I have labeled this position *comfort*. Ironically, the public debate over comfort was often ambivalent about the increasing number of consumer goods that actually made dwellings into places where time could be spent in a pleasurable physical state. The rhetoric of much advice literature of the time argued that comfort was much more than ease; it was a distinctively middle-class state of mind that elites with aristocratic tendencies and consumers enslaved to novelties such as parlor stoves could not begin to understand. As the apologists for middle-class comfort tried to define a distinctive approach to consuming household goods, the new kind of genteel parlor became a particular focus of their concern and advice.

Pushed and pulled between an interest in the pleasures and properties of fashionable living and a fear of its consequences, including economic collapse and the disintegration of what we now call "family values," middle-class families expressed the ambiguities of their identity in a variety of ways, although this text focuses in particular on certain consumption choices. The confusion did not prevent middle-class families from creating parlors. Typically, they positioned themselves somewhere between domesticity's ethos of anticonsumption and gentility's ethos of pleasurable consumption and graceful use, creating "comfortable theaters" for self-presentation. In middle-class houses, the parlor was the site where these two discourses clashed most visibly; the dining room was another space where the conflict between domesticity and gentility was manifested as the act of eating became the ritual of dining.[2] Debates over what constituted an appropriate parlor, and over whether middle-class people should even have one, echoed throughout the era and were reflected in the decor and use patterns of the room.[3]

The original edition of this book, titled *Culture and Comfort: People, Parlors, and Upholstery, 1850–1930*, was a big, heavily illustrated text intended both to document the contents of an exhibition of the same title and to stand as a work of scholarship after the five-month run of the exhibition at The Strong Museum in Rochester, New York. I created chapters to fill a variety of purposes, from explaining the specific elements of window coverings to establishing the sources of the parlor ideal, in an effort to serve the multiple constituencies of readers interested in Victorian material culture. I wanted to offer an interpretive account of a particular moment in the material culture of American Victorianism. However, there was no reference book for textile furnishings of the second half of the nineteenth and the early twentieth centuries, and little had been published on the subject. I needed to provide a basic guide to identifying the textile furnishings that were fundamental to the appearance of middle-class interiors between 1850 and 1930 yet were now misunderstood, undervalued, uncataloged, and disappearing fast because of their inherent fragility and the unintentional disregard of museums and collectors. I believe that the exhibition and the original edition of *Culture and Comfort* were successful in encouraging the preservation of these cultural artifacts, an outcome in which I have found real satisfaction.

I also faced the knotty problem of defining what a work of material culture studies should be. Although standards for excellence had been established in architecture and decorative arts, following formulas taken largely from art history, archaeology, and folklife studies, my work combined forms of evidence and ways of thinking that had been used to good purpose in social history (particularly as practiced by a few history museums like The Strong Museum), cultural anthropology, and that genre of art history concerned with reception and aesthetic experience as a social phenomenon. I also decided to give full scholarly attention to objects that had become, in their time, common—even ordinary. Most of the pieces that drew my interest in the collection of The Strong Museum and other museums were neither "high style" nor "folk," as I understand those terms. Rather they were part of a new middle-class material vernacular that tried to blend the conventions of gentility and domesticity, the two great poles of cultural meaning that I have labeled "culture" and "comfort," as they were made manifest through coded design and materials in individual objects and assemblages of consumer goods.

All these factors shaped the original text, as did the exhibition deadline. The result was a book that many readers seem to have found provocative and useful but that was, simply put, too long for easy use in college courses. (It was much too heavy to read in bed too.) In addition, the book went out of print less than a year following its September 1988 publication date. The original *Culture and Comfort* is now rare enough to turn up occasionally in the catalogs of book dealers, which is why I was pleased and surprised when Mark Hirsch, of the Smithsonian Institution Press, approached me about creating an abridgement of the original edition. He felt, and I soon concurred, that a shorter text focused on the central argument might have a place in college courses on American social and cultural history and on material culture studies. It took me several years to turn to the project, but Mark continued to support the idea. Thanks to a Career Development Grant from the College of Humanities at the University of Utah, *Culture and Comfort* has a second life. Its new subtitle, *Parlor Making and Middle-Class Identity, 1850–1930*, reflects the tighter focus of this shorter text. I offer my thanks to the institutions providing photographs for this new edition, to Teddy Diggs of Diggs Editorial Services, and to the staff of the Smithsonian Institution Press for making this new, streamlined edition look so good. This abridgement of *Culture and Comfort* also has been made possible by an agreement with the trustees of The Strong Museum, which holds the original copyright; I thank them for their cooperation.

During the process of creating the original book and serving as the principal team member for the exhibition, I benefited from the hard work and goodwill of my colleagues at The Strong Museum. They include museum conservator Richard Sherin, my fellow historian William Siles, curators Susan Williams and Patricia Tice, designers Kevin Murphy and Kenneth Townsend, and the staff members of the museum's library, the Office of Publications and Technical Services, the Office of the Registrar, and the

Exhibits Department. Two of my colleagues at The Strong Museum were especially critical to what was occasionally a difficult process as the exhibition deadline approached. Putting out the first version of *Culture and Comfort* was a test not only of my stamina but also of the commitment and goodwill of Harvey Green, Vice President for Interpretation, and Kathryn Grover, the head of the Office of Publications and Technical Services, and their support staff, particularly administrative secretary Judy White. Subsequently, the book received several awards, including the Charles Montgomery Award of the Decorative Arts Society, which I regard as testimony to the good work of everyone involved. The original edition of *Culture and Comfort*, and the exhibition of the same title, received support from the National Endowment for Humanities (NEH) both for exhibition planning and implementation and for publication subvention. I would be remiss if I did not comment on the critical role that the NEH's Office of Museum Programs has played for many years in fostering excellence among museums. Its reduced funding is a tragedy for history museums in particular, since these institutions are least likely to attract private money to support substantive research.

I find the pleasure that Victorian Americans took in the material world around them, and the intricacy of the systems of conventional meanings-in-things that they manipulated for social ends, endlessly interesting. The roots of my fascination are admittedly personal; echoes of Victorian culture survived in my extended family all through my childhood. However, my ability to translate my intuitive interest in middle-class life in the nineteenth century into a scholarly form results from my graduate training, particularly my contact with Rodris Roth of the National Museum of American History of the Smithsonian Institution; Kenneth L. Ames, then head of the Office of Advanced Studies at the Henry Francis du Pont Winterthur Museum; George Basalla of the Department of History at the University of Delaware; and Richard L. Bushman, then of the University of Delaware, who supervised the dissertation out of which this book grew.

I must offer a brief caveat to this new edition. I have worked hard to leave the original text's arguments alone, even where my feelings about aspects of them have changed. I would be more cautious now about using the term *vocabulary* when discussing meaning-sets of artifacts. The easy, even reflexive, use of the metaphors "material culture as language" and "material culture as text" has implications that I don't think are supportable, although I continue to argue that constellations of artifacts are structured, and culturally positioned, ways of communicating some kinds of critically important cultural information. Material culturists have made significant headway in understanding how the artifacts do their cultural work. Yet much research remains to be done, which should cheer students considering working in material culture studies, a community of scholarly interest that was "blurring genres" before genre-blurring became fashionable. I hope that readers who subsequently turned to their own projects after reading *Culture and Comfort* learned something from the strengths and weaknesses of the original edition (weaknesses for which I take sole responsibility) and that new readers will find useful insights in this abridgement. I wish them good fortune and hope that they get as much pleasure out of interrogating the intractably silent artifact as I do.

# Symbols and Sensibility

In her 1881 advice book *Home Decoration*, Janet Ruutz-Rees informed her readers that bare doorways, walls, and window frames distressed the refined sensibility. "Some rooms seem to be all doors," she wrote. "In whatever direction one turns, the eye is confronted by an opening; and it is becoming very usual to drape the entire room in a way that shall make such necessities, as far as possible, parts of an harmonious whole." Draperies, Ruutz-Rees pointed out, allowed "the skillful hiding of defects . . . , the softening of angles, and happy obliteration of corners."[1] *American Etiquette and Rules of Politeness*, an inexpensive manners book published around the same time as *Home Decoration*, explained the "Value of Etiquette" by using the same vocabulary: "That culture only is valuable which smooths the rough places, harmonizes the imperfections, and develops the pure, the good, and the gentle in human character. . . . Politeness in the hourly intercourse of life . . . smooths away most of the rudeness that otherwise might jar upon our nerves."[2]

It is no accident that the author of a book on interior decoration and another of a book on manners chose to use similar language and concepts—"harmonizing," "smoothing," "softening" the defects or "rough places"—to describe the effects of both upholstery and etiquette. Both interior decoration and manners were believed to express the progress of civilization; both were described with a vocabulary that revealed a popular taxonomy, a way of choosing language that reflects the presence of some cultural framework for organizing many kinds of human experience.

**Figure 1.** Unidentified parlor, Rochester, New York, about 1900. Courtesy, The Strong Museum, Rochester, New York.

This book investigates the culture commonly known as "Victorian" by exploring how middle-class people furnished the rooms called parlors, one of several spaces (the other being the dining room) intended to serve as the setting for important social events and to present the civilized facade of its occupants (Fig. 1). Its conventions of furnishing represented two poles of thought about the appropriate character of the parlor—its domesticity ("comfort") and its cosmopolitan character ("culture"). In this text, the terms *culture* and *comfort* concisely designate two complex collations of ideas, attitudes, and assumptions that together represent a critical tension in Victorian culture. *Culture* is used here as shorthand for the cultivated worldview of educated, genteel, and cosmopolitan people whose habits of consumption (including furnishing a gala parlor) were intended to create an expressive social facade. On the other hand, *comfort* not only signals a group of ideas and beliefs associated with a pleasurable physical state but also designates the presence of the more family-centered values associated with "home," values emphasizing domesticity, perfect sincerity, and moderation in all things. Social commentators claimed true comfort to be a distinctively middle-class state of mind.

Together, aspirations toward culture and comfort composed a cultural framework that set the terms for questions about personal cultivation and social progress. They also framed questions about consumption, including both dress and household furnishings. Such questions focused particularly closely on the act of setting aside space for and devoting family resources to the making of a parlor. The ideal parlor of culture presented a family's cultivated facade, but the ideal parlor of comfort at once discounted the value of that appearance. In fact, middle-class commentators insisted that the room be homey, not theatrical. Similar tensions existed in the realm of manners. Was a parlor-person pious and domestic or a cosmopolite, an American aristocrat?

Between 1850 and 1910 parlor contents were commercially available to everyone who had money for furnishings; yet parlors in ordinary households retained their association with gentility, a set of personal attributes that was supposedly beyond the reach of commerce. People preferred to set aside spaces for formality when possible, although they adapted their own "gala apartments" to such special uses as funerals and the display of Christmas trees. In Anglo-America, the term *parlor* had long been used to describe what was also called the "best room" in a house, but this room was supposed to retain the identity of a family sitting room even as it also served more public and formal uses. For ordinary consumers, the problem lay in how to combine the domestic and the gala, how to create a "comfortable theater" for middle-class self-presentation.

Victorianism, as Daniel Walker Howe has defined it, is the Anglo-American, transatlantic, bourgeois culture of industrializing Western civilization.[3] Not all nineteenth-century Americans were Victorians. Many immigrants, for example, certainly were not Victorian, nor were generations of their working-class descendants. Yet even though Victorian Americans did not call themselves by this name, they knew who they were, and Victorianism embraced a set of symbols to which all other cultural groups in the nation responded. Non-Victorian Americans had on some level to be conversant with this dominant culture even if they retained their own cultural forms. They could scarcely avoid participating in some of its aspects, especially those associated with the burgeoning consumer society. The domestic goods that proliferated so dramatically after 1850 potentially served as a means of participating in Victorian culture. To own a home and purchase the proper furnishings for it meant that one shared, in some measure, the culture's vision of the formal characteristics of respectable family living.

"Home" was one of Victorian culture's most important and complicated symbols, a web of ideas, objects, and images that was powerful partly because it seemed so basic, even mundane. The apparently familiar word *home* is itself complex, bearing meanings that are both psychological and locational. To be "at home" not only means being present in one's place of residence but also implies being at ease in some place or in the company of a like-minded person or group of people. To cultivate and demonstrate good manners, in the words of one nineteenth-century advice writer, was to be "at home" in all society.[4] *Home* also can connote a particular geographical place, as large as a nation-state. However, Victorian Americans, like their descendants today, usually thought of home as an actual physical site, composed of a building and its furnishings and peopled by the members of a family. Popular prints, sheet music, advice literature, and fiction all attest the concreteness of the ideal—a single-family residence, separated from its neighbors by a green strip of lawn or the fields of a farm.[5]

The corporeal quality of the symbol of "home" even extended into the realm of popular religiosity. In the 1879 best-seller *The Complete Home: An Encyclopedia of Domestic Life and Affairs*, Julia McNair Wright wrote: "Between the Home set up in Eden, and the Home before us in Eternity, stand the Homes of Earth in a long succession. It is therefore important that our Homes should be brought up to a standard in harmony with their origin and destiny. Here are 'Empire's primal springs;' here are the Church and State in embryo; here all improvements and reform must rise. For national and social disasters, for moral and financial evils, the cure begins in the Household."[6] The concept of "Heavenly Home" domesticated the "Pearly Gates" into a white picket fence surrounding a site where a person could be reunited with deceased relatives and create anew the earthly family circle. The Reverend W. K. Tweedie elaborated on these connections in a collection of pious essays titled *Home; or, The Parents' Assistant and Children's Friend* (1873). Chapter 3 was an exegesis on "Names for Home," including "the Eden of Home," "God's First Church," "A Miniature of Heaven," "a Copy of Heaven," and "a Nursery for Heaven."[7]

In popular books of household advice throughout the nineteenth century, the concept of the Christian household was a powerful shaper of discussions of home life, enhancing the symbolic meaning of "home" by blending religiosity and domesticity. Catharine Beecher, devoting a chapter apiece in her *American Woman's Home* to "The Christian Family" and "A Christian House," argued that the "family state" was designed "to provide for the training of our race . . . with chief reference to a future immortal existence"; it was, she felt, "the aptest earthly illustration of the heavenly kingdom." As its "chief minister," each woman required "a home in which to exercise this ministry." Beecher believed that the physical qualities of each house should support "a style of living . . . conformed to the great design."[8] Hence, the private dwelling, rather than the public church building, became the most important sanctuary, and its contents also could serve as religious symbols.[9]

"Home" as a specific physical place implied ownership, possession, and permanence. In a world of little employment stability for ordinary people without guaranteed pensions or financial security, such practical considerations necessary to family survival underlay the physicality of the symbol of "home." Richard L. Bushman has observed that while the complicated exchange network of rural American society between 1750 and 1850 provided some level of subsistence for almost everyone, "property and children were the only means of support when strength and health eventually failed."[10] Yet urban living increasingly became the dominant mode, whether by choice because it offered comparatively high wages and freedom or by necessity because some laborers could not sustain themselves in the rural economy. Families, Bushman has argued, began to "erect defenses in their urban homes against layoffs, wage cuts, illness and old age" through the uses that they applied to their dwellings. Workers who did not bounce from city to city accepted heavy mortgages and sacrificed their children's educations to be able to own a small house in the city. Through a variety of strategies—accepting boarders, providing shelter for relatives, and taking into the home piecework such as shoe finishing—families made the house the "urban surrogate for the self-sufficient family farm." Such strategies were not confined to working-class families; middle-class families also resorted to taking in boarders and working out of their houses as financial circumstances required.[11] The home in this particular context provided a real alternative, in economic terms, to the dangerous, unreliable, "outside" world of commerce and work.

The Victorian understanding of the economic and social roles occupied by men and women continued and further embellished the conventional distinction between home and the world beyond its doors. In the nineteenth century, the old conception of separate but complementary "spheres" of work for men and women in preindustrial economies was incorporated into a new kind of domesticity, one in which women became the guardians of the finer human feelings as well as the administrators of the household. In this vision of appropriate domestic life, "home" became not the resource for minimum subsistence but the space for psychological refuge from the rigors of economic life as well as the proper site for expression of familial love and guidance.

## DOMESTIC ENVIRONMENTALISM

During the first half of the nineteenth century, one aspect of popular thinking, widespread enough that it was regarded virtually as common sense, attributed great power to the family environment in the shaping of personal—and, by implication, national—character. This determinism was often expressed in the works of widely published authors who addressed themselves to women: Lydia Sigourney, the author of *Letters to Mothers* (1838); Harriet Beecher Stowe, the prolific author of domestic fiction and advice; Emma Willard, advocate of women's education; and Sarah Josepha Hale, the editor of *Godey's Lady's Book*, among others. The family, they argued, was the strongest and best antidote to the temptations and poisons of the commercial world. Although men provided the means of each family's material existence, women set the tone of that existence. As a mother, each woman nurtured the development of proper character in her children. A mother did this not only to enable them to succeed as adults but also to ensure the very future of the American republic. Sigourney urged each reader to consider her vital role as a "barrier" to what the author perceived as a "torrent of corruption" and public disorder. Each middle-class mother could be "like the mother of Washington, feeling that the first lesson to every incipient ruler should be 'how to obey.' The degree of her diligence in preparing her children to be good subjects of a just government, will be the true measure of her patriotism." [12]

Other authors of domestic advice and fiction argued that the tone of family life set by women was fundamental because the State itself was, as Stowe put it, "but a larger family." [13] Almira Seymour, a lesser-known author who published a small collection of essays titled *Home: The Basis of the State*, argued that domestic reform—that is, the proper ordering of "the hidden source of all growth and expansion . . . the organization of the Family, the institution of Home"—provided the bulwark against the chaos that rapid industrial and social change threatened. [14]

Popular thinking about child rearing and domestic life in pre-Civil War America continued to stress the example set for young children by the behavior and good character of family members. But by the 1830s, discussions of domesticity and society were infused with a second strain of deterministic thought that assigned to the house's physical setting and details the power to shape human character. This "domestic environmentalism" conflated moral guidance with the actual appearance and physical layout of the house and its contents. [15]

The same authors who stressed the concepts of the Christian family and republican motherhood also described the operation of the domestic environment on individual sensibility. Beecher cautioned that although the "aesthetic element must be subordinate to the requirements of physical existence . . . it contributes much to the education of the entire household in refinement, intellectual development, and moral sensibility."[16] An article titled "The Domestic Use of Design," published in the *Furniture Gazette*, a London-based trade journal with a transatlantic readership, offered a full account of the power of decor:

> There can be no doubt that altogether, independently of direct intellectual culture, either from books or society, the mind is moulded and coloured to a great extent by the persistent impressions produced upon it by the most familiar objects that daily meet the eye. . . . That a carefully regulated and intelligent change of the domestic scenery about a sick person is beneficial is obvious, and yet there are few who correctly apprehend to how great an extent the character, and especially the temper, may be affected by the nature of ordinary physical surroundings. . . .
>
> What architecture is to the mass, furniture in its domestic application is to the individual; and though the cathedral may produce an immense impression on a crowd, and even for the time on the human minds composing it, it will often happen that a comparatively utterly insignificant article in the house really does more in the way of impressing, or even moulding, the human intelligence with which it is in almost persistent contact.[17]

The indirect, gentle influence that objects were thought to exert on the individual sensibility was very much like the kind of influence that authors of tracts and fiction about domesticity expected women to have on their families inside each private dwelling. In the household, worldly goods served as the communicative medium for higher ends. One example of how this communicative chain was believed to function—from women to things, from things to family members and selected outsiders—can be found in one of Stowe's lesser novels, *We and Our Neighbors*. Describing the preparations of the newlyweds Eva and Harry Henderson for a series of "social reunions" in their small house on an unfashionable New York City street, Stowe digressed to explain how the character of a woman was made manifest in her home: "Self begins to melt away into something higher. . . . The *home* becomes her center, and to her home passes the charm that was once thrown around her person. . . . Her home is the new impersonation of herself."[18] Selection and arrangement of possessions personified the nature of the woman who served as "priestess and minister of a family state," and interiors became material equivalents of the moral state of the household.[19]

The increasing emphasis on the positive influence of rooms and personal possessions on character had the effect of tying the formation of character to correct habits of consumption. The advice writer Clarence Cook argued in 1878 that the family "living room" (he objected to "parlors") was "an important agent in the education of life. . . . It is no trifling matter, whether we hang poor pictures on our walls or good ones, whether we select a fine cast or a second-rate one. We might almost as well say it makes no difference whether the people we live with are first-rate or second-rate."[20] This linking of consumption to the expression and formation of character helps explain the vehemence of much nineteenth-century domestic advice literature on interior decoration. Decor did not simply express character but helped to create it. Victorian consumers understood that objects were culture in tangible form and that possessions inappropriate to the social class of the family who owned them were a potential source of danger because they sent conflicting messages to both their owners and outsiders. The debate on this point was most strongly expressed in the opposition of "aristocratic" and "middle-class" models of parlor decoration and domestic comfort in both advice literature and a genre of popular fiction that may be called "moral tales of furnishing." The same authors who offered advice on the domestic economy of true comfort also often wrote these parables, which appeared in women's magazines and even in the form of lengthy novels.

The relationship of home to the commercial world was paradoxical, however. Although the conventions of domesticity emphasized the absolute separation of the domestic and business worlds, we have seen that real considerations of labor and calculations of economic advantage and future security were tied to house ownership. On another level, touching even those families who could not own their own houses, furnishings were also marked by an ambiguous tension between their symbolic value and their commercial origins. The continued vitality of domestic environmentalism as one component of Victorian popular thought was supported by this connection to the emergence of mass consumer culture. As Gwendolyn Wright has suggested, the ideal house was steadily viewed as a place for promoting family privacy, protection, and security despite its increasingly complex ties to consumer culture.[21] The products of industrialization and commercialization, from factory-made furniture to commercially canned soup, permeated and, I argue, enriched the site that was supposedly the haven from these forces during the last quarter of the nineteenth century.

Thus the proliferation of industrially produced and commercially marketed consumer goods does not require that their symbolic richness be necessarily cheapened or, as Siegfried Giedion has suggested, "devalued."[22] Whereas *society* is the set of institutions that groups of human beings develop in order to keep daily life operating with some degree of smoothness, *culture*, in the sense that anthropologists use the word, lies in the realm of the mind. Culture is a historically transmitted "pattern of meanings," as the anthropologist Clifford Geertz has put it—"a system of inherited conceptions" about the nature of the world, "by means of which men communicate, perpetuate, and develop their knowledge about and attitudes toward life." A culture expresses meaning by manipulating symbols; in so doing, it expresses to itself, as much as to outsiders, what it thinks is important to know about life.[23]

The commercialization of objects that served as the vehicles for symbolic meanings was one of the fundamental ways in which Victorian culture worked, the means through which its forms became the dominant mode of cultural expression in the United States in the nineteenth century. The objects that bore meaning within the overarching symbol of "home"—its various furnishings—generally predated Victorian culture, although their availability had been limited to families of means. The processes of commercialization—the creation of a national framework of distribution, marketing, consumer credit, and sales—made versions of these furnishings readily available to the ordinary members of American society. Victorian culture's longevity and vitality were due in part to this process. Such commercialization moved symbolic values throughout the culture, inviting broader participation in already established conceptions.

## SYMBOLS AND SENSIBILITY

The building, the miniature Eden of its grounds, many of the objects that filled its rooms, and even the family members residing in it all potentially served as aspects of the complex symbol of "home" because the meaning of each could be enriched by complicated chains of association. Victorian Americans used commercially produced objects to create rich personal connections to larger spheres of cultural meaning, a process that continues among contemporary consumers. Some of the associative chains engendered by particular objects that people own and carefully save are strictly personal or even idiosyncratic, the product of individual experience: the handful of beach pebbles and shells collected on a vacation always suggests that time to the person who has saved them, but they are meaningless to outsiders. By contrast, symbols that predominate in a culture capitalize on agreed-upon sets of associations. These conventional meanings are culturally produced and reinforced through a wide variety of channels, including the popular media, informal learning from family members or associates, and formal instruction in schools and other institutions. Many chains of association blend the personal and the conventional: a miniature Statue of Liberty purchased on Liberty Island blends the qualities of patriotic icon and personal memento. A formal photograph of a woman holding a baby can be understood as a depiction of unique individuals (my grandmother, my father as a baby), but its meaning is enhanced if the photographer capitalized on common knowledge of the visual conventions for depicting the Madonna and the infant Jesus. Using the conventions makes the photo meaningful for viewers who do not know the people in the photo, and it adds possible layers of interpretation for family members.

In Victorian culture, "home," with its complex chains of association, made cultural symbols out of domestic objects that were utilitarian and common. As conventions of culture, these domestic symbols seem generally to have been understood by Victorian Americans, although some individuals might have understood more nuances of meaning than others. In an analysis of Victorian mementos of mourning, Lawrence Taylor has used the subjects and imagery of sentimental mourning poetry in *Godey's Lady's Book* to demonstrate how series of symbolic associations were believed to work. "This increasing importance of ritual objects—from locks of hair and empty cradle to gravestones—was a natural outcome of the prevalent 'theory of associations.' Put simply, objects, by virtue of their cultural form and/or specific history, were thought to be packed with meanings" for those individuals with "sensitive souls, or souls made sensitive by the impress of a properly ritual setting, whether church, cemetery, or museum."[24]

Sentimental poetry and fiction do not demonstrate all the ways in which such chains of association worked in connection to artifacts such as furniture, but at the time, they probably helped to perpetuate certain conventional associations. "The Old Arm-Chair," a four-stanza poem by Eliza Cook, appeared in the popular magazine *Godey's Lady's Book* in March 1855; it illustrates how associative thinking was structured, as well as how popular literature supported the process. In the poem, an armchair served as a symbol within the larger symbol of home and neatly encapsulated its own range of meanings. The poem ascribed to this single piece of furniture a chain of associations that many, if not all, of the readers could have appreciated.

### The Old Arm-Chair

I love it, I love it; and who shall dare
To chide me for loving that old arm-chair?
I've treasured it long as a sacred prize;
I've bedewed it with tears, and embalmed it with sighs;
'Tis bound by a thousand bands to my heart;
Not a tie will break, not a link will start.
Would ye learn the spell? a mother sat there,
And a sacred thing is that old arm-chair.[25]

Cook's poem in *Godey's* exemplified the melding of personal and conventional associations, explaining that her deep feelings for the chair stemmed from its previous ownership by "a mother," a particularly honored social role. The next verse revealed that "a mother" was Cook's own mother, who had given her daughter religious instruction from the chair and who had passed through the stages of her life in it. Personal memory was embedded in the chair.

In childhood's hour, I lingered near
The hallowed seat with listening ear;
And gentle words that mother would give,
To fit me to die and teach me to live.
She told me shame would never betide,
With truth for my creed and God for my guide;
She taught me to lisp my earliest prayer,
As I knelt beside that old arm-chair.

'Tis past! 'tis past! but I gaze on it now
With quivering breath and throbbing brow;
'Twas there she nursed me; 'twas there she died;
And memory flows with lava tide.
Say it is folly, and deem me weak,
While scalding drops start down my cheek;

> But I love it, I love it, and cannot tear
> My soul from a mother's old arm-chair.[26]

The poem moves from an explanation of a conventional association, the honor of motherhood, through a chain of personal meanings. A *Godey's Lady's Book* reader of 1855 would have been able to bring additional associations to the poem, especially the link between religion and domesticity. The symbol "home" incorporated both connotations, as suggested in a common genre of print that depicted families praying or reading together around a parlor center table. This particular example, "Home Made Happy," was the frontispiece of *Golden Sheaves*, a collection of largely pious essays, poems, and tidbits of fiction intended for reading aloud (Fig. 2).

Objects can express symbolic meaning in several ways. They can impart messages in a comparatively direct manner. The narrative content of a popular print such as this frontispiece from *Golden Sheaves* is quite clear; it is intended to trigger a set of popularly shared associations about the relationship of family life and moral growth and the emotional as well as physical closeness of the family circle (and to imply that the book is a vehicle for their attainment). A verse such as "The Old Arm-Chair" can sug-

**Figure 2.** "Home Made Happy," chromolithograph, unidentified artist. Frontispiece, H. A. Cleveland, comp., *Golden Sheaves, Gathered from the Fields of Ancient and Modern Literature* (1872). The image of a family gathered around a center table suggested both the appropriate use for this book and the setting where such happy moments would be best spent. Author's collection.

gest a set of less obvious, culturally specific associations—the connection, for example, of a type of chair with mothers. Objects also can express symbolic meaning by possessing qualities that people consider analogous to larger cultural values.[27] For example, the soaring architectural space of a church is associated with the feelings that worship is meant to inspire—awe, smallness in the face of divine truth—and the church's grandeur and size also "describe" the qualities of the Almighty. A set of lace curtains in a parlor window carried no overt message, as did a transfer-printed platter celebrating Lafayette's visit to America. However, the way those curtains diffused and softened sunlight, the delicacy of the textile, and the patterns the curtains might cast on the parlor walls or the carpet all suggested the refined character of the parlor and the propriety of "softened" behavior there.

In this way, some symbols may be interpreted best as an expression of sensibility, the distinctive form in which a culture's mental perception or awareness of itself is manifested. This awareness can exist in a realm of direct sensory perception, a recognition that is often expressed through actions or aesthetic choices rather than speech.[28] Much of the sensory information that people receive is not easily described in words, nor is it processed at the level of conscious awareness.[29] Experience with things crosses a boundary between different modes of experience, between visual and tactile understanding and language.[30] However, the act of choosing, even if it is often an inarticulate process, always makes a statement about one's personal and cultural values.

Exploring the history of sensibility and its symbols requires that past sensory perception for objects, often now bereft of their original contexts, be reconstructed. Efforts to recover sensibility are necessarily partial, but we can determine some of the meanings that some people ascribed to sensory experience by comparing the language used to articulate valued cultural concepts with the language used to describe objects. When certain descriptive terms cut across categories of experience, they are arguably evidence of a particular way of organizing the world—what the anthropologist Daniel Biebuyck has called "semantic taxonomy."[31]

## SYMBOLIC LANGUAGES: FURNISHINGS AS RHETORICAL STATEMENTS

As they are found in sentimental fiction and books of furnishing advice, the nuances of use and meaning associated with domestic objects and

**Figure 3.** "Drawing Room," stereograph in the Popular "Five Cent" Series published by Stevens Bookstore, Lewiston, Maine, about 1870. A few stereographs, such as this view showing one-half of a typical pair of middle-class parlors (the viewer is "standing" in one parlor, looking into a second one), may have been published to initiate new consumers into the mysteries of furnishing modern parlors. Courtesy, Smithsonian Institution; private collection.

household furnishings are sometimes astonishingly complex. Not every person could have appreciated equally all the possible chains of association connected to the domestic artifacts of a household. Probably people were variably compelled by some meanings and unaffected by others. Furnishings in the Gothic style might have contained deep meaning for very pious people, suggesting the link between religion and domesticity; for others, they might simply have conveyed a shallow set of associations with a specific church building.

However, popular literature (including fiction, poetry, and advice books) and popular imagery (published prints, pictures in periodicals, and photographs) provide considerable reason to believe that many ordinary Americans were seriously interested in learning the conventional meanings of things in the nineteenth century (Fig. 3). Entire chapters of domestic manuals were devoted to explicating the meaning of finger rings or the "language of flowers" (a term used in the period). Richard Wells's *Manners, Culture, and Dress,* an advice manual that was reprinted often in the 1890s, listed in one chapter the meaning of 318 flowers and plants presented as gifts. A deep-red rose signaled "bashful love"; an iris signaled "melancholy." The language of flowers, Wells pointed out, was "no new thing," having originated in the ancient East.[32] The nuances of Victorian domestic life lay in this juxtaposition of cultural associations and personal experiences—for example, in the juxtaposition of the *idea* of "the mother's chair" with the chair favored by one's own mother, or the *idea* of bashful love with the roses in a backyard garden.

As the interest in the "language of flowers" suggests, Victorian Americans were taken with the possibility of nonverbal, expressive "languages" structured by "grammars." They found one such highly nuanced "language" in the practice of etiquette. As Mrs. H. O. Ward, author of *Sensible Etiquette*, noted, "Society has its grammar as language has, and the rules of that grammar must be learned."[33] In 1903, the author of *Social Culture* declared, "Manners constitute the language in which the biography of every individual is written."[34] Owners of stylish furnishings also understood the symbolic, communicative possibilities of the furnishings and consciously used them to make symbolic assertions that could be understood, with varying degrees of clarity and comprehension, by people who confronted them. In a fundamental way, carefully planned rooms were designed to be rhetorical statements expressing aspirations, what a person believed or wished to believe.[35]

Historians have long interpreted architecture as rhetoric.[36] The exclusively neoclassical public building campaign in the first decades of American independence is a case in point. American intellectuals, aware that their buildings would be judged by posterity and believing that a nation's public buildings and monuments were a statement of its character, found classicism "a perfect style to express the pastoral ideal" of republican virtue.[37] Thus, Greek Revival buildings were a rhetorical statement of belief. Furniture is rhetoric too. The domestic critics of parlor furnishings in Victorian America also understood and were troubled by the rhetorical ends to which consumption of furnishings was put. Like critics of clothing fashions, they recognized that as the commercialization of society proceeded and as attractive clothing and domestic furnishings became available to new groups of people, no correspondence was guaranteed between what a person "said" he was through the "language" of his possessions and what he really was; one could no longer tell the players without a program.

The use of objects as a structured form of communication is analogous more to spoken language than to literacy, more to speech than to text, in that it is highly repetitive (furniture and buildings communicate a relatively constricted range of ideas) and relatively imprecise.[38] We can think of users of this language of objects as being more or less successful in the act of communicating through their manipulation, as being "artifactually competent" just as they were competent as speakers. Because Victorian culture's symbols were so often "real" in the sense that they were material and were often available for ownership by individuals, we can describe the process of gaining knowledge, fluency, and ease in their manipulation as a process of gaining competence in communication. Communicative skill was demonstrated through domestic furnishings, by people ranging from new consumers just learning the basic elements of furnishing to "professional interpreters," interior decorators.

The expanding universe of available consumer goods was like the universe of words available in a language. The choices made by individual consumers, choices that might have been highly idiosyncratic or highly conventional, were comparable to the ordering of the vocabulary they used in speech. In the furnishing of houses, then as now, ordinary consumers were provided with a constantly evolving range of choices, but specific room types were governed by a "grammar" that indicated how comprehensible statements were to be made. Some of the customs of furnishing had function as their basis—dining rooms require tables, for example. But many of the nuances of furnishing each type of room had other sources, historical in origin and metaphorical in content. In the nineteenth century, for example, dining room furnishings continued to employ a masculine iconography of the hunt, even though few of the men who headed dinner tables in these settings ever brought dinner home to their families in such a direct manner.[39] Images of the violence of the hunt, the conquests, and the abundance resulting from skill at hunting reflected the sense of self as well as the economic competence that good masculine providers were supposed to have. Placed inside a family's house, such images were also a carefully contained reminder of the difference between the harsh world outside the home and the softer one within its walls.

Although each type of room could have been furnished in infinitely various ways, certain elements were essential so that any given room would be understood as one of its type—a parlor, a dining room, or a library, for example. People who furnished a room made selections based not only on the constraints of economics and the dimensions of interior space but also on an understanding of what that room was supposed to include and signify. Ordinary consumers studied "ideal" statements that existed in the world—hotel parlors, photographers' studios, rooms opened for auctions in the houses of rich people, or the "model" interiors at world's fairs— and also followed cues in a variety of printed sources including novels, magazines, and by the 1890s, mail-order catalogs. They tried to re-create these ideals to the extent that their time, money, space, and understanding would allow. Depending on their resources and competence, the rooms they made "paraphrased" the parlor ideal more or less exactly.[40]

Other terms have been attached to the process by which individuals who are not perceived as social tastemakers make consumption decisions. Most typically applied is the term *emulation:* "the endeavor to equal or surpass others in any achievement or quality . . . the ambition to equal or excel."[41] Thorstein Veblen associated *emulation* with the process of "social comparison of persons with a view to rating and grading them in respect to relative worth or value," what he termed "invidious comparison."[42] Viewing consumption decisions solely as a competitive process is, however, too narrow. For ordinary people, consumption for the purposes of parlor making might have been less competitive than demonstrative. By working toward some attainable version of a parlor, they proclaimed membership in the respectable middle classes.

The idea of paraphrase seems particularly appropriate, however, because it implies that when a message is restated, it experiences some change, often in the direction of compression or economy; it is reduced to its most concise elements.[43] Indeed, paraphrase of the parlor sometimes involved ingenious compromises in the use of the established parlor vocabulary. At the lower end of the furniture-buying market, the purchase of a single inexpensive lounge, with its intricate interplay of wood frame and rich-looking, brightly colored carpet upholstery, could serve as a paraphrase of an entire parlor suite. The idea of paraphrase is also useful in analyzing the economics of the design and production of less expensive lines of consumer goods. The production of inexpensive upholstery demanded, by the last quarter of the nineteenth century, that those elements indicating an object's style and its adherence to aesthetic standards, such as the use of tufting, be pared down to some minimally acceptable level yet still be made available.

## DECORATIVE ARTS AS SYMBOLS: UPHOLSTERY

Within this study of parlor making and use, one type of parlor furnishing serves as a focal point because it seems particularly expressive of the tension between culture, the desire for cultivation and cosmopolitanism, and comfort, the desire for middle-class domesticity. *Upholstery* defined in its traditional sense—all the loose textile furnishings of rooms, draperies as well as seating furniture—was used often and ingeniously in Victorian parlors. The levels of detail employed on seating furniture and the myriad forms of drapery suggest that both professional upholsterers and ambitious do-it-yourselfers found furnishing textiles rich in expressive possibilities. Further, upholstery in all its forms was increasingly available over the course of the nineteenth century to new groups of consumers.

What Victorians labeled the "decorative arts"—furniture, textiles, ceramics and glass, silver, and all the other ornamental yet ostensibly functional objects that filled their rooms—were an integral part of the group of symbols contained within the larger symbol of "home." The visual complexities of the decorative arts were the source of both pleasure and, among design reformers, discomfort. As utilitarian objects, their perfected materials and workmanship and increased serviceability were products and emblems of advancing technology. The variety of their forms reflected civilization's improved understanding and a quasi-scientific categorization of domestic activities. Their forms and their aesthetic qualities also expressed the highest human intellectual faculties, just as did the "fine arts" of painting and sculpture. As the anonymous author of "A Visit to Henkels' Warerooms in Chestnut Street above Fifth" in the August 1850 issue of *Godey's Lady's Book* noted: "Few things are better calculated to give pleasure to the patriot than those evidences of advancement, which are witnessed here and there in our country, in those arts that unite physical comfort with intellectual pleasure. . . . Upholstery and cabinet-making . . . merit, we think, a high regard, as they call into action many of the most ingenious faculties of him who engaged in them practically."[44] In the view of this domestic patriot, the decorative arts were admirable for the inventive solution they offered to the relationship between the practical mechanical arts, domestic comforts, and the "intellectual pleasure" that the fine arts were capable of providing.

Because the decorative arts bridged the realms of practical work and art, they also offered the possibility of creating long, complex chains of cultural associations and meanings in addition to the personal associations that such objects could develop in the context of the private house. In this, rather than in the historical associations alone that "Gothic revival" or "Renaissance revival" furnishings bore in their ornamental detail, lies much of the Victorian *popular* fascination with furnishings. Ownership of decorative objects presented the possibility of the private house as a "memory palace" of culture, where the potentially dangerous outside worlds, not just of commerce but also of secular knowledge, could be tamed and made domestic by bringing them under the softening hand of familial influence.

The chain of historical and cultural associations attached to one type of furnishing—textiles—illustrates this point. All forms of household textiles, from simple domestic dress cottons to elaborate furnishing damasks, were the objects of considerable fascination throughout the nineteenth century because the industrialization of textile production changed their availability and cost so profoundly. The process of producing even simple sheeting for household use had always been time-consuming, making all textiles comparatively expensive. Historically, beautiful printed, pile, and pattern-woven textiles used both for dress and for furnishing enjoyed an association with wealth and power because their production was so labor- and skill-intensive and because some of the raw materials, such as silk and threads made from precious metals, were scarce and expensive. In the mobile courts of feudal Europe, textiles—like precious metals and ivory—were an easily portable and tangible sign of the wealth and power of a prince.[45] This state of chronic scarcity and expense began to change with the invention of the spinning jenny in 1770. Mechanization of spinning and weaving affected the daily lives of ordinary people in profound ways, altering the nature of the family as an economic unit as well as changing the experience of work through the setting of the textile mill in the 1820s and 1830s.[46]

Throughout the first half of the nineteenth century, textile technology was as vibrant an arena for innovation as small computers are today; many talented individuals in both Britain and America devoted their lives to textile innovations. Like the computer industry, textile technology was also the object of considerable appreciation and comment because of its effect on ordinary lives. In 1836 Daniel Webster considered "the use of the elastic power of steam, applied to the operations of spinning and weaving and dressing fabrics for human wear" as "the most prominent instance of the application of science to art" for the benefit of mankind. In 1860 another author interested in technological progress could still call the manufacture of domestic cottons "a most beautiful and complicated art."[47]

Other, peculiarly American aspects to the public interest in textiles made textiles a particularly meaningful part of domestic consumption. The eighteenth-century debate about the effects of fashion and luxury on the citizens of the colonies and the young republic, which decried domestic consumption of foreign "finery," had often focused on imported textiles for furnishing and clothing rather than on other imported consumer goods. Textile production and consumption had first been politicized through the Stamp Act controversy, when nonimportation and nonconsumption resolutions directed against English goods led to the craze among fashionable young women for holding "spinning bees" and to the fad among local high society for wearing garments of homespun fabric at their public events. Boosters of domestic textile production developed a "rhetoric of homespun" that linked household spinning and weaving to republican virtue well into the nineteenth century. The editor of the *Niles Weekly Register* noted in 1821:

> We never reflect upon the progress and prospects of that portion
> of the national labor which is applied to household manufactures,
> without feeling our hearts warmed with a national pride; for all the
> virtues, moral, religious and political, are interested in it. Tens of
> thousands of amiable, respectable and lovely young women . . . of
> those ranks and conditions in life which, a few years since, almost
> as much despised a distaff as they did a field-hoe, are now engaged
> to drive away the diseases and distresses of inanity, and keep them-
> selves in health and cheerfulness, render themselves good wives,
> and estimable mothers, while they add to the comforts and conve-
> niences of their parents, and make a "plentiful house" by a diligent
> attention to spinning, weaving, bleaching, dyeing, etc.[48]

The dramatic proliferation of factory-woven plain household textiles after the introduction of the power loom in America in 1815 was accompanied by an equally dramatic decline in their prices. Between 1815 and 1830 the price of a yard of unbleached shirting material dropped from forty-two to seven and a half cents.[49] The author of *Eighty Years' Progress in the United States* (1867) described the drop in textile prices in common parlance: "The price of a good calico is now twelve yards to a bushel of wheat. Forty years ago it was one yard for a bushel of wheat. The quality of goods at the same time has improved in a greater ratio. The handsome prints that now re-place the 'factory checks' of that day, show as great a change as does the price."[50]

The first successes of fully mechanized textile production affected the cost of plain and printed fabrics for clothing and for such basic domestic uses as bed linens. The development of the lace net loom and the jacquard loom attachment in the first decade of the nineteenth century began the process of adapting mechanized production to fabrics for drapery and up-holstery. Bobbin net grounds for laces that could be embellished by hand embroidery were produced by machine beginning in 1809. Entire lace cur-tains were made by machine by the 1840s. Machine-made tapestries for upholstery uses were in production in Great Britain by the 1850s; carpet

upholstery—tough, brightly colored, and inexpensive—was a common-
place on inexpensive furniture by 1870.[51] The development of new classes
of factory-woven furnishing textiles such as velvets and plushes with sturdy
and inexpensive cotton grounds brought further change to furnishing textile consumption. Although most production remained European until
the 1890s, and although many beautiful furnishing fabrics continued to
be largely handmade and expensive, ordinary consumers gained access to
a range of furnishing fabrics that had, in the scope of living memory, been
reserved for individuals of wealth.

A careful study of upholstery can illuminate the continuing power of
conceptions of parlor life established decades earlier, conceptions that
seem to have survived even when the context that inspired their initial articulation no longer exist. Many surviving upholstered chairs still seem
"uncomfortable" to modern eyes, yet were they ever meant to be comfortable? Or did they serve other functions more important to parlor makers,
symbolic functions or uses that expressed some connection to eighteenth-
century ideals of self-presentation? If upholstery is one medium that em-
bodies the tension between culture and comfort, do changes in its forms
and uses also help chart evolution in these two poles of thought?

This book follows Americans' interest and understanding of parlor furnishing from their early exposure to it in a variety of commercial settings
to their growing ability to imagine and then realize themselves creating
and living in such spaces in their own homes. It traces the effect of two
competing models of domestic life on the development of the middle-class
parlor and the ways in which consumers learned the fundamental vocabulary for furnishing these spaces. The complexities of the concept of comfort are explored, including the cultural limits on getting comfortable and
the rationale behind the popularity of spring-seat upholstery. The book
explores the sensibility that found meaning in the formal visual and tactile
qualities of upholstery and examines how such preferences were one facet
of larger patterns of thought embracing the concept of "refinement." It
analyzes how the upholstery trade interpreted these aesthetic preferences
and notions about seated comfort. Within the economic compromises that
manufacturers were able to achieve in design and production, they made
parlor furnishings that satisfied the sensibilities of Victorian Americans
and were accessible to a broad range of incomes. Finally, *Culture and Comfort* discusses the replacement of the parlor by the modern living room.
Surprising continuities and significant changes became apparent by the
1920s, evidence that Victorianism waned slowly and unevenly in early
twentieth-century America.

# CHAPTER ONE

# Imagining the Parlor

In 1853 the New York daguerreotypist M. M. Lawrence opened his new heliographic establishment on the upper floor of 381 Broadway. Prospective clients first entered a 25-by-40-foot "reception room," described in *Humphrey's Journal of Photography* as "furnished with rich, heavy Brussels carpet . . . the walls handsomely papered, window shades, and appropriate lace curtains, gilt cornices and ornaments, rosewood furniture, upholstered and covered with green velvet." Gentlemen waiting for admission to the "operating room," the site of the actual picture making, remained in this elegant interior. Women, however, were invited to prepare themselves for their portraits in a 25-foot-square "ladies' parlor," which was "carpeted with rich tapestry . . . walls covered with richest blue velvet and gold paper—rose wood furniture, covered with blue and gold brocatelle—reception, easy and rocking chairs, tete-a-tetes, &c. . . . Marble-top centre table, rose wood book-stand."[1]

M. M. Lawrence furnished the reception room and the ladies' parlor of his photography studio as if they were a pair of drawing rooms in a well-to-do private household. Beginning around 1820, a new kind of interior space—publicly accessible "commercial parlors" like Lawrence's—proliferated in several types of businesses frequented by ordinary Americans. Beyond their business purposes, these interiors were an important intermediary between the sources of tasteful furnishings and the new consumers deeply interested in having parlors and in furnishing them appropriately. The abundant sources of advice taken for granted by contemporary homeowners—the mass magazines and books brimming with color photographs of exemplary rooms, the cable-television decorating shows, and even the model interiors in furniture showrooms—were not available to Victorian homeowners. Thus commercial parlors not only supplied furnishing information in three dimensions and glowing color but also provided the experience of simply being in a parlor. In so doing, they implied that parlor gentility was accessible through the great engine of American commerce—and that the temporary inhabitants of the rooms were themselves (or could become) "parlor people," comfortable with the room's social ceremony and at home in its special milieu.

The commercial parlor predated the agencies typically given greatest credit for changing and educating public taste: the department store and the international exhibition.[2] At least a century before the 1851 Crystal Palace Exposition, a "consumer revolution" had been under way; citizens with new means to purchase what historian Neil McKendrick has termed "decencies"—and, in time, luxury goods—were also eager seekers of information to guide their consumption.[3] Between 1830 and 1880, they found model parlors in hotels, on steamboats and railroad cars, in photographers' studios, and in the meeting rooms of various voluntary associations. These "public parlors" in commercial spaces captured the imagination of at least those segments of the public that were middle class and urbane in their aspirations, if not yet in their actual means.

The commercial parlors in hotels, steamboats, photography studios, and railroad cars usually were not copied exactly by aspiring parlor makers, although many of them could have been reproduced. They were model interiors that allowed people to try on the idea of having a parlor; they were settings in which people could picture themselves. The model interior between 1830 and 1880 was also not necessarily created with the goal of forming or changing taste, although some creators of these interiors, such as George Pullman, believed that the spaces they furnished would make their clientele more refined. Most of the model rooms played a role in the creation of consumer demand merely by providing an experience— that of being in a carefully decorated room that looked like a parlor and suggested its suitability for similar purposes. Commercial parlors stimulated demand by provoking a process of imagining, providing access to a setting that allowed one to imagine owning and using such a room.

How might this process of individual imagination have taken shape in the minds of thousands of individual consumers? Before demand for ownership of objects can be aroused in the minds of potential buyers, they not only must learn that the objects exist but also must perceive the possibility of owning the objects as *real*. Per capita income or productive capacity must be sufficient, and there must also be a change in attitudes about spending. People must believe that spending income on consumer goods can make an actual difference in their lives, either in terms of greater physical comfort or as an avenue for expressing one's self or modeling new kinds of social relationships. Finally, they must perceive that the possibility of economic and social mobility is real—that society is fluid, to some degree, without the restraints of ironclad castes.[4]

Using furnishings to make social claims was not confined to relatively flexible social structures; as historian Penelope Eames has argued, furnishings expressed political power in England, France, and the Netherlands between the twelfth and fifteenth centuries.

> When social and political power was exercised through continuous contact between the seigneurial lord and his men of every rank, as it was in the feudal societies of the Middle Ages, that power was sustained, re-enforced and advertised by ceremony. Court ceremonial was structured by elaborate rules of precedence and behaviour in which the position of each individual, in any given situation, was apparent, not only in what he *did*, but by what he *used* in terms of his clothing, his food and his furnishings. Certain forms of furniture, and indeed furnishings in general, reflected those degrees of honour, or precedence, which were termed *estate* . . . [and] which might govern use, form, ornament and fabric.[5]

In the court life of Burgundy during this period, the degree of excellence permitted in specific furnishings—the number of shelves permitted in the stepped buffets used to display the concrete wealth of plate owned by the lord or the number of coverings on state beds—was regulated by written rules. These rules for furnishings were the equivalent of sumptuary laws for clothing by rank.[6] Possession of clothing or furnishings of particular quality was not simply a function of wealth but was a reflection of castelike social status. Imagining ownership—the creation of desire and hence of demand—was beyond the realm of possibility for most individuals.

By the eighteenth century, however, aspirations to own fashionable furnishings became realistic for new groups of people, a circumstance that coincided with changing concepts of decor. The idea of furnishings as a created setting for the display of social power was indeed medieval; however, as royalty consolidated its claims to power and since lords were no longer required to maintain portable households in order to retain control of their holdings, concepts of architecture and decor also changed.[7] The idea of creating self-consciously decorated rooms as personal settings for the display of cultivation (a highly refined form of social competition), in addition to political power, clearly had its roots in the seventeenth century, yet it gained force in the eighteenth century. It attained its highest refinement in the French concept of *civilisation* but also held sway in the British empire and colonial territories.[8] It is possible to think of the tastefully decorated salons of men and women of cultivation as extensions of their dress, which also, within the dictates of fashion, became more personally expressive. Thus, the habit of mind that perceived furnishing as a means of expressing social status (whether real or desired) was long-standing, but by the second half of the eighteenth century, it was linked firmly to the developing notion of changing fashion and "taste," an association that remained strong through the nineteenth century.

The motivation to furnish was in place as Victorian culture developed, but processes of consumer access to information about durable goods such as furniture were underdeveloped until the last decades of the nineteenth century. By the 1870s, furniture producers and various kinds of professional mediators (decorators, home economists, and retailers) stepped up their efforts both to make information about furnishings available and to influence consumer taste. Furniture trade periodicals such as *The American Cabinetmaker, Upholsterer and Carpet Reporter*, new in the 1870s and 1880s, were part of this effort. These professional periodicals demonstrate that furnishing trades continually introduced "decorative novelties" to keep consumers active in the marketplace, which suggests that the wheels of consumer interest had been set in motion and had been well greased some decades earlier.[9]

Another information source new to the late nineteenth century was the "model room" created by furniture manufacturers or interior decorators for commercial demonstration purposes. This seems to have been a product of the 1876 Centennial Exhibition in Philadelphia. Before this time, furniture warerooms were conglomerations of merchandise organized by price line or type. Although many exhibitors retained the old techniques of typological display of goods, a number of model rooms at the Centennial seem to have suggested to furnishing manufacturers the efficacy of presenting what would now be termed "a total look." Grand Rapids, Michigan, furniture companies, particularly Berkey and Gay, were the first to set up "rooms" offered for sale on the show floor (although the company's marketing strategy was aimed at sales not to individual consumers but to store owners during the semiannual furniture markets).[10]

Popular decorating advice books and articles were also largely a product of the 1870s and later, although earlier domestic economy manuals often included a chapter on furnishing.[11] Specific decorating advice in mass magazines appeared sporadically until the 1870s and usually omitted illustrations or included pictures of single objects out of context. Mass publications sometimes included images of exemplary parlors, as when *Gleason's Pictorial Drawing-Room Companion* published an engraving, cartoonlike to modern eyes, of the elaborate parlor of a New York merchant in 1854 (Fig. 4). Occasionally, the costume prints in magazines also included enough details of room furnishing to provide useful information to alert readers. But extensive illustrations of domestic interiors did not appear in periodicals until the 1890s.

For consumers, information on personal fashion—clothing styles, modes of hairdressing, and the like—seems to have been the easiest of all types of advice to obtain and the most widely disseminated, even among those who could not read or afford to subscribe to magazines with fashion plates. For example, information about new styles in clothing and hairdressing was readily transmitted through face-to-face contact among social classes in the mingling of street life. On her first visit to New York in 1832, British actress Fanny Kemble commented on the quality of clothing worn by lower-class people, including the African Americans whom she saw "parading up and down" on Broadway, "most of them in the height of fashion, with every colour of the rainbow about them."[12]

However, such casual mingling did not extend to socializing within the houses of the fashionable, at least in cities. New members of the middle classes there probably knew less about the style of living of the wealthy (who received their fashion news directly from European émigré craftsmen and shop owners and through networks of contacts with Europe) than did rural Americans, who entered the houses of small-town leading citizens for special occasions such as funerals. Over the course of the nineteenth century, city neighborhoods that had once contained an economic cross section became increasingly stratified and too large to encourage socializing among elites and the professionals, the substantial merchants, the small-businesspeople, and the "respectable" skilled artisans who constituted the middle class. The upper classes and the lower classes likely intermingled in the homes of the wealthy more often than did the rich and the middle classes, since working-class people were employed as domestic help.[13]

**Figure 4.** "A Parlor View in a New York Dwelling House," engraving after a drawing by A. Kimbel in *Gleason's Pictorial Drawing-Room Companion*, November 11, 1854. The brief article accompanying this image described the parlor as "the interior of an apartment in a magnificent mansion uptown, where one of the most eminent of our merchants has surrounded himself and family with all the elegancies and luxuries to which years of successful enterprise entitle him. . . . The room looks like a fitting abode of a man of refinement—a drawing room where a lady of elegant manners and educated tastes might appropriately receive her guests." Courtesy, The Strong Museum, Rochester, New York.

Ordinary Americans with modest incomes and aspirations to fashion did occasionally gain admittance to the homes of the fashionable. One of the most important ways may have been the household auction, which provided not only furnishing information but also the possibility of ownership of goods that would otherwise have been beyond their means. The story "A Bargain: Is a Penny Saved, Twopence Got?" in an 1854 issue of *Gleason's Pictorial Drawing-Room Companion* described a New York City auction preview in "an elegantly furnished private mansion" owned by a man named Lyons. "[The house] looked as if the owners had only gone out for morning calls, and might be expected back at any moment. The curtains, mirrors, suites of elegant furniture, set forth in the catalogue . . . were arranged as if for an ordinary reception day, instead of the press of an ignoble crowd,—second-hand furniture men, small boarding-house people, ladies, porters, idle spectators, and busy-bodies thronging around."[14] The heroine of the story, a country girl visiting city friends, was appalled at the crowds, who "swarmed from the kitchen to the servants' rooms," "scanned the furniture," "tried the springs of the sofas and chairs," and "plunged themselves up and down in the library chairs." She was chided, however, by an acquaintance who described the benefits of auction sales:

> "That's it, you see," Mr. Allen said. . . . "That's the way so many people of moderate means have their houses so handsomely furnished. A man of taste like Lyons or yourself, collects books, and pictures, and furniture, to be dispersed eventually after this fashion. The next owner 'declines housekeeping' in turn, and the things being a little more tarnished by removal or use, are purchased a shade cheaper by a class a grade lower in the scale, and so *decencus averni.*"[15]

Household auction catalogs confirm that these sales offered the public contact with beautifully planned and furnished parlors, as well as elegantly appointed dining rooms and chambers. A catalog for a sale of "Handsome Household Furniture" in New York City on April 22, 1841, described the "Front Parlour" furnishings as including a "large pier glass," "royal Wilton carpet," "2 rosewood couches, covered with fawn coloured striped satin, with figured blue silk border," two divans to match, and "4 chairs, with stuffed backs, to match, with figured blue chintz covers for all." The windows were curtained with "very elegant window curtains, fawn colored, with blue trimmings"; all the furnishings were listed as being "good as new, made by Ellcau." An 1853 sale of "Genteel Household Furniture," also in New York City, included in its inventory of the front parlor an eight-piece suite upholstered in "crimson plush," "rich tapestry Carpet," and two windows with gilt cornices from which hung "very rich crimson and maroon drapery and lace window Curtains, &c." The room was also furnished with a variety of mirrors, candlesticks, sofa tables, and two "Ptgs Landscape and cattle."[16]

For most Americans, however, commercial parlors provided incipient parlor makers with their first contact with consciously "designed" interiors—or even with as simple a novelty as spring-seat upholstery and lace curtains. In her popular novel of 1854, *High Life in New York*, Ann S. Stephens described one such encounter in the parlor of the Howard Hotel through the eyes of the book's "author," the Connecticut farmer Jonathan Slick. Invited to take a seat on a "cushioned bench," Slick did not demur. "'Wal,' sez I, a bowin, 'I don't care if I du, just to oblige you;' so down I sot, but the cushion give so, that I sprung right up on eend agin, and when I see it rise up as shiney and smooth as ever, I looked at her, and sez I— 'Did you ever!' 'It's elastic,' sez she, a puckerin up her mouth. 'I don't know the name on it,' sez I, 'but it gives like an old friend, so I'll try it agin.'"[17]

We cannot enumerate how many people developed a taste for parlor life through their contact with parlors in commercial buildings, but articles and advertisements in newspaper and magazines suggest that the public was very interested in these rooms. The presence of a properly genteel parlor or a parlorlike setting became a selling point for photographers' studios, hotels, and steamboat and railroad lines. Parlors in commercial spaces were an integral part of a web of ideas and images about the rapid advance of civilized living in America as a result of commercial activity, a set of ideas that crystallized in the popular notion of "palaces of the people." The New York City "dry goods palace" of the period from 1845 to 1875 was one specific architectural type whose exterior featured palatial iconography. The prototype was A. T. Stewart's "Marble Palace" (1846) on Broadway and Chambers Street, the largest and most famous dry goods palace of the period.[18] Hotels and other commercial buildings, the kinds of steamboats commonly called "palace steamers," and railroad cars such as "Wagner's Palace Parlor Car" also were "palaces of the people" whose parlors were publicly accessible rooms of state. In a series of articles on new "first-class hotels" in America in the early 1850s, publisher Frederick J. Gleason associated the proliferation of hotels with "the advancements of civilization and refinement in our growing country" and claimed in 1852, "Nearly every city in this Union boasts of a first-class hotel, which though devoted to the accommodation of the public, is yet equal to a European palace."[19] In 1854 journalist Reuben Vose articulated the popular equation between commerce and civilization's progress, an equation that supported the creation of New York City as a "city of palaces," when he claimed, "Commerce is the great civilizer of nations, and where merchants flourish, there all that adds charm to social existence will be found in the greatest abundance."[20]

The commercial palace and its related interior space, the commercial parlor, were visible symbols that carried real power among commercially minded Americans. By frequenting these places, middle-class Americans could become "parlor people," even if only for a short time; they could imagine themselves possessing that space. Vose deliberately described the pleasures of taking a seat in the "marble hall" of New York's Fifth Avenue Hotel in terms of imaginary ownership:

> If slightly fatigued a seat may be occupied in the hotel, and before him will pass more of the real beauty and wealth of the nation than in any other spot in the city. Here we recover from the toils that recur with every rising sun. Here as we gaze on the wealth of the world we feel at "home." *Yielding to the illusion of the place, and to a suggestive imagination, we often fancy that we are the happy owner of all that glides in beauty before us — except the ladies.*[21]

Contemporary commentators even blamed the American taste for hotel living at least partly on the public's enthusiasm for the spurious gentility that access to hotel parlors offered, the very access that Vose found so seductive in his imaginings of financial success.[22]

Commercial parlors were created and recognized as such because they featured furnishings that, placed in any kind of space, seemed unequivocally to denote the presence of a "parlor." During the first half of the nineteenth century, a specific set of elements came to be viewed as essential to such a room: carpets, window draperies with lace curtains, a parlor suite, "reception" or "fancy" chairs, a center table, a piano, and a decorated mantel, along with smaller objects such as framed pictures. Moreover, certain terms for fabrics, carpets, and even wood types were so emblematic of ideal parlor decor that they provided a descriptive shorthand for authors or journalists who described rooms—terms such as specific adjectives ("damask" or "satin") and coded descriptions such as "richly carved" for furniture and "velvet" for carpets. Finally, to attain the parlor ideal fully, the room had to give the appearance of having been furnished all at once; even if furnishings did not match exactly, the room should seem to have been furnished in a coordinated—hence more expensive—manner. *Humphrey's Journal* noted of M. M. Lawrence's elegant heliographic establishment: "Every article here is selected with the greatest care to uniformity."[23]

Although the largest and most elaborate parlors in commercial spaces expressed a scale of expenditure that was beyond the means of most consumers, the elegant interiors of first-class hotels, steamboats, and the largest photographers' studios still used a vocabulary of furnishings that was comprehensible to middle-class consumers at least through midcentury. A description of the ladies' drawing rooms of Girard House in Philadelphia in 1852 set out the coded terms of this vocabulary:

The floors are covered with painted velvet carpets, that echo no footfall; the curtains, yellow damask, relieved by rich lace hangings, and the most costly trimmings; sofas, lounges, etageres, tables, rosewood, *inlaid;* the sofas, &c., seated and backed with yellow satin, the chairs entire gilt, and yellow satin. The walls, from which gigantic mirrors blaze and multiply on every side, are decorated, and each parlor furnished with a massive chandelier of new style.[24]

The decor of the Girard House, though grand, seems very close in appearance to that of the parlors in Mrs. Israel Pemberton Hutchinson's Philadelphia home, on Spruce above 10th Street, as they appeared in this description of ten years earlier:

Their rooms are the most beautiful I ever saw. *All* the furniture [is] from Paris of the most costly description and admirable taste and keeping. The front room is in rosewood and some rich fawn colored stuff for drapery and sofas, with immense mirrors and splendid chandelier, candalabra [*sic*], lamps, bronze ornaments, etc.; the back room, which is the dress room, is in blue and white damask and gold. The woodwork of chairs is massy gilt, the chandelier, candelabra etc. ormolu of exquisite taste and execution.[25]

Thus the first commercial parlors seem to have taken their appearance from their domestic counterparts in the homes of wealthy Americans. Because they were new kinds of places—ones in which socializing was an element of the "product" being sold, whether accommodations, transportation, or photographs—there existed no real precedent in America for what spaces that commingled social and commercial functions in this fashion should look like. However, the parlor in well-to-do private houses in the late eighteenth and first decades of the nineteenth centuries served as a social space that brought together sizable groups of the "best people," a select company rather than the more constricted domestic group that socialized in the middle-class parlor later in the nineteenth century. Some of the first commercial parlors may have served this same function.[26] Because the "best men" of communities such as New York and Boston were also the first to finance first-class hotels and steamboat companies, they seem to have chosen to furnish their commercial parlors along familiar lines, hiring firms that also provided furniture for their residences. Later commercial parlors probably took their decorating cues from the public interest in these first rooms.

## HOTELS AS MODEL INTERIORS

The public rooms of city hotels were perhaps the most influential form of commercial parlor between 1830 and 1860. In urban settings, the power of fashion was greatest, and consumers could directly translate the room-making information that such interiors provided. The range and number of public rooms in good hotels varied. Francis J. Grund, a German scientist and mathematician who wrote a travelogue in 1837 about his trip to the United States, considered a typical hotel in a larger American city to contain "besides the bar a ladies' and a gentlemen's drawing-room, a number of sitting and smoking rooms for the gratuitous use of boarders, a newsroom, and one or two large dining-rooms."[27] With the exception of the bars and service areas such as barbershops, hotel public rooms were analogous to specific-use rooms in the homes of upper-middle-class and wealthy Americans—for example, the reading room or newsroom was similar to the library of a private house. Grund noted that the "elegantly fitted up" public rooms were intended to "supply, in a measure, the want of private parlours," which were few in number and expensive in hotels.[28]

As Vose's fantasy of "owning" a public room suggests, nineteenth-century hotels appear to have been more open for the public's perusal, use, and informal instruction in civility than are such spaces today. Anthony Trollope was astonished at the number of local people who passed time in hotel public rooms: "[There] is always gathered together a crowd, apparently belonging in no way to the hotel. . . . In the West, during the months of this war, the traveller would always see many soldiers among the crowd,—not only officers, but privates. They sit in public seats, silent but apparently contented, sometimes for an hour together."[29] He considered such spontaneous but companionable crowding into public places a peculiarly American characteristic.

In this social meeting-place role, the hotels Trollope described were continuing a function that taverns had served in the eighteenth century, but with changes in their scale, appearance, and pretensions. Eighteenth-century inns were generally private houses that had been converted into public lodgings, but between 1790 and 1830, entrepreneurs in East Coast cities opened larger structures built specifically as inns in order to meet the needs of increasing numbers of transients. These larger inns filled the role of the eighteenth-century inn as a social gathering place with "gaudy Long Rooms and Bar Parlors," rooms that could be leased for social events such as balls.[30]

Not only did the appearance and size of hotels change, but the way people thought about them also seems to have evolved. The notion of the "palace hotel" developed, denoting a first-class hotel offering individual accommodations for guests, a variety of special services, and leasable space for public social gatherings. The first published appearance of the term "palaces of the people" in reference to hotels probably occurred in a Washington, D.C., newspaper article about the opening of that city's National Hotel in June 1827.[31] The first-class hotel was a publicly accessible site that could still be associated with social ceremony and power and a kind of public civility—and best of all, this social power and refinement was located in the world of commerce, a sphere of activity that seemed open to every man.

Between 1830 and 1860, large hotels were constructed in all major American cities and in communities with aspirations toward size and commercial greatness. In 1836, for example—the same year that John Jacob Astor opened the Astor House, the first palace hotel in New York City— Buffalo, New York (population 16,000), welcomed the opening of the American Hotel, which was built in the "Grecian" style including a center stained-glass dome. Civic boosters freely acknowledged that the presence of a first-class hotel was associated with the progress of civilized living in America and believed citizens should be educated by them. Frederick Gleason, publisher of *Gleason's Pictorial Drawing-Room Companion*, was a particularly avid hotel enthusiast. In 1852 the periodical presented a series of descriptions of palace hotels and views of their facades, "not only for the amusement of our readers, but also for their real benefit."[32] Foreign visitors also observed the power of the hotel as a concrete symbol of aspirations for a society that was both open and refined. In the 1860s Trollope wrote that Americans were still obsessed with hotels: "They are quite as much thought of in the nation as the legislature, or judicative, or literature of the country; and any falling off in them, or any improvement in the accommodation given, would strike the community as forcibly as a change in the constitution, or an alteration in the franchise."[33]

The Tremont House of Boston, which opened in 1829, is generally considered to have been the first palace hotel. Its architectural plan and details, its provisions for privacy and security, its pioneering inclusion of systems for heating and rudimentary plumbing, and the size and grandeur of its public rooms attracted so much interest that a book was published containing its plan and selected details, along with a brief history and description of the interior finishes.[34] The Tremont's public rooms included two parlors for receiving new arrivals, two more "appropriated to the use of families," two sets of rooms for parties and clubs, six parlors attached to suites of rooms (promptly taken by permanent residents), and a large reading room with an attached "public Drawing-room for gentlemen."[35] The reading and drawing room was free to hotel guests; "a small annual sub-scription" allowed any male citizen to use it as a library and club.

No images of the Tremont's first public parlors appear to have survived, if any were made. The general appearance of its interior and that of other pre-Civil War palace hotels can be pieced together, however, through what is known about the tradespeople who provided fittings for both hotels and domestic interiors in major American cities. Twenty-one cabinetmakers, upholsterers, and importers of carpets, mirrors, and lighting devices sup-plied furnishings for the Tremont as well as for the houses of the well-to-do Bostonians. Hotel furnishing was not yet a separate specialty in the furniture business. Because the hotel was paid for by a stock company of the "better men" of the city, its furnishings probably reflected their upper-class preferences, informed through contact with imported furnishings and publications. Sherlock Spooner, one supplier, advertised his firm in the 1829 Boston city directory as "constantly manufacturing every article in the CABINET, CHAIR, AND UPHOLSTERY hue." He offered "Spring-seat Rock-ing Chairs, Couches, Sofas, Mahogany Chairs, Music Stools" and a range of specialized tables "in superior style."[36] Another supplier, upholsterer and furniture merchant William Hancock, included a woodcut of a fancy Gre-cian couch in his advertisement that same year. Several examples of furni-ture made around 1830 with Hancock's paper label, including an elegant sofa with upholstered cylindrical arms, survive in the collections of the Metropolitan Museum of Art.[37] The Tremont House parlors in 1830 may, in fact, have looked much like the large parlors of around 1824 depicted in Henry Sargent's painting *The Tea Party* (Fig. 5).

The furniture of the La Pierre House, a palace hotel that opened in Philadelphia in 1853, was supplied by George J. Henkels's sizable furniture warerooms, which normally provided furniture for middle- and upper-class households in the Philadelphia area between 1850 and 1876.[38] Hen-kels's stock of furniture fell well within the canons of middle-class taste as interpreted by *Godey's Lady's Book*, which promoted the firm's current offer-ings in several articles in 1850.[39] A sixteen-page catalog for Henkels's warerooms, dating from around 1855, suggests the types of furnishings that the public rooms of the La Pierre—a ladies' parlor, a "reception par-lor," another parlor for gentlemen, the main dining room, and several tea rooms—might have contained.[40] With the exception of a group of com-paratively inexpensive "Plain style" furnishings (probably late neoclassical "pillar and scroll" style) and a passing mention of "Elizabethan" style on the title page, the listed furniture was all based on fashionable French re-vival styles. The catalog offered "Drawing-Room" furniture as a type dis-tinct from "Parlor Furniture." Although the range of forms offered in each

**Figure 5.** *The Tea Party*, oil on canvas by Henry Sargent, Boston, Massachusetts, about 1824. Courtesy, Museum of Fine Arts, Boston; gift of Mrs. Horatio A. Lamb in memory of Mr. and Mrs. Winthrop Sargent.

of these lines was the same, the lines were distinguished by cost and degree of ornamentation. Drawing room furniture (which may have been imported) was offered in the "antique" style, an interpretation of sixteenth-century furniture highly carved with grotesque animal and plant imagery. The French called the style of such furnishings "Renaissance."[41] The drawing room "Trio Tete-a-Tete" in the group ("elaborately carved, Satin covering") was offered at the breathtaking price of $350. Less expensive ($60 to $75) but still fashionable "Tetes" listed under "Parlor Furniture" were offered in a plainer (probably less highly carved but retaining the basic shapes and ornament of the style) version of the antique style or in the popular Louis XIV taste. All three options offered customers tête-à-tête sofas, matching armchairs, ladies' chairs, and side chairs—the grouping of forms that, sold together, composed the typical seven-piece parlor suite of the 1860s through the 1880s. "Consol" and "Center" tables, étagères, and reception chairs rounded out the basic parlor line.

More is known about the appearance of the draperies in the La Pierre public rooms, thanks to an illustrated article that appeared in the February 1854 issue of *Godey's*. The magazine touted the "celebrated depot" of W. H. Carryl, which supplied curtains, furniture coverings, window shades, and "all kinds of parlor trimmings" for the La Pierre (Fig. 6). The magazine published the plates as one of a series of images of "parlor window drapery" furnished by Carryl over the course of several years. The article marked no difference between the kinds of draperies used in houses and those used in commercial parlors, and the materials and forms listed correspond to middle-class interior decoration. In the parlor and tearoom were "heavy green lambrequins" whose "rich bullion fringe" was praised for being so close in appearance to real gold bullion that "it would take a practiced eye to detect it." Reading and drawing room curtains were made in brocatelle, an upholstering fabric that, at midcentury, was either all wool or had a linen warp and a wool weft and was woven in damask patterns with the figures formed by the warp in a satin weave. This was a sturdier, middle-class substitute for more expensive brocaded fabrics and damask made of silk.

The parlor window drapery in *Godey's* ("Fig. 1" in that magazine) was claimed to be "nearly identical" in style to the window treatments found in the principal drawing room of the La Pierre. The windows were "draped with crimson, garnet, and gold brocatelle, finished by heavy cornices and the richest corresponding decorations," along with "exquisite lace curtains, as in the plate, falling below." "Fig. 2" represented the draperies of the "elegant suite of parlors on the second floor," which were "curtains of brocatelle, crimson, yellow, and green and gold, equally rich and suited to the style of the apartments, as in the drawing-room below." *Godey's* congratulated Carryl for the part his curtains played in giving the hotel "a cheerful welcome and homelike feeling."[42]

Interiors that probably closely resemble the public parlors of first-class hotels in the mid-nineteenth century are to be found today in what was,

**Figure 6.** "Fashion Plates for Decorating Parlor Windows," engraving in *Godey's Lady's Book*, February 1854. Courtesy, The Winterthur Library: Printed Book and Periodical Collection.

until the 1940s, a summer residence in Portland, Maine. Known as the Morse-Libby Mansion, or the Victoria Mansion, the brownstone Italianate villa was constructed between 1858 and 1861 by Ruggles Sylvester Morse, a self-made man whose entire career was devoted to hotels.[43] Morse was born in Leeds, Maine, in 1813, but family history (otherwise undocumented) holds that he left the state in the early 1830s to work first at the Tremont House in Boston and then at the Astor House in New York. A father-and-son team named Boyden, who managed the Tremont and later the Astor, may have brought the evidently able young man along as an assistant manager. After a brief sojourn to California to look for gold in 1849, Morse wound up later that year and in 1850 as an employee of the

St. Charles Hotel in New Orleans, perhaps serving as manager. Between 1853 and 1870, Morse became proprietor of the Arcade, the City, and the St. James Hotels in that city.

Morse, who died in 1893, became a wealthy man through the hotel business, so much so that he was able to own a house in New Orleans, a plantation some miles outside of town, and the Portland villa. It seems safe to assume that Morse's tastes (and those of his wife, who was also a Maine native) were formed by his knowledge of hotel decor, especially in his adopted city. The floor plan of the house, with its grand central staircase and large drawing and reception rooms, the elaborate and brightly colored rococo revival interior painting and architectural details, and the furnishings in the French taste all recall the descriptions of first-class hotel parlors, especially the description of the Girard House in Philadelphia. Two photographs of the drawing room from the end of the Morse era (taken in about 1890) show wall-to-wall carpet of a large rococo pattern, with a center medallion of roses, and chair upholstery of satin with bullion fringe and, on the seats of gilt reception chairs, what was probably a brocaded silk (Fig. 7). The windows were hung with lace undercurtains and with satin valances and draperies embellished with fringe and tiebacks in contrasting colors. A slightly later photograph, of the reception room during the ownership of the house by the Libby family (who left the interiors substantially unchanged), shows a button-tufted easy armchair in the French taste as well as a *bourne*, or ottoman—a large, round, fabric-covered couch designed to occupy the center of a room. The *bourne* was a French innovation, its design a reflection of the "Turkish taste" that was an element of French decor throughout the nineteenth century.

What is also striking about the public rooms of the Morse-Libby Mansion, as they are depicted in the photographs, is the absence of personal memorabilia and the restrained use of ceramics and other decorative accessories. When these appear, as in the mantel garniture of the reception room, it is because they are considered elements of the decorative scheme. Along with this absence of personal knickknacks, the scale of the rooms, their exuberant decoration, and their French furnishings suggest their fundamentally public character. At the same time, they are furnished with what, to the mid-nineteenth-century sensibility, were recognizably parlor furnishings.

Public parlors in hotels also seem to have served as sites for parlorlike entertainments. Some evidence suggests that the kinds of socializing that took place in the public parlors of the Tremont House may have been much like the convivial receptions and tea parties given in large private

**Figure 7.** Drawing room, Morse-Libby Mansion, Portland, Maine, by unidentified photographer, about 1890. The photograph is damaged, which accounts for the horizontal breaks across the image. Courtesy, Victoria Mansion.

houses. *Sayings and Doings at the Tremont House in the Year 1832*, a two-volume miscellany of dialogs, sentimental and comic stories, and "letters" written pseudonymously by "Costard Sly," described several social gatherings in the hotel's public parlors, including formal calls and large parties. The participants were residents of the hotel and other Bostonians. A story called "No Mistake about That" described a large after-theater party in "a magnificent saloon, (the ladies' dining and drawing rooms in the TREMONT had been thrown into *one*,) brilliantly lighted, and so forth,—and already occupied by a large party of ladies and gentlemen,—their friends and acquaintences [*sic*];—of course, the most approved fashionables of Boston."[44] Another story, "A Second Scene in the Ladies' Drawing Room," drew all the characters in the book together for a party whose tone was decidedly domestic. The participants provided their own amusements: "The doings were simple—common-place enough. There was some dancing—some singing—and a good deal of eating and drinking between heats."[45]

An 1858 *Illustrated London News* article on life along the Mississippi River devoted considerable space to a description of social life at the St.

Charles Hotel. Its author's comments suggested that such socializing was simultaneously public and commercial in character yet "domestic" enough to be suitable for the wives and daughters of planters.

> The most prominent public building in New Orleans is the St. Charles Hotel, an edifice somewhat after the style and appearance of the Palace of the King of the Belgians at Brussels. During the twelve days I remained under its hospitable roof it contained from seven hundred to seven hundred and fifty guests. . . . The southern planters, and their wives and daughters, escaping from the monotony of their cotton or sugar plantations, come down to New Orleans in the early spring season, and, as private lodgings are not to be had, they throng to the St. Louis and St. Charles Hotels, but principally to the St. Charles, where they lead a life of constant publicity and gaiety. . . . After dinner the drawing-rooms offer a scene to which no city in the world offers a parallel. It is the very court of Queen Mab, whose courtiers are some of the finest, wealthiest, and most beautiful of the daughters of the south, mingling in true Republican equality with the chance wayfarers, gentle or simple, well-dressed or ill-dressed, clean or dirty, who can pay for a nightly lodging or a day's board at this mighty caravanseri.[46]

To this commentator, as to "Costard Sly," hotel parlors presented interesting possibilities for social life in a new setting, among a commercially fostered version of "select company."

More modest hotels, in both the largest urban centers and provincial cities, also tried to provide their clientele with elegant parlors for socializing. Anthony Trollope noted that all the hotels he frequented during his 1861 visit, even in the West, contained the complete range of public rooms—"two and sometimes three" ladies' parlors [which in the West were rarely used, he noted], as well as "reading rooms, smoking rooms, shaving rooms, drinking rooms, [and] parlors for gentlemen in which smoking [was] prohibited."[47] In 1848 the Waverly Hotel in Rochester, New York, contained "Reading, Receiving and Bar Rooms" on its first floor, "public Drawing Rooms," private parlors and bedrooms, and the dining room on its second, and a leasable ballroom or lecture hall on its fifth floor. The local newspaper commented: "All are remarkable for their neatness, order and convenience, and are furnished in elegant style. . . . The whole arrangement of the house is such that all will feel at home."[48]

But was it possible for a middle-class American to be properly at home in the commercial parlors and sitting rooms of hotels? Although only a small percentage of American families probably lived in hotels, their number was significant enough to inspire comment among European travelers and American commentators. These observers disagreed about the effects that hotel living—and its gentility—had on the domestic sentiments of their residents, especially women. Francis Grund thought boarding "commendable on the score of economy" both for single men and for newly married couples, not only because it permitted marriages to take place "a little sooner than their means would otherwise allow them" but also because it saved expenses for servants as well as rent.[49] Thirty years later, the author of *Eighty Years' Progress of the United States* claimed that hotels provided "an unrivaled combination of the applications of human ingenuity to the improvement of domestic life" with their "splendid furniture, elaborate food, economical yet liberal housekeeping, labor-saving machinery."[50]

Even when hotel life seemed close enough to more traditional domestic arrangements to be safe and suitable for women, the open character of hotel parlors created special etiquette problems. How could residents negotiate the important middle-class ceremonies of daytime social calling, dining, and evening entertainments in parlors and dining rooms that were public? These concerns were common enough that the sensible Miss Eliza Leslie, author of domestic economy manuals and cookbooks, offered several chapters of very specific advice on "Deportment at a Hotel, or at a Large Boarding House" in *The Ladies' Guide to True Politeness and Perfect Manners* (1864). Her commentary illustrates the real difficulties that socializing in public parlors sometimes entailed while demonstrating that hotel parlors were indeed used for the same purposes as their domestic counterparts. Leslie devoted particular attention to the problems of social calling and parlor pastimes:

> In a public parlour, it is selfish and unmannerly to sit down to the
> instrument uninvited, and fall to playing or practising. . . . If you
> want amusement, you had better read, or occupy yourself with some
> light sewing or knitting-work. . . . Should a visitor come in to see
> one of the boarders who may be sitting near you, change your
> place, and take a seat in a distant part of the room. . . . It is best for
> the visited lady to meet her friend as soon as she sees her enter the
> room, and conduct her to a sofa or ottoman where they can enjoy
> their talk without danger of being overheard.[51]

Other commentators worried that hotel life was dangerous because resident families were also members of the middle classes, on whose domestic sentiments the continuing development of republican virtue depended.

**Figure 8.** "How We Sit in Our Hotel Homes," engraving in *Harper's Weekly*, December 26, 1857. This illustration accompanied the story by "William Brown," "American Homes in New York Hotels." Courtesy, The Winterthur Library: Printed Book and Periodical Collection.

Like the even more modest boardinghouses, family hotels provoked this kind of criticism in both editorials and moralizing short stories. For example, in the supposedly factual account "American Homes in New York Hotels" by "William Brown" in an 1857 issue of *Harper's Weekly*, newlyweds encountered firsthand the negative effect that living at the "St. Thunder Hotel" had on domesticity (Fig. 8). Even the new styles of fashionable furniture had a bad effect on their lives: the spring bed was so noisy that it prevented sleep, and an untied spring poked through the yellow-and-purple brocatelle cover of the showy but shoddy spring-seat sofa, ruining the bridegroom's trousers.[52] In "Boarding Out," published in *Harper's Weekly* that same year, the author pinpointed access to parlor life as a common yet spurious motive for choosing the hotel "mode of living."

Apart from the convenience of travel, the most common motive which persuades to the mode of living alluded to is economy. But it is quite clear that this idea of economy is founded upon a false standard of the necessities of life. If the tastes of our people were better regulated, and mere show was not preferred to substance, there would be less resort to the hotel or boarding-house on the plea of money-saving. If gingerbread furniture, damask curtains, tapestry carpets and a French cook are essential to happiness, there is no doubt they can be secured in greater perfection and at a less price by the gregarious hotel system than by individual effort. Such luxuries, however, as we all know, are not essential to happiness, and however permissible as superfluous enjoyments, they certainly are too dearly paid for when at the expense of domestic virtue and happiness.[53]

To these critics, hotel parlors and their "superfluous" luxuries dangerously blurred the necessary separation between the domestic haven and the world outside. Hotel parlors appeared domestic on the surface, yet they exposed young women, in particular, to lives of "publicity and indolence" rather than to the privacy, permanence, and well-regulated round of household management that a home offered, attributes that encouraged moral development. The parlors were nothing more than a facade, "a theatrical mockery of society, where the characters and scenes, always varying and shifting, can only present a passing show and produce a temporary excitement."[54] The "passing show" of the hotel parlor and the opportunity to participate in the facade of commercial gentility were, of course, precisely what Reuben Vose and the mixture of planters and traders at the St. Charles enjoyed.

## STEAMBOATS AND RAILROAD CARS AS MODEL INTERIORS

Contemporary reporting and commentary about the glamorous interiors of eastern and western river steamboats and coastal packets appeared in the mid-1820s, soon after fare competition for profitable passenger traffic began on the Hudson River and the Long Island Sound/Providence-to-Boston Lines. Initially, this kind of genteel travel was expensive—the elegant Hudson River paddle steamers, which had "a bar and a ladies' cabin and perhaps a band of music," charged up to three dollars for the trip from New York to Albany. By the 1840s, however, even fancy boats charged as little as one dollar for the same route.[55]

The history of Hudson River steamboat travel, which at its peak involved regular runs by approximately one hundred vessels, demonstrates the ways in which line operators made use of the growing preoccupation with fashion and creature comforts in their competition for passengers. Between 1825 and 1864, competition often centered on the issues of safety and speed as improvements in boat and steam engine design decreased upstream running time from seventeen hours to around seven.[56] Yet as early as 1825, Hudson River steamboat companies had begun to advertise the accommodations they offered as an added inducement to passengers. Some lines experimented with the concept of the "safety barge," a towboat arrangement that featured the same range of public rooms and amenities that would soon be offered by first-class hotels. In 1825 an advertisement for the Steam Navigation Company's barges the *Commerce* and the *Lady-Clinton* noted that each was "fitted exclusively for passengers, with a dining Cabin of nearly 90 feet in length, a deck Cabin for the accommodation of ladies, a range of state rooms for private families, a reading room, and all the usual accommodations found in the best steam boats."[57]

By the late 1830s, paddle steamers plying the western lakes and rivers also featured parlorlike public rooms and even separate sleeping cabins for passengers who could afford a higher fare.[58] Steamboats tended to have at least one large, general-use room known almost uniformly as the "saloon," a popularization of the term "salon," which was used to describe very large reception rooms in grand houses. Saloons were also features of early oceangoing steam vessels; some of these interiors were so notable that they were depicted on the transfer-printed china series "The Boston Mails" of about 1842. Although constrained by limited space, the need to provide sleeping berths, and furniture that had to be stable during rough weather, the rooms illustrated in this series paraphrased parlors as much as possible by using upholstered couches built into the wall (called banquettes), mirrors, carpets, and decorative mantels and woodwork. Sometimes the main saloon served as men's sleeping quarters and featured convertible furniture. The gentleman's cabin on the *Empire State*, which entered service on the Fall Riverline in 1848, doubled as the dining room; its berths were concealed from passengers by the use of "drapery of different colors mixed with lace shades," mimicking window fashions for houses.[59]

Ladies' parlors also doubled as sleeping quarters, except on boats large enough to have separate staterooms. In her short story "Mrs. Pell's Pilgrimage," Mrs. C. M. Kirkland described the ladies' cabin on a Hudson River steamer as containing rocking chairs and settees, which doubled as sleeping couches. An illustration accompanying the story depicted the backdrop of an elaborately draped doorway and wall-to-wall carpet.[60]

In keeping with parlor furnishing conventions, the main saloon of the *City of Boston*, one of the Norwich and New York Transportation Company's small fleet of steamers used on Long Island Sound in the early 1860s, was furnished with wall-to-wall carpet, center tables under gas chandeliers, and a large set of furniture designed in some variation of a "Louis" style (Fig. 9). The furniture, shown in "summer dress" with

**Figure 9.** Main saloon, *City of Boston*, by unidentified photographer, about 1865, reproduced in J. Gardner, "The Development of Steam Navigation on Long Island Sound," *Historical Transactions 1893–1943: The Society of Naval Architects and Marine Engineers* (1945). Courtesy, The Steamship Historical Society Collection, University of Baltimore Library.

striped slipcovers, included a type of circular sofa that was designed as an expanded version of a parlor sofa.[61]

Just as first-class hotels in the antebellum period were christened "palace hotels," the biggest and best of the domestic steamboats were dubbed "palace steamers." Describing a trip on the *Bay State*, which ran between New York and Newport from 1847 to 1863, Philadelphian Sidney George Fisher wrote that its interiors were "another wonder of modern art": "The saloons, cabins & staterooms are all painted and gilded in the most splendid style & sumptuously furnished. Brilliant Saxony carpets, chandeliers, marble tables, sofas, armchairs of every pattern, well-cushioned and covered with the richest stuffs, silk curtains, French china, cut glass, mirrors fill every apartment."[62]

The Great Lakes also was home to a fleet of increasingly luxurious passenger steamboats from 1838 to 1857, when financial panic forced many lake shipping lines into bankruptcy. By the time prosperity returned, railroads had obviated the need for these large and expensive vessels. The *City of Buffalo*, admittedly the most luxurious as well as the last of the breed, was the object of much public curiosity during its construction. Before the inaugural voyage, the boat was opened to public inspection, and the local press published a lengthy description of its appointments.

> The ladies' private cabin, on the after main deck, is excellently arranged; it is handsomely furnished with rich brussels carpets, rosewood furniture, upholstered with fine plush. . . . Passengers, upon going on board, enter a fine reception room furnished with sofas, marble-topped tables, etc., and in the centre is a pretty fountain. . . .
>
> Proceeding up the grand stairway, at the first landing, on the floor, we notice a large brass buffalo, and overhead a handsome mirror and splendid landscape painting. This introduces us to the grand cabin, lighted by sky-lights, and a splendid stained glass dome at the further end. On either hand the doors open up into the state-rooms. The cabin has an arched ceiling, which, together with the panels, are ornamented by gilt moundings, the white and gold making a very rich appearance. This cabin is like a gallery as we look into the cabin below. Several splendid chandeliers light it by night, the centre one of which is double, the lower portion lighting the ladies' cabin. The furniture is of richest rose-wood, with damask and plush upholsterings; the carpets are costly brussels, and the "tout ensemble" magnificent.[63]

The description of the decor of the *City of Buffalo* closed with the note that all carpets and upholstery had been purchased from A. T. Stewart and Co. of New York. Appropriately, the first and most famous "dry goods palace" in the United States provided the interior fittings for this palace steamboat.

Thinking back on his riverboat piloting days, Mark Twain was aware of the symbolic power of "floating palaces," especially in communities far from cities. He reminisced that Mississippi steamboats were "indubitably magnificent" when compared with midcentury "superior dwelling-houses and first-class hotels in the [Mississippi] Valley."

> To a few people living in New Orleans and St. Louis they were not magnificent, perhaps; not palaces; but to the great majority of those

populations, and to the entire populations spread over both banks between Baton Rouge and St. Louis, they were palaces; they tallied with the citizen's dream of what magnificence was, and satisfied it.

Their interior fittings, from the "far receding snow-white 'cabin;' porcelain knob and oil-picture on every state-room door" to the ladies' cabin with its "pink and white Wilton carpet, as soft as mush, and glorified with a ravishing pattern of gigantic flowers" provided visitors "a bewildering and soul satisfying spectacle!"[64]

According to an 1889 history of railroading in America, the comforts available on steamboats inspired George Pullman to attempt to upgrade sleeping and travel accommodations on his trains.[65] By the 1840s, as railroad lines grew longer and the possible length of trips was extended, passenger cars began to be equipped with more elaborate creature comforts.[66] As early as 1842, a fancy railroad car containing upholstered seats, curtains, and carpeting was placed on public display in Rochester, New York, and received notice in local papers. The *Rochester Evening Post* described four of the six cars, destined for service on the Auburn and Rochester Railroad, as containing separate rooms for ladies, with "luxurious sofas for seats and . . . a washstand and other conveniences."[67] Following the practice of hotels and steamboats, most railroads provided separate accommodations for women by the mid-1840s, in the form of either a small ladies' parlor in a section of a passenger car or an entirely separate ladies' car. These areas usually contained a sofa in addition to the typical bench seating.[68]

First-class passenger cars appeared on trains by the late 1830s, and luxury sleeping cars and parlor cars had proliferated by the 1850s. The latter usually appeared on short lines between large cities and cost one to two dollars per day more than normal coach fares, although access to parlor cars was sometimes offered free on competitive routes. In a large advertisement for its western routes, the Chicago, Burlington and Quincy Railroad offered passengers from Buffalo the use of "B. & Q. Palace Drawing-Room Cars, with Horton's Reclining Chairs," at no additional charge.[69] Parlor cars featured reclining chairs for passengers as early as the mid-1850s, when the Illinois Central Railroad introduced its new "Gothic" stateroom cars.[70] The design of reclining chairs on railroads was related to the design of barber chairs, as well as to patent reclining chairs for domestic interiors.

Even ordinary railroad cars were embellished with window curtains and decorative painting, and they featured comforts that were associated with parlors, especially spring seating. Most probably, these rail cars gave many

Americans their first contact with luxurious-looking, deep-colored pile upholstery fabrics in the form of sturdy mohair plush, one of the most popular furniture covers of the late nineteenth century. Beginning in the 1850s mohair was chosen by railroad companies for seating because of its resistance to dirt and its long-wearing qualities. In an 1881 technical manual for the textile trade, the entry under "mohair" noted: "The best mohair plushes are almost indestructible. They have been in constant use on certain railroads in this country for twenty years without wearing out."[71] Wool and mohair plushes (the latter were also called "Utrecht velvet") had been used on some good-quality furniture throughout the century; mohair gradually supplanted wool because of its superior luster and colors as well as its sturdiness. Yet until the 1880s, plush made from mohair was still comparatively expensive because it was imported. By the 1890s, domestically woven mohair plush had become a luxury fabric for ordinary people and was featured in the parlor-suite offerings of the Sears, Roebuck and Co. catalogs.[72]

Fancy railroad cars captured the public's imagination, just as steamboats had several decades earlier, because they combined symbols of refined living and domestic comfort with mobility. The humorist Benjamin Franklin Taylor described parlor cars, which he called "flying drawing-rooms," as "home adrift" and pronounced "flying bedrooms" (sleeping cars), with their ingenious planning, to be "among the crowning achievements of railroad travel."[73] Even Americans who could not afford to pay for travel in "flying bedrooms" or "flying drawing-rooms" were able to get a firsthand look at these interiors through public exhibition of the newest and fanciest cars. In 1876 the Jackson and Sharp Company of Wilmington, Delaware, sent two such cars, built for private clients, to the Centennial Exhibition in Philadelphia for display. One, the "Brazilian car of State," contained a drawing room with "a sofa and two tete-a-tete chairs, covered with silver bronze leather with claret rep puffing (a loosely pleated decorative technique used on both seat fronts and backs) and silk fringe and tassels" and window curtains of "green figured rep," one of the most popular fabrics for middle-class interior decor in that decade.[74]

The decorated interiors of railroad cars continued to represent popular furnishing taste through the last decades of the nineteenth century (Fig. 10). Their elaborate, dark woodwork, button-tufted seats, portieres, and figured carpets reflected ordinary Americans' preferences for parlor furnishing and expressed the popular understanding of upholstered refinement and comfort. In fact, railroad upholstery so powerfully epitomized the aesthetics of middle-class parlors of the late nineteenth and early twen-

**Figure 10.** "Pullman Sleeper on a Vestibuled Train," engraving in Thomas Curtis Clarke et al., *The American Railway* (1889). Courtesy, The Strong Museum, Rochester, New York.

tieth centuries that later furnishing advice books sometimes used it as a case in point of "old-fashioned" bad taste. *The Modern Priscilla Home Furnishing Book* of 1925 dubbed the common parlor-furnishing practices of its readers' youths as "the Early Pullman period of home decoration."[75]

## PHOTOGRAPHERS' STUDIOS AS MODEL INTERIORS

The appointments of the two elaborate parlors in photographer M. M. Lawrence's New York City portrait studio were remarkable, as demonstrated by the description in *Humphrey's Journal of Photography* quoted at the beginning of this chapter. But these parlors were not unique among photographers' studios. By the late 1840s, many daguerreotype operators went to great expense to create separate reception areas that included lavish draperies, suites of upholstered furniture, wall-to-wall carpeting, large mirrors, and center tables. Some, such as Ball's Great Daguerrian Gallery of the West in Cincinnati, furnished reception rooms with pianos to encourage informal parlor musicales among waiting patrons. Mr. Ball's gallery was the subject of a half-page illustration and descriptive article in *Gleason's Pictorial Drawing-Room Companion* for April 1, 1854 (Fig. 11). The gallery consisted of five rooms, the largest of which was the "Great Gallery," which displayed paintings, prints, allegorical figures representing the arts, and a handsome selection of Mr. Ball's half- and full-plate daguerreotypes. The author of the article described the decor as "replete with elegance and beauty."[76]

Articles describing and praising such photographers' studios appeared in both middle-class periodicals and photographic journals such as *Humphrey's Journal of Photography* and the *Photographic Art-Journal* throughout the 1850s. They tended to focus on the most elaborate and elegant studios as examples of what could be achieved by photographers of vision and ambition. However, parlor making among photographers spread through all but the cheapest studios from the 1840s to the 1860s in cities and larger towns across the United States. In the *Rochester Daily Advertiser* for March 3, 1848, the daguerreotypist T. Mercer advertised the opening of a new set of "Branch Daguerrian Rooms" to accommodate the rapidly expanding city:

> These Rooms are fitted up in a style of unusual splendor—are supplied with every thing the extravagant could desire, the luxurious sigh for. After naming *Sofas, Divans, Ottomans,* and *French Chairs,* comes one of ELDER's splendid *Golden Pier Tables,* with a Glass, (the

**Figure 11.** "Ball's Great Daguerrian Gallery of the West," engraving in *Gleason's*, April 1, 1854. Courtesy, The Strong Museum, Rochester, New York.

first completed in Rochester) in which, 'tis said, the *Fair*, look more lovely still, and assume that pleasing expression so much coveted by Artists, and their friends. Carpets of downy softness are spread beneath the feet, and hush the noisy tread. Statuary from Italy, of *pure marble*, adorn the Rooms at various points; the walls are hung with some of the finest works of Art, both of pencil and engraver.[77]

Only after extolling the beauty of the receiving room did the advertisement mention "*premium* DAGUERREOTYPES," taken by Mercer himself, for a fee ranging from one to twelve dollars each depending on the size of the image and the case chosen for it.[78]

By the 1860s, Rochester photographers emphasized the range and prices of photographic practices available in their studios: ambrotypes, photographs on paper, "Imperial" enlargements that could be painted over and transformed into "oil portraits." Attractive rooms, though still important, were no longer a novelty worth much advertising copy. Powelson's "new and elaborate Photographic Rooms" in 1864 simply encouraged prospective patrons to "take a look at the new Gallery, which is acknowledged by everyone to be the best fitted up, finest carpets and most elegant furniture, the most commodious toilet room for the ladies to be found in the country."[79]

By the 1870s, the efforts of ordinary studio photographers working in provincial cities to provide elegant parlors for waiting patrons had become so common that the activity was burlesqued in the photographic advice literature. H. J. Rodger's *Twenty-Three Years under a Sky-Light*, published in 1872, was directed both to photographers and to prospective customers. Rather than presenting technical advice, Rodgers used anecdotes on good and bad clients encountered in his business to address etiquette questions related to behavior in the studio and to advise both photographers and patrons on how to obtain the best possible portraits. He depicted the commercial portrait photographer as a long-suffering working stiff whose patient efforts at presenting a genteel public face were frequently tested by onslaughts from boors, rubes, and ignoramuses. In one such anecdote, Rodgers illustrated the trials of keeping up a refined reception room by describing the entry of a group of young men: "They step carefully over the door rug, and having approached the middle of the room, wipe their feet on the Brussels carpet. . . . When told that they must wait five or ten minutes, and after roughly handling specimens of art, especially selections framed in gold-leaf, they 'set down,' elevating their muddy *under-standings* (which are suitable for a Connecticut River fishing smack) into the best and most expensive upholstered chair."[80]

Historians estimate that three million daguerreotypes were made annually through the 1840s. This suggests that the experience of passing time in a photographer's studio was common by then; it grew even more ordinary in the next decade. Photographers encouraged their prospective patrons to visit newly redecorated studios for inspection and to pass a pleasant hour or two in the reception rooms.[81] A properly decorated studio located in St. Louis in 1851 was praised as "a most agreeable place to spend a leisure hour," and an 1848 advertisement for the Emporium Daguerreotype Gallery in Rochester invited "ladies and gentlemen" to visit the gallery "whether they desire to sit for portraits or not."[82]

Both commercial pressures and social aspirations led to the creation of quasi-public spaces that used the material vocabulary of gentility—the artifacts of the parlor—to attract and keep business. Historian of photography Richard Rudisill has offered the hypothesis that such settings "allowed the photographer to control his clients more effectively" because the setting differed from their homes "only in degree."[83] Indeed, some advice literature directed to photographers proffered similar arguments. M. A. Root's influential photography advice book *The Camera and the Pencil* (1864) devoted a whole chapter to the "Fitting Up of Heliographic

Rooms." He noted that the experience of waiting needed to be pleasant in order to awaken "proper moods" in sitters and suggested that furniture that reproduced Hogarth's curving "line of beauty" was most effective to this end.[84] Six years earlier, in a series of articles for the *American Journal of Photography* entitled "Expressing Character in Photographic Pictures," E. K. Hough had noted, "Almost every operator is ambitious of having what is called a 'nice place,' and he fits up his room as richly as he can afford, but he usually makes one fatal mistake: he puts his wealth and beauty in his reception room, while his operating room is left comparatively unfurnished, and comfortless, with the dirty paraphernalia of the art scattered about, and a strong disagreeable smell of chemicals."[85]

Getting the best out of sitters was only one motive for parlor-making activity, however. Photographers sought to attract and hold patrons for repeat visits, even offering their reception rooms as an agreeable and socially acceptable site for spending leisure hours. The illustration of Ball's Great Daguerrian Gallery showed clients socializing and enjoying an informal musicale. Additionally, photographers, by displaying their own work alongside art in parlorlike settings, suggested that photographs were both artistic and appropriate elements of parlor decor. Photographers thereby guided new habits of consumption by suggesting that photographs themselves were genteel, as was the photographer who owned the parlor setting.

## THE MODEL ROOM AT EXPOSITIONS AND FAIRS

Attendance at fairs—international expositions, mechanics' fairs, and state and county fairs—was a regular event for Americans in the second half of the nineteenth and the early years of the twentieth centuries.[86] The Centennial Exhibition in Philadelphia clocked ten million visits in 1876, whereas the White City of the World's Columbian Exposition of 1893 in Chicago recorded about twenty-five million. Fair-goers learned what has been termed "the lesson of things" as they passed through the enormous buildings that categorized the works of man by country of origin, by degree of transformation through man's hand, from raw materials and agricultural products to consumable goods, and by a work's place along the scale of human intellectual achievement, from mechanical and applied arts to the perceived apex of civilization, the "fine arts," which often were exhibited in separate buildings.[87]

Household furnishings exhibited in international expositions were displayed as merchandise with visible prices as early as 1855.[88] The organization of these manufacturers' exhibits was much like that in stores of the period: simple groupings by category or displays of material abundance, such as "waterfalls" of textiles.[89] Even displays of furniture sometimes followed this simple, abundant style of display. Gardener and Co.'s exhibit of perforated veneer seating furniture at the Centennial was organized as a pyramiding cascade of chairs.[90] Published images of exemplary furniture, household accessories, and textiles from the numerous illustrated accounts of fairs also tended to concentrate on isolated objects or groupings, with no backdrop to suggest appropriate sites for their display at home. The accompanying texts usually concentrated on simple descriptions of materials and techniques of manufacture, their costliness, and their design.

The notion of the overtly didactic or exemplary model room setting was not completely alien to fairs before the Centennial. Beginning with the Sanitary Fairs of the 1860s, "New England Kitchens" were a popular attraction, exposing visitors to settings that were furnished with a miscellany of "colonial" furnishings and memorabilia and were populated by women in quaint costumes. The New England Kitchen at the Centennial consisted of two buildings that contrasted a colonial kitchen of 1776 with a "modern" one of 1876. The colonial kitchen was dominated by a large fireplace whose mantel shelf was covered with candlesticks and other paraphernalia. It was furnished with spinning wheels, cradles, a settle, and various pieces of furniture with "Pilgrim century" provenance, such as a small desk "which John Alden brought over with him on the Mayflower." Ironically, the idea of constructing a separate colonial kitchen building seems to have been realized first not in the United States but in the "primitive woodland village" built for the International Exhibition in Vienna in 1873. This village included furnished examples of Hungarian and Austrian regional architecture, populated with residents in appropriate native costume, as well as several ethnic restaurants.[91]

However, model room settings created specifically for the purpose of selling their contents were an innovation of the Centennial. These vignettes were created by elite British, French, and American furniture and interior decoration firms. For example, the Philadelphia decorating firm of Smith and Campion exhibited four settings—a parlor, a library, a dining room, and a bedroom. Although only a few examples were illustrated, several books of commentary on the Centennial Exhibition discussed what was, by all accounts, a new approach to selling and displaying furnishings: "An interesting feature of the Exhibition is the method which the upholsterers, decorators, and furniture-dealers have chosen by which to display their goods to the best advantage. This method consists in dividing the sections allotted to them into rooms, which are afterwards fitted up as parlor, library, boudoir, dining-room, or any special apartment."[92]

James D. McCabe, the author of a lengthy illustrated history of the Centennial, noted that "makers of the finest grades of furniture in New York and Philadelphia went to great expense" in re-creating "rooms of the usual size, which were handsomely carpeted, provided with curtains, doors, frescoed ceilings and walls, and superb gas fixtures and mantel-pieces. The rooms were open on one side. With the homelike surroundings thus provided the furniture showed to the best possible advantage. It was of the most elaborate description, and was richly upholstered."[93]

The room that may have represented the height of taste and luxury to the popular imagination (although the firm received no prizes) was a Turkish/French-style "boudoir" exhibited by the Philadelphia upholstering supply firm Carrington, deZouche and Company. The room was a tour de force of button tufting in cretonne (unglazed cotton fabric usually printed with the same floral designs as glazed chintz), reflecting the kind of fabric-swaddled interior that had made its appearance in France as early as the first decade of the nineteenth century.[94] A black-and-white plate of the room appeared in Walter Smith's *Industrial Art*, volume 2 of *The Masterpieces of the Centennial Exhibition, Illustrated*, and was reproduced three years later in Frank H. Norton's *Illustrated Historical Register of the Centennial Exhibition, Philadelphia, 1876, and of the Exposition Universelle, Paris, 1878*, this time in glowing color (Fig. 12).[95]

Some observers found these model rooms fascinating because they seemed to offer a peek into the mysterious households of the rich (settings that lost their mystique, if not their attraction, through the publication in the 1880s of vanity books such as *Artistic Houses*).[96] One visitor noted enthusiastically that the rooms offered "glimpses of the surroundings of the classes who set the fashions" that could be had in no other way. "We look into the most private apartments, the boudoirs and bed-chambers, which are so artfully arranged as to suggest occupancy. Bric-a-brac and knick-knacks are disposed about in studied carelessness so as to make the effect as natural as possible."[97] The rooms were theatrical sets awaiting the entrance of fashionable people, and the observer was a consumer-voyeur.

## PARLOR MAKING BY VOLUNTARY ASSOCIATIONS

Between 1830 and 1880, other kinds of commercial parlors occasionally appeared in cities in the form of assembly rooms and "drawing rooms" attached to theaters.[98] However, a particularly telling form of parlor making that was public but not commercial was undertaken by voluntary associations for their own use. Some men's clubs, such as the Athenaeum of

**Figure 12.** "Interior Decorations: United States," chromolithograph by Cosack and Co., Buffalo, New York, published by the American News Company, New York City; plate tipped into Frank H. Norton, *Illustrated Historical Register of the Centennial Exhibition, Philadelphia, 1876, and of the Exposition Universelle, 1878* (1879). Courtesy, The Strong Museum, Rochester, New York.

Philadelphia, were organized by members of social elites, but others were largely made and occupied by groups of young workingmen and took the form of reading rooms, athenaeums, or parlors. The "New York Athenaeum" rooms, described in detail in the *Daguerrian Journal* of November 15, 1850, were typical. For the modest fee of twelve dollars per year, the member gained access to "three very spacious apartments" located under the galleries of the Academy of Design in New York City. Although the "great size and height" of the rooms made them unusual, the anonymous author felt that these qualities heightened "the imposing effect of interiors devoted to social intercourse." He went on to marvel at the effect of the coordinated decor (executed by "Mr. Patterson of London"): "We are familiar with immense concert halls and public ballrooms, but our residences are generally too small to admit of very spacious saloons or drawing rooms. In addition to this peculiarity, the colors used in the furniture and decoration are harmonious; the prevailing tint of one of the apartments being green, of another crimson, and the third neutral." The author described the reading room as having green flocked wallpaper, "heavy green curtains," and floral-patterned carpets that "had a costly look."[99] The descriptions suggest that contact with this kind of planned interior, the kind that might be found in well-to-do households, was a new and pleasant experience for the author; it was perhaps decor he might try to re-create on his own at some future date.

The urge to create and congregate in such respectable-looking interiors was so strong that by the 1850s, associations of fire fighters, groups long known for their roughness and competitive brawling at the scenes of fires, also made for themselves what seem to modern eyes to be astonishingly elaborate and expensive session rooms. An illustration from the *Illustrated London News* series "Transatlantic Sketches" depicted a "Parlour Belonging to New York City Firemen" (Fig. 13). Not only were the firefighters depicted as top-hatted, waistcoated gentlemen, but their setting was no ordinary drinking establishment. Rather, it featured many of the elements that by this time were recognized as essential for a parlor, its decor inflected by the masculine interests of its makers. "C. M."—the author Charles Mackey—noted that firemen's parlors were furnished "with a degree of luxury equal to that of the public rooms of the most celebrated hotels."

> At one of the central stations, of which I send you a sketch, the walls are hung with excellent portraits of Washington, Franklin, Jefferson, Adams, and other founders of the Republic; the floor is covered with velvet-pile carpeting, a noble chandelier hangs from the

**Figure 13.** "Parlour Belonging to New York City Firemen," engraving in *Illustrated London News*, January 23, 1858. Courtesy, Museum of the City of New York.

centre, the curtains are rich and heavy, and the sideboard is spread with silver claret-jugs and pieces of plate, presented by citizens whose houses and property have been preserved from fire by the exertions of the brigade; or by the fire companies of other cities, in testimony of their admiration for some particular act of gallantry or heroism which the newspapers have recorded.[100]

The reporter was impressed by the willingness of volunteer firefighters, "mostly youths engaged during the day in various handicrafts and mechanical trades, with a sprinkling of clerks and shopmen," to participate, on behalf of the company, in "an amount of expenditure which is not the least surprising part of the 'institution,'" money that went to uniforms, to decorated fire equipment, and to "furnishing of their bunk-rooms and parlours at the fire stations."[101] Although the brawling and spontaneous street processions depicted in the article have been considered expressions of working-class, urban folk culture, the same firemen expressed their claims to respectability by adopting clothing associated with status, such as top hats, and by creating for themselves a genteel setting that incorporated the standard trappings of a parlor as well as a sideboard, a symbol of respectability borrowed from the dining room, here used to display the company's award silver. In comparing the furnishings to those of a hotel, Mackey may have offered a clue to the model followed by the fire company in its parlor furnishing. This parlor was not unique, however. Fire companies in other cities, such as the Active Hose Company in Rochester, New York, in the 1870s, also seem to have created elaborate parlors for themselves.[102]

### A WORLD FULL OF PARLORS

The appearance of the parlor in steamboats and trains is partly due to the increase in the number of Americans traveling during the first half of the nineteenth century for business and pleasure. Improvements in transportation technology and the development of canals, better roads, and railroad-track beds encouraged long-distance travel by making it less grueling. Finding some way to accommodate travelers on long journeys without stopping for overnight lodgings made sense to companies, since they could make money on the service and offer the fastest trip.

The increased presence of women and children travelers was also a factor in the process of making such mobile and commercial "domestic interiors," and at least part of the traveling public's interest in the interior arrangements of such vessels was stimulated by the presence of women and children on board. An account by Thomas L. McKenney of a barge trip up the Hudson River in 1826 praised the "ladies cabin and apartments" not only because they contained "splendid" furnishings but also because a woman thus had "all the retirement and comfort which the delicacy and tenderness of her sex requires."[103] Apart from the practical considerations associated with tending to small children or women's special sanitary needs, the concern of operators and commentators may have been stimulated by the increasing power of the cult of domesticity. Internal public transportation of such an unprecedented physical scale needed to be made suitably domestic, in both its actual physical arrangements and the associations carried by the decoration of at least some of its interior spaces. But the realities of domestic life sometimes overwhelmed steamboat gentility. The English actress Fanny Kemble complained that the atmosphere of the ladies' cabins was far from genteel, despite their parlor pretensions, because so many women with small children were confined there in bad weather: "What with the vibratory motion of the rocking chairs and their contents, the women's shrill jabber, the children's shriller wailing and shouting, the heat and closeness of the air, a ladies' cabin on board an American steamboat is one of the most overpowering things to sense and soul that can well be imagined."[104]

Separate women's parlors on steamboats (by the late 1820s) and railroad cars (from the 1840s) and separate family parlors and women's dining rooms in hotels also allowed women to relax their public decorum temporarily while also offering segregation from the coarse behavior of many traveling men, particularly from the men's drinking of ardent spirits and their use of tobacco. European travelers such as Fanny Kemble in the 1830s and Charles Dickens in the 1840s were particularly appalled at the public behavior of "these very obnoxious chewers of tobacco." Kemble complained: "It has happened to me after a few hours' travelling in a steam-boat to find the white dress, put on fresh in the morning, covered with yellow tobacco stains; nor is this offensive habit confined to the lower orders alone. I have seen *gentlemen* spit upon the carpet of the room where they were sitting, in the company of women, without the slightest remorse."[105] This separation was not absolute—women could and did participate in mixed-sex social life in the saloons of steamboats, on railroad coaches, and in the large parlors of hotels. In his 1873 *World on Wheels*, Benjamin Franklin Taylor even suggested that women not be provided with separate accommodations because "women sprinkled through the cars keep a train upon its honor, if not upon the track, and elevate the lumbering things from a common carrier to an educator."[106] But given the typical behavior of traveling men, women may have been grateful that they could escape to the ladies' parlors on steamboats and railroad cars, their mobile islands of domesticity.

Some of the businesses that engaged in the practice of making parlors—steamboat companies, hotels, and photographers—do not seem to have much in common. However, all of these businesses were engaged in trying to sell their services or products in an intensely competitive market. After 1825, for example, five different steamboat lines were already competing for the passenger traffic between New York City and Albany. Selling comfort and genteel surroundings in a travel setting (when most travel was a dirty, uncomfortable, tiresome process at best) offered something apart from basic transportation, something that could create the competitive edge for a steamboat line. Hotels such as the Tremont House of Boston offered a rare service to travelers and some city residents: comfortable, clean, and genteel accommodations. To attract a clientele with money to spend, these hotels provided an experience that was, for America in the 1820s and 1830s, uniquely urbane and refined. Finally, the photographer's studio was a commercial setting that grew out of a combination of factors. The pressures of economic and professional competition and the artistic aspirations of some photographers stimulated parlor-making efforts, as did the willingness of Americans (including middle-class women with leisure hours to spend) to patronize such refined commercial settings.

Commercial parlors also grew out of the domestic-environmentalist assumption that the appearance of the refined interior would discipline and civilize its clientele, an assumption that also justified the expenditures to create parlors. The most articulate statement of this position appeared quite late, in an "interview" from the early 1890s with railroad-car builder George Pullman.

> Putting carpets on the floors of cars, for instance, was considered a very useless piece of extravagance, and putting clean sheets on the beds was even more an absurdity in the minds of many. They said that men would get in between the sheets with their boots on. But they did not. So it was with the more elaborate and costly ornamentation and upholstery which has been steadily developed. It was criticised . . . as useless extravagance—a waste of money on things which passengers would only destroy. It has not proved to be the case. I have always held that people are very greatly influenced by their physical surroundings. Take the roughest man, a man whose lines have always brought him into coarsest and poorest surroundings, and the effect upon his bearing is immediate. The more artistic and refined the mere external surroundings, in other words, the better and more refined the man. This goes further than the mere fact that people will be more careful in a beautifully decorated, upholstered and carpeted sleeping car than they would were not such surroundings above them. It goes, when carried out under other conditions, to the more important matter of a man's productive powers and general usefulness to himself and society.[107]

## THE SELECT COMPANY IN THE WORLD OF COMMERCE

An explanation of the development and proliferation of public parlors in commercial spaces between 1830 and 1880 is incomplete without reference to the symbolic and rhetorical power that commercial parlors had precisely because they were both commercial and genteel. Victorianism, the bourgeois culture of industrialization and commercialization in Anglo-America, did not suddenly appear full blown, wielding a new and untried vocabulary of symbols. Instead, the culture emerged, and demonstrated its power, through the commercialization of already existing symbols, as well as through the articulation of new symbolic forms peculiar to a modernizing, commercial world. Two powerful metaphors permeated descriptions of the commercial spaces under investigation here—the palace and the parlor. The palace, the symbol of the concentration of royal power, existed outside the world of commerce, in the realm of power divinely ordained and inaccessible to ordinary people. When Americans appropriated the symbol of the palace to describe the "palace hotel," the "palace steamboat," or the "dry goods palace," they were grafting an old symbol onto a new situation, suggesting the simultaneously leveling and uplifting effects of democratic society ("every man a king") and of commercially derived wealth. The parlor, the second symbol transplanted into the commercial sphere, was the site of formal social ceremony in the household and was the room that most clearly bespoke the notion of gentility—of personal cultivation in appearance, etiquette, and education. The commercial parlor represented the commercialization of the concept of gentility, and its presence in commercial "palaces" may explain why elegant, gala furnishings rather than homey, modest versions of parlor decor appear to have been preferred.

Middle-class gentility also required appropriate settings in which it could be expressed. The parlors in the best hotels were locations for entertainment and social ceremony for guests, residents, and outsiders; they were a commercial version of the beau monde of cultivated people. At the same time, ladies' parlors in particular provided a domestic haven that buffered women's interactions with the broader public in commercial spaces and provided an interim solution for a society still looking for a place, in both the psychological and the spatial sense, for women in the public sphere. Finally, because anyone with enough money and desire could create a commercial parlor, as photographers did, anyone could attempt to imply membership in the world of refinement and cultivation.

For several decades after 1830, most first-class hotel parlors (and probably the more modest examples of respectable hotels) were essentially large-scale versions of the fashionable drawing rooms in private houses.[108] But beginning in the 1850s, some commercial parlors grew more grand and less homelike. The public rooms of some first-class hotels and the most lavish steamboat interiors became so elaborate that their original relationship to domestic parlor furnishing became blurred. For example, with the remodeling of the *Isaac Newton* and the *New-World* in 1855, the grand saloons of Hudson River palace steamers began to take on a theatrical appearance, extending through several decks with gallery-level promenades.[109] The interiors of the most elaborate hotels, such as the Palace in San Francisco and the St. Nicholas in New York, were, as Russell Lynes has called them, fantasy settings.[110]

Americans experienced difficulties in controlling the uses of the public parlor because, democratically, it was open to uncultivated individuals, from tobacco chewers to ill-behaved photographers' clients. Americans also expressed ambivalence about the effects that some commercial parlors had on domestic life because some members of the middle classes seemed to relish parlor life, even in hotels, over a more sparse yet more private domestic environment. Still, commercial parlors served to stimulate interest in creating gala parlors in the private households of new members of the middle classes. In a world that provided few models for interior decor, commercial parlors introduced people to the essential artifact vocabulary—the forms of parlor furniture, carpets, draperies, and wall decoration. They also showed the observant the nuances of that vocabulary—matching color schemes and the use of certain woods, fabrics, and as the Connecticut farmer Jonathan Slick discovered, even the newest techniques of upholstery construction. Public parlors both expressed the aspirations of commercializing American society and provided models for the aspirations of new participants in Victorian culture, creating demand by priming consumer imagination during the first decades of public parlor making.

# CHAPTER TWO

# The Comfortable Theater

## Parlor Making in the Middle-Class
## Victorian Household, 1850–1910

The word *parlor* is rarely used to describe a type of room anymore, and when it is, it is usually used to refer either to hair-cutting businesses that have no particular pretense toward high fashion or to deliberately quaint restaurants that specialize in serving ice cream. As a descriptive term, *parlor* has little in the way of cultural power.

This was not always the case. As commercial parlors in hotels and other quasi-public places suggest, for Victorian Americans, the word *parlor* carried a wealth of associations. In ordinary discourse, *parlor* usually denoted a space within a private household where families could present their public faces. The room was used for the purposes of social ceremony—the place in which calls and social visits by friends were received and the setting for entertainments such as tea parties and musicales. For many families, parlors were also the location of such traditional rites of passage as small weddings and laying out the dead, for meetings of women's clubs, for the display of the Christmas tree, for courting, and for visits from local dignitaries. Over the course of the nineteenth century, even as critics decried parlors as "ceremonial deserts . . . useless and out of place in the houses of nine-tenths of our Americans," average people who wanted to be identified as members of the middle class focused some of their energy and financial resources on making a parlor for themselves.[1] Setting aside a specific room for the purposes of social rituals and furnishing it for that use—once a prerogative only of families of means—became an activity that denoted membership in, or aspirations to belong to, the most important culture-defining group in nineteenth-century America.

If the term *parlor* alone has little meaning today, one has only to add the descriptor "Victorian" to achieve quite a different effect. In the popular imagination, Victorian parlors were "stuffy," "crowded" with useless and bizarre objects, and "dirty" because of the dust their myriad contents collected. They were also "uncomfortable," which is the most damning kind of modern criticism. In her memoir of middle-class life in Pittsburgh at the turn of the century, Ethel Spencer found fault with this very stiffness of her family's parlor from the perspective of the 1950s:

> The house was square. To the right of the central hall as one entered was the library and to the left the parlor. The parlor went through many transformations and toward the end of our occupancy of the house it became a living room, but in our childhood no one could have lived in it happily. It was meant for occasions— for formal calls, for receptions, for Sundays, but not for everyday living. No one could have relaxed in its overstuffed rocking chair of vast proportions or felt at home with its tall china lamp, a Victorian monstrosity of the first order.[2]

Indeed, as the second half of the nineteenth century passed, parlors were stuffed full of increasing numbers of things. As Clarence Cook complained in 1878, "What with easels, chairs not meant for use, little teetery stands, pedestals, and the rest of the supernumerary family filling up the room left by the solid and supposed useful pieces, it is sometimes a considerable test of one's dexterity and presence of mind to make one's way from end to end of a long New York drawing room."[3]

This multitude of things was often hard to clean, and maintaining a parlor required a certain degree of dedication. Although many middle-class women relied on the services of at least a visiting laundress, most cleaned their own houses. But for incipient parlor makers in the second half of the nineteenth century, anticipated maintenance problems seem not to have stifled the impulse to furnish and embellish. For example, when Mr. and Mrs. George Ware Fulton built and furnished their Second Empire–style "dream house" near Rockport, Texas, in the mid-1870s, they purchased furniture, drapery, and carpets for most of the rooms from companies in Cincinnati and New York. The parlor was furnished in a manner reflecting typical conservative upper-middle-class good taste for the time: a seven-piece suite and several "window chairs" (low-backed chairs intended to sit inside a bay window) covered in silk, along with a number of other fancy chairs, wall-to-wall Brussels carpeting, and cretonne window lambrequins. The Fultons furnished their parlor this way despite the fact that all the furnishings were in constant peril from the ravages of moths, beetles, roaches, and Gulf Coast humidity and mold. In a letter written when she and her husband were out of town, Mrs. Fulton reminded her daughter to shake out the lambrequins and handle the parlor furniture weekly to discourage vermin. (Residents of the Gulf Coast still tell visitors that constant use and handling of textiles is necessary to prevent infestations.)[4]

Housekeepers in the urban Northeast did not have to worry about weevils in their lambrequins, but they faced their own special trials, particularly soot from burning coal and gas. Spencer recalled that her mother "spent hours pinning ten-foot long [lace] curtains to stretchers when they had to be washed—which was about twice a month in those days of uncontrolled smoke."[5]

Despite the unrelenting labors involved in maintaining parlors and the criticisms of parlors as coldly formal, uncomfortable spaces that wasted family resources and saw little daily use, it seems clear that thousands of Americans devoured and acted on the parlor furnishing advice found in books and women's periodicals. For these consumers, the equation between comfort and ceremony in the parlor was balanced in favor of as much formality as their limited resources could muster. Middle-class American families who made such rooms often chose to use rooms other than the parlor—the kitchen, the dining room, a second parlor, or a sitting room—as the place where they gathered daily. Sometimes the motivation for limiting parlor use to special occasions was associated with practical concerns; it was expensive, for example, to heat an extra room. However, most families who saved their parlor for social purposes seem to have been motivated by the desire to give due respect to the scale and gravity of the events they knew were expected to take place there.

The middle-class parlor between 1850 and 1910 was the descendant of two different kinds of "best rooms" of the eighteenth and the early nineteenth centuries. In *The Decoration of Houses* (1897), Edith Wharton and Ogden Codman Jr. described this "mixed ancestry"—the gala apartment and the "family sitting room"—and its consequences:

> In modern American houses both traditional influences are seen. Sometimes, as in England, the drawing-room is treated as a family apartment, and provided with books, lamps, easy-chairs and writing tables. In other houses, it is still considered sacred to gilding and dis-

comfort, the best room in the house, and the convenience of all its
inmates, being sacrificed to a vague feeling that no drawing-room is
worthy of the name unless it is uninhabitable. This is an instance of
the *salon de compagnie* having usurped the rightful place of the *salon
de famille;* or rather, if the bourgeois descent of the American house
be considered, it may be more truly defined as a remnant of the
"best parlor" superstition.[6]

In many pre-Georgian American house plans of the seventeenth and eighteenth centuries, the name "parlor" designated one of two principal rooms
on the house's ground floor, the other being the hall. Like all rooms in such
houses, the parlor was a multipurpose space. It was where the family's best
possessions, including the best bed in the household, were stored and displayed. Although company was received there, the parlor was not what
might be termed a "gala apartment," a room designed only for socializing.
Beds disappeared from parlors in more expensive homes during the second
half of the eighteenth century, but in modest houses they continued to be
found there well into the nineteenth century.

The second source for the parlor of the mid-nineteenth century was a
result of new cultural imperatives. Beginning with the popular spread of
the Georgian house plan in the eighteenth century, well-to-do Americans,
proponents of the cultural ideal called gentility, also increasingly favored
interior arrangements that more rigorously separated "public" (social) and
more private regions of houses (Fig. 14). This preference was associated
with the elaboration of etiquette, the formal code for social behavior, and
a new conception of the role of entertainment and display in households.

Planning for special-use rooms in houses, called the art of distribution,
had been perfected by French architects in the late seventeenth century. In
house plans, the major categories of human activity were segregated, and
each specific function was allotted its own domestic space.[7] In grand
houses, architects planned several kinds of public rooms to serve the needs
of gatherings of varying size and intimacy. The architect Alexandre Jean-
Baptiste Le Blond said of salons in 1710, "[Here] people of quality are
received and one may dine on grand occasions." "Grand cabinets" (later
called *appartements de société*) were "very glamorous reception rooms of
moderate size, where one could expect to find select company" in less formal circumstances than in salons.[8]

Fascinated with the ingenious French plans, English architects adapted
these room divisions in the eighteenth century, but the requirements of
English society were somewhat different. Robert Adam's plan for Syon

PERSPECTIVE VIEW.

CHAMBER PLAN.

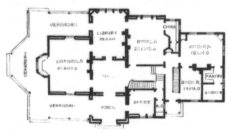

PLAN OF PRINCIPAL FLOOR.

**Figure 14.** "Design No. 19," engraving in Calvert Vaux, *Villas and Cottages* (1864). Victorian house plans typically included several rooms designed to meet the requirements of middle-class social life—parlors and dining rooms—on the first floor at the front of the house. In this plan the library was probably intended to serve as a family sitting room. Bedrooms and rooms for housekeeping— kitchens and pantries—were typically placed upstairs or at the back of houses. Courtesy, The Strong Museum, Rochester, New York.

House, remodeled in the early 1760s, included both private and public dining rooms. Next door to the public dining room was "a splendid withdrawing room for the ladies, or *salle de compagnie*, as it is called in Paris." Next to this was the gallery, "an admirable room for the reception of company after dinner, or for the ladies to retire to after it" and, finally, a circular "saloon" for public entertainments along the lines of balls or very large receptions.[9] The concept of the "drawing room" or "parlor" in fashionable English houses of the late eighteenth and early nineteenth centuries combined the functions of the "with-drawing room" and the "gallery" (a term that was not used in America). It was closest in concept to the French *appartement de société* and was intended as a location for the display of social graces and personal cultivation. The function of the French *salon* had been split between Adam's saloon and the public dining room.

Members of the economic and social elites in America probably gathered their ideas about the function and contents of parlors both from their connections to English gentry and from time spent in France or in the company of French visitors to America. The French conception of what might be called the "social geography" of gentility seemed particularly seductive, however, and Francophiles in the last decades of the eighteenth century, such as Philadelphian Samuel Powel III, attempted to reproduce it. A native of Philadelphia, Powel was reared as a gentleman and traveled in Europe for seven years before his marriage in 1769. He served as mayor of Philadelphia during the Revolution, and his house was the site of lavish entertainments both for members of the Continental Congress and for officers of the British Army.

When Powel returned from his European sojourn, carrying with him a collection of furnishings (now lost), he promptly remodeled his house on Third Street. The new front rooms on both floors reflected his understanding of the public facade of a gentleman; the presence of his children and evidence of domestic work were noticeably lacking. The first two floors of the house's primary block, facing the street, were devoted completely to "parlors" that were drawing rooms and an impressive second-floor ballroom for evening entertainments—rich suppers, music and dancing, card playing, and lively conversation. Sleeping and daily living were confined to the third floor of this block and to a simply furnished rear wing. The denizens of parlors such as Powel's were members of a "select company," not a cross section of the entire society nor a close-knit family group but instead men and women of similar social class and breeding.[10]

By the mid-nineteenth century, the old term *parlor* was still in use in the United States. Yet even in middle-class households, ideas about the function of parlors—and about the nature of the possessions appropriate for such rooms—had evolved toward the concept of the "drawing room," devoted to the presentation of an elaborated public self. Neither personal accounts nor published furnishing advice of the era consistently used the term *parlor* as distinct from *drawing room*. Books that used the term *drawing room* sometimes seem to have been addressed to audiences who must have had enough rooms and resources to feature a gala space devoted only to entertainment. Other terms, including *salon* and *sitting room*, also occasionally appear. The term *sitting room* presents another exercise in analyzing the ambiguities of domestic architectural terminology and actual patterns of use. In houses with adequate space, "sitting room" referred to a separate room that saw daily, casual use as a center for reading, sewing, and other family activities, as opposed to the parlor's more formal function as a site for social ritual. Case studies of room use indicate that the "sitting room" could be a back parlor, equipped with older, simpler furniture. Often the dining room or kitchen doubled as the sitting room if a house did not possess enough rooms. In these instances, families still chose to reserve their parlors for formality.

Through the second half of the nineteenth century, the word *parlor* seems to have been commonly understood as *The Century Dictionary* defined it in 1890: "a room in a private house set apart for the conversational entertainment of guests; a reception-room; a drawing-room ... In the United States, where the word 'drawing-room' is little used, *parlor* is the general term for the room used for the reception of guests."[11] Even in households that could not set aside a room for only occasional use, the parlor was the center of formal sociability. Catharine Beecher described it as the space "reserved for the reception-room of friends, and for our own dressed leisure hours."[12] The authors of *Beautiful Homes; or, Hints in House Furnishing*, an 1878 advice book directed toward new consumers of household furnishings, explained the purpose and appearance of the parlor by referring to the older understanding of the term. For members of the "middle classes," the parlor served "both as reception-room and that chosen apartment, which in olden times was the 'best room' of our grandmothers."[13]

For middle-class families, the modern parlor now had to be presentable enough to serve as the family's *appartement de société* even if it doubled as the sitting room. However, advice literature made plain that separate rooms were preferable: "With these requirements, it is in the parlor therefore that we find the choicest treasures that the house can afford, that will tend to the hospitable entertainment of guests," Mrs. C. S. Jones and Henry T. Williams wrote in *Beautiful Homes*, "just as in the sitting-room or living-room are gathered the dearest tokens of love of the family circle."[14] Noah Webster's 1882 edition of the *American Dictionary of the English Language* noted this double usage when it described the parlor as the room "which the family usually occupy for society and conversation, the reception-room of visitors, &c. . . .; sometimes, the best room of a house, kept for receiving company, as distinguished from the sitting room of the family."[15]

The impulse to make modern parlors in middle-class households gathered momentum steadily after 1830 and continued into the twentieth century, moving down through the economic strata as far as incomes allowed the purchase of appropriate furnishings. Architectural advice books published in the middle decades of the nineteenth century reveal that parlors became an important factor in space and room-use planning even for very modest structures. In Victorian house plans for large and small suburban "villas," apartment houses, rowhouses, and many farmhouses, cooking was separated from eating by the inclusion of a dining room. A range of other private activities took place in the back regions of houses—sleep, care of clothing, and children's play. A front hall provided a psychological buffer zone between the outside world and the domestic realm. And, ideally, the plan denoted a space that the family could reserve specifically for the presentation of its dressed-up social identity—the parlor.

Calvert Vaux's *Villas and Cottages* (1864) provided designs for suburban and rural houses in varying degrees of grandeur and expense, but almost all included a parlor. The related rooms, and the language that Vaux used in naming each, reveal something about how the owners of each house might be expected to spend their time in the spaces. Small houses had a parlor and a living room (which was sometimes also the dining room); large houses had a parlor, a living room, a study or a drawing room, a morning room, and a library.[16]

Even house-plan books addressed specifically to audiences with limited incomes revealed the importance placed on setting aside valuable domestic space for the purposes of the parlor. One such plan book was S. B. Reed's *House-Plans for Everybody*, first published in 1878 by Orange Judd and Co., the New York publisher of the weekly newspaper *American Agriculturalist* (which, at its peak of popularity in the late 1860s, had a circulation of 160,000).[17] *House-Plans for Everybody* was one of a variety of inexpensive advice books aimed at the lower-middle and middle classes, especially those living in rural areas. The book was a particular success for the firm, remaining in print at least until 1900. It was distributed by both Sears,

Roebuck and Co. and Montgomery Ward and Co., whose catalog for spring and summer 1895 described *House-Plans for Everybody* as a "useful volume" for "persons of moderate means." It sold for $1.10 plus postage.[18]

Reed's little book consists of forty house plans arranged in order of increasing expense. Considerable space was devoted to modest single-family dwellings; ten of these were estimated to cost $1,100 or less to construct. Although the houses were often very small, the interiors were marked by the division of space into tiny rooms, with their specific functions labeled. Parlors appeared as early as Design V ($650), which included an 11-by-11-foot "Kitchen or Living-Room" and a 13-by-14-foot "Parlor." Reed understood that having differentiated room spaces was more important to his rural and small-town audience than were generous, open spaces: "Conventional modes of living have established a system of household arrangement and economy requiring for every home of even moderate refinement, a house with a front hall, a parlor, a dining room, and a kitchen on the first floor, and a liberal suite of chambers on the second story."[19]

Within Reed's small houses, several architectural features helped define any particular room as a "parlor." Mantels were important (even though most of the houses would actually have been heated by stoves) because the hearth was a symbol of happy family life. In the comments for Design IX, a "Country or Village Cottage," the parlor had a "marble shelf" but was warmed by a "radiator" beneath, which communicated heat from the stove in the adjoining room.[20] Bay windows (available in prefabricated form for fifty to sixty dollars complete) were a second important parlor feature. Reed noted in passing not only that such windows would add space to parlors but also that a bay window "indicates refinement."[21] Indeed, architectural details such as bays or elaborate mantels could provide important cues about the type of decor appropriate in a room and were the focus of much furnishing effort and attention. However, parlors could in theory be made anywhere that a space could be found for them.

A variety of other sources attest to the development of what might be termed "parlor consciousness" in both new members of the middle classes and individuals aspiring to that respectable, if not always well-defined, identity. Interest in having a modern parlor was not only an urban phenomenon, although the sources of news about changes in furnishing tastes were located in cities. The desire to make modern parlors reached into the economic and social elites of small-town and rural America by the 1820s and slowly moved into less urbane groups in such communities. In the 1850s and 1860s, women's magazines such as *Godey's Lady's Book* and *Peterson's* published articles that made explicit the assumption that their readers included women living "at a distance from cities, who wish to send orders" for up-to-date furnishings.[22]

The 1850 *Godey's* article "New Furniture" carefully listed the contents of the modern house room by room. The most up-to-date parlors or drawing rooms contained sets of "sofas and ordinary chairs, covered with satin damask, crimson and black, deeply tufted or knotted" or with velvet, plush or haircloth covers over rosewood frames. Modern parlors also incorporated "lounging or arm-chairs," pianos, sofa tables with oval marble tops, and étagères, which required explanation because of their newness. These freestanding sets of shelves were meant to be filled with "elegantly bound books and *bijouterie* [decorative accessories such as vases and ceramic figures] of all descriptions."[23]

"New Furniture" diagrammed the conventions or "vocabulary" of furnishing middle- and upper-class urban households, some of which would remain essentially unchanged for the rest of the century—at least at the level of popular, rather than fashionable, taste. Its description of old-fashioned parlors noted with evident scorn that some of the solid citizens of rural communities still did not understand modern tastes in furniture: "Now, this may cause divers groans from 'honest country folk,' where chairs, a bureau, a looking-glass, and a table, are still considered the essentials of parlor furniture; and a sofa or centre-table luxuries, that call forth the remark from visitors, that 'Squire Smith, or Major Jones's people are living quite too stylish!'"[24] In a fictional description of the rural owners of a new frame house, Mrs. C. M. Kirkland described the family's "parlour," which she clearly considered typical, as containing white "curtains" (from the description, actually decorated window shades) "with netting and fringe half a yard deep," a shelf of books, a rag carpet, and "the best bed, with volumes of white drapery about it." The special character of this old-fashioned parlor was confirmed by the fact that the kitchen was the room "in which the family usually lived."[25]

Perhaps because published information about the modern way to furnish parlors usually emanated from cities, differences in the tastes of ordinary urban and rural parlor makers were not extreme by the second half of the nineteenth century, at least in areas no longer subject to the roughness of frontier living or to extraordinary geographical or social isolation. In their abilities to create modern parlors, ordinary consumers in rural communities differed from their comparable urban peers chiefly in their initial difficulties in obtaining access to goods (problems that improved transportation systems and the arrival of the mail-order business eventually solved) and, among smaller farmers, in a shortage of cash (a chronic problem in the rural economy generally) with which to purchase consumer goods from faraway places. The penetration of the rural market by a national or regional consumer culture drew more people into a network of similar middle-class tastes and is one of the most important results of the commercialization of society. Once only elites had been cosmopolitan, with access to national and international information about changing tastes in fashions. Over the course of the nineteenth century, ordinary people also became cosmopolitan in a modest way through the popular ideas, tastes, and goods of middle-class consumer culture.

As the western territories were settled in the second half of the nineteenth century, respectable families created up-to-date parlors for themselves in rough places where steamboats and railroads permitted shipping but where social calling, one of the most important behaviors associated with the room type, was an impossibility. Recall how the Fulton family made determined efforts to transplant a middle-class parlor typically found in the East to Texas. They were not alone. The Kohrs family, a prosperous ranching family in Deer Lodge Valley, Montana Territory, outfitted a "magnificently furnished parlor" in their log ranch house with furniture purchased in St. Louis in 1868; it was shipped as far as Fort Benton by steamer.[26]

*The Household*, a monthly magazine published between 1868 and 1903 in Brattleboro, Vermont, provides additional evidence that less prosperous rural women were interested in and knew about the furnishing practices of the urban middle classes by the 1870s. Published correspondence from *The Household*'s readers and frequent firsthand accounts (some probably fictionalized) of parlor making indicate that farmwives knew what such rooms ought to contain. Each issue included descriptions of homemade upholstered furniture, curtains and mantel lambrequins, "tidies and antimacassars" (ornamental needlework pieces used to protect furniture surfaces), and parlor ornaments such as homemade bracket shelves. Many of these articles suggested that attractive parlor furnishing could be attained without having to purchase all the elements ready-made. In one article, "How We Furnished the Parlor," the narrator helped a neighbor create a parlor with fifty dollars and elbow grease. The money was spent largely on upholstery fabrics (for curtains, shelf and mantel drapery, and chair cushions) and a twelve-dollar lounge. It represented the accumulation of years of savings that the farmwife had originally designated for a "raw silk [parlor] set"; she knew that a parlor suite was an essential component of conventional parlor furnishing.[27]

*The Household* also encouraged "parlor consciousness" by grouping its articles under room names, including "Drawing Room," "Parlor," "Library," and "Dressing Room." These "departments" also suggested the appropriate activities for each space. Although the majority of *The Household*'s audience probably did not have more than a single parlor or sitting room, to organize content in this way addressed the ideal dimensions of social activity or women's work that took place in each. The "Drawing Room" section represented personal refinement and social interaction, containing brief essays of a sentimental or moralizing nature with titles like "Memory's Treasures," fiction of the same tone, and some discussion of the arts. It also included advice on etiquette; these articles bore such titles as "Courteous Manners" and "Visitors and Visiting." The "Parlor" concentrated on the life of the family, including articles for or about children and suggestions for pastimes, with titles along the lines of "Games for Winter Evenings." It offered instructions for guessing games with a literary bent— "The Shakespeare Game," the "Game of Mythology," and another called "Poetical Pot Pie." The "Library" division promoted self-improvement with articles on literature and music. Finally, the "Dressing Room" was the location of general advice on housework other than cooking (sewing in particular) and instruction in "fancywork" and homemade interior decoration. Through its organization, *The Household* provided readers with both practical household advice and a vision of the possibilities that having rooms strictly for social purposes might offer.[28]

Etiquette and "parlor pastime" books, compared with personal reminiscences of parlor life as it was actually lived in a variety of urban and rural places, reveal the conventions of parlor use and the ways these ideas differed from actual use patterns in the decades after 1850. In the first decades of the nineteenth century, prosperous families of the American elites continued to furnish beautiful parlors used as the settings for entertainments for the "select company," just as Samuel Powel's parlor had been used. In a diary entry for March 4, 1839, Sidney George Fisher described one such event and its participants:

> At 9 went to a small, but very beautiful recherché [refined] party at Mrs. Geo: Cadwalader's. It was made for Mrs. Harrison. The rooms are very rich and splendid, & also in excellent taste, tho I think too costly for our style of living and habits. Walls & ceiling painted in fresco by Monachesi [a Philadelphia portrait painter], curtains, chairs white & gold, beautiful carpets. etc.etc., in two large rooms, brilliantly lighted, and filled with about 50 well-dressed and well-bred men & women, sitting in quiet talk, made a pretty scene. The supper was in the same style of sumptuous elegance, without profusion. They have been accustomed to this thing all their lives, and do

it with ease, propriety & grace. Very different from the gaudy show, crowded glitter and loaded tables of certain vulgar people here, who by mere force of money have got into a society to which they are not entitled by birth, education or manners.[29]

In discussions of parlor social life, most nineteenth-century etiquette books echoed Fisher's description of a beau monde ideal of parlor decor, entertainments, deportment, and social grace. Underlying their advice is the concept of the parlor as a theatrical location for personal display, the same concept that guided the remodeling and use of Powel's front rooms. Books that offered advice on etiquette described a world of parlor entertainment—receptions, musicales, and tea parties—that Fisher would have recognized.

However, using etiquette books as a guide to actual habits of middle-class living, especially in the second half of the nineteenth century, requires some caution. Manners books are a highly stylized genre of domestic advice literature, marked by repeated plagiarism over very long periods of time. For example, *Social Culture*, a 1903 etiquette manual common enough in libraries to suggest its wide circulation, borrowed heavily from Emily Thornwell's *The Lady's Guide to Perfect Gentility* of 1856, which in turn cribbed much of its material from *Etiquette for Ladies; with Hints on the Preservation, Improvement, and Display of Female Beauty*, first published in Philadelphia in 1838 and reprinted as late as 1856. *Etiquette for Ladies*, which contained several untranslated French terms and mentioned social life in Paris several times in its pages, may be a translation and American reprint of an earlier French work, as yet untraced.[30] Thus perhaps much of the advice of etiquette books on the forms of social life is best considered as an expression of the range of social and personal possibilities that ordinary Victorian Americans envisioned in the mastery of etiquette and domestic ritual. Such books represented a vision of the expressive possibilities of formal social life.

Yet etiquette books did describe at least some parlor social behavior as it really happened. The survival of large numbers of calling cards and card receivers certainly supports the particular attention devoted in these books to formal calling, an aspect of parlor ritual that had become more important in the first half of the nineteenth century.[31]

The instructions in manners books indicate that calling was considered an urban activity, since it consisted largely of brief social visits, impractical and unnecessary in small communities or among rural households. The author of *Etiquette for Ladies* explained (using the term "visit" where other books used "calling"), "Visits are a very important part of Etiquette: they are not merely the simple means of communication established by necessity, since they have at once for their object, duty and pleasure, but they enter into almost all acts of life." The author described several categories of visits: "on new-years-day," "of friendship," and the "half-ceremonious" and "ceremonious" visits of formal calling.[32] Formal calls ("ceremonious visits") were very brief. They sometimes entailed simply leaving a card and were largely a means of maintaining social acquaintance; "half-ceremonious" calls were more friendly visits. In all kinds of calls, authors informed their readers, visitors were received in the "reception room" of the house, the parlor or drawing room where the occupants of the house, usually the women, waited, occupying their time with reading or doing fancywork. Many advice authors recommended that their readers set aside regular afternoons for being "at home" to callers so as to avoid missing visits while they themselves were out calling.

The authors of *American Etiquette*, an 1886 volume that may have a more authentic "voice" than *Etiquette for Ladies* because it seems to contain fewer plagiarized passages, tried to clarify the rituals of calling by explaining them in terms of social efficiency. The "system of calls," they wrote, was "one of the necessary inventions of polite society in thickly populated localities . . . where the circle of acquaintances is large [and] less time can be devoted to each. . . . the social machinery is necessarily more complicated." The authors described a number of calling occasions, all of which were acted out in the parlor: general formal calls ("a mere device for keeping up acquaintance"); formal calls for special occasions, such as after a party; "morning," that is, daytime, calls; "evening calls," which were limited to friends of the family; "calls of congratulation"; and finally, "friendly calls," brief visits among friends.[33]

Reading about the practice and etiquette of calling, we find it difficult today to have any real sense of its nuances and meaning for participants. However, as described in *American Etiquette*, the categories of "calling" were very much like a description of the occasions on which individuals today would pick up the telephone; it seems no coincidence that the use of the telephone has been designated "calling." Telephone calls, however, can be made when the caller is in a disheveled, less-than-presentable state; parlor calls required both controlled self-presentation on the part of the caller and an appropriate setting for the recipient of the call. Calling and other parlor activities—formal receptions, tea parties, balls, and other evening gatherings that etiquette books devoted considerable space to describing—may become more comprehensible if the parlor is thus viewed as a space that contained the necessary props, held in readiness, for formality. These props offered myriad possibilities for one's temporary self-transformation into a parlor person.[34]

Around midcentury, another type of parlor social activity, the parlor pastime, developed its own genre of advice book. Parlor pastimes encompassed a range of games and activities including guessing and word games, amateur theatricals and similar entertainments, and activities that used toys and objects to amuse, instruct, and encourage conversation among both children and adults: stereopticons, scrapbooks and photo albums, and board games. Such pastime books can be grouped into two types. Dating largely from the 1850s and 1860s, the first emphasized adult activities. Some, such as Catharine Harbeson Esling's *The Book of Parlour Games*, featured old games (what may now be called folk games, such as "Blindman's Buff" and kissing or courting games) with rules set in print. They relied heavily on practical jokes and even on physical humor. Such pastimes lay outside the rules for polite deportment as outlined by manners books. Others, such as Frank Bellew's *The Art of Amusing* published in 1866, emphasized genteel theatricals but were still directed to adults.[35]

Some parlor pastime books went so far as to suggest that such activities were necessary because formal parlor entertainments were often so dull. (Fisher's diary entry comparing Philadelphia's genteel elite with the local parvenus also suggests that the lengthy and anxious preparation involved in presenting oneself in the parlor, along with the handicap of a less cosmopolitan education and worldview, was too wearing for self-made members of the prosperous middle classes.) The author of one pastime book noted, "We have seen a whole party of estimable people sit round the room for hours together in an agony of silence, only broken now and then by a small remark fired off by some desperate individual, in the forlorn hope that he would bring on a general conversation."[36] Another observed, "There are not many refined miseries keener than the sufferings of a hostess who, in the fullness of her heart or from some conventional necessity, invites a few friends to spend a social evening at her house, and as a result sees them at last seated in a dismal semi-circle, all apparently animated, or rather deadened, by a full purpose not to enjoy themselves."[37]

Whereas manners books usually described a world in which no children disrupted the smooth execution of parlor social ritual, the second type of parlor pastime book, which developed in the 1860s and 1870s, often described gatherings in middle-class households, where young and old mingled. The authors of these books suggested that such parties had long precedent: "It is a good old custom in New England, on Thanksgiving evening, for old and young to join in merry games," Caroline L. Smith, or

"Aunt Carrie," wrote in *The American Book of In-Door Games, Amusements, and Occupations* in 1873. "And now we are glad to see the same custom extends even to the Christmas holidays."[38] The games and activities described could take place whether or not visitors were present. Some were far from genteel. One game, recommended to give "life to a quiet company on a stormy winter evening," according to Aunt Carrie, was "menagerie," in which each participant was given the name of an animal to imitate on signal.[39] Along with charades and tableaux, authors also recommended arithmetical puzzles, "The Game of Twenty Questions," games of memory, and "Musical Games or Home Dancing," including versions of musical chairs.[40] Diaries sometimes confirm that adults and children amused each other with such puzzles and riddles on long evenings and also drew pictures for each other, but these activities actually seem to have taken place in rooms all over the house.[41]

Manners books and manuals of instruction for familial parlor pastimes from the second half of the nineteenth century thus described two poles of parlor social activity that correspond to the dual origins of the Victorian parlor—the drawing room and the multiuse parlor/sitting room of the hall/parlor-type house. Yet in the daily rounds of real life, use seems to have been more complicated than both kinds of advice literature suggest. Because the piano was there, parlors were the location of informal dances in the evening and of group singing (including the singing of hymns on Sunday). Because they were not in constant use, parlors were a good place for a private conversation, a solitary cry, or courting. All these activities, along with the more usual social gatherings, took place in the formal parlor of Grove Hill in Virginia, according to the memoir of occupant Lucy Breckenridge.[42]

Common and important rituals, which people had long understood as part of family and community traditions, continued to be staged in the new style of gala parlor. One such practice was the laying out of the dead for viewing. Here the room became an appropriate setting, as the most ceremonious room of a house, for a traditional ritual whose importance eclipsed that of other social ceremonies in mid-nineteenth-century parlor life (Fig. 15).[43]

The range of more lighthearted social activities, such as weddings, that were held in a family's parlor varied depending on the amount of space in the house (Fig. 16). Victorian Americans nonetheless tried to keep one room from being used daily by the family. In larger households, a formal parlor or drawing room could be devoted only to the entertainment of callers and guests; in these houses, a family sitting room served as the everyday gathering place. For example, the formal parlor of the Tucker

**Figure 15.** "Decoration of Flowers, at the Funeral of Clara Jane Treat, Residence of Dr. N. Q. Tirrell, East Weymouth. On Sunday April 16, 1876," stereograph by unidentified photographer. Courtesy, The Society for the Preservation of New England Antiquities.

**Figure 16.** "Back parlor of the Otis House, for the wedding of Mary S. Otis and Fred W. Baker, June 19, 1889," by unidentified photographer, Rochester, New York. A handwritten note on the photograph mount states "Back Parlor—married under the horseshoe—all white and green in back parlor." The open doorway offers a glimpse of the dining room, its table set for the reception afterward. Throughout the second half of the nineteenth century, weddings often took place at home. Photographs of such parlor ceremonies support the advice offered by Florence Hartley, the author of *The Ladies' Book of Etiquette* (1860): "When the wedding takes place at home, let the company assemble in the front drawing-room, and close the doors between that and the back room. In the back room, let the bride, bridegroom, bridesmaids, and groomsmen, the parents of the bride, and the clergyman, assemble. . . . then open the doors and let the ceremony begin." Courtesy, The Strong Museum, Rochester, New York.

family of Wiscasset, Maine, was the site for temperance society meetings and similar ceremonious occasions, but children were not allowed to spend time in the room unsupervised or to sit on its eight-piece parlor suite (Fig. 17).

Some houses were planned with a pair of parlors, connected by wide doorways often fitted with sliding pocket doors. In this situation, a family might have a "front parlor" or "best parlor," the most formal and showy room, and a "back parlor." The back parlor could serve as a family sitting

**Figure 17.** Richard Holbrook Tucker seated in the parlor of his house, Castle Tucker, in Wiscasset, Maine, 1894. Courtesy, Castle Tucker.

room, but the spaces could also be combined and used as one large space for the purposes of entertaining. Harriet Beecher Stowe's *We and Our Neighbors* (1875) chronicled life in a middle-class household on an "unfashionable" street in New York City and described what was probably the typical pattern of the shifting use for double parlors, from informal family space to a setting for formal calling. The protagonists, Harry and Eva Henderson, kept house with the help of a cook-housekeeper and a part-time maid, the cook's daughter. Their house had a pair of small parlors, one of which doubled as a sitting room in the afternoons and evenings. At the couple's weekly "at homes" on Thursday evenings, the doors between the parlors were opened to accommodate the larger group, the room received special decorations, a tea table was set up, and the furnishings were rearranged to encourage conversation. Eva also received occasional formal calls in the front parlor in its everyday arrangement.[44]

Even modest households could be equipped with two parlors, with one reserved for special occasions such as courting or visits from teachers. In a memoir of growing up in a Catholic family in Buffalo, New York, Alice Hughes Neupert recalled the decoration and customary use of the small front and back parlors around 1880:

> The front parlor was for state occasions only, and for entertaining priests, nuns, and important visitors such as Charles Deuther, organist at St. Patrick's Church. . . . The two front windows were hung with lace curtains and lambrequins or valances of dark red velvet heavily fringed and ornamented with long cords and tassels at the side. In each corner was a large easy chair, one with a paisley covering and the other a newer style of cinnamon brown. If you pushed a button on this latter chair, a foot stool slid out. The other corner of the room held a dark chair with a high back, upholstered with *high* green satin. It had slender arms, and we were never supposed to sit in it. There was a marble topped table in the center on which stood a carrara marble statue of "winter" . . . another little silver dish for cards and a bound book of *Great Musicians*, that smelled sort of leathery.[45]

The front parlor also contained the family's prized piano, over which hung a large print of Beethoven.

> Now the back parlor. In those days the carpeting of the double parlors was always the same, as well as the wallpapering. These carpets . . . were small patterned with dark red and yellow roses and much greenery. Because the back parlor was used more, this carpet was saved by putting a crimson colored rug with a gray border over it, which gave a cheerful aspect to the room. I remember a table cornerwise with a cover made of scarlet flannel, black fringe and black cut out dragons at each corner. This table also held a lamp and teakwood box which smelled like cinnamon and held a turtle that could move its legs. There was also a Chinese ornament made with brown and yellow shells. There were two side windows in this room hung

with straight lace curtains. In one window hung the bird-cage with a Kentucky Cardinal in it. . . . The other window held the gold-fish bowl that never contained less than four little fish flashing around. . . . In the center stood a great square black heating stove that furnished the heat for the two parlors, the front hall, and the bedroom off the back parlor. . . . One corner of this back parlor held a whatnot which was used for a bookcase. . . . On the top shelf there was a piece of amethyst colored quartz that we were never al-lowed to touch. In the corner near the dining room door was a sofa, horsehair, of course, that my mother had when she was first mar-ried. It was not large, and there was a throw over it of some kind of Roman striped material and a large yellow painted velvet pillow with yellow painted roses at each corner. . . . After supper when there chanced to be company we all went into the back parlor where the stove was. Edgar and I would take down one of Dr. Kane's books [the family owned a six-volume set titled *Dr. Kane's Trip to the Arctic*], sit on this sofa, and pretend we were looking at the pictures, but in reality we were whispering awful things about the company.[46]

This passage not only suggests the special character of the front parlor but also is rich in detail about the compromises that average families necessar-ily made in both furnishing and preserving parlors. Some furniture was so special that it had to be saved, especially if the family could not afford to replace it easily. Potential despoilers such as children were not allowed to use it.[47] Mrs. Neupert's mother, Mrs. Hughes, also had to use furniture from the early, leaner years of her marriage—the haircloth-covered sofa—to be able to furnish both parlors completely. Not only was the sofa in the back parlor older, but its haircloth was exceedingly sturdy and could withstand use by Alice and her brother; it was there they sat during parlor evenings. Mrs. Hughes also preserved the matching carpet of both parlors by protecting the carpet in the back parlor with an additional rug. Because the back parlor had the heating stove, it seems to have doubled as the ev-eryday sitting room for the family.

In some middle-class families, the parlor was reserved for special occa-sions such as Sundays or holidays, and the dining room doubled as the family sitting room. Alice Steele's memoir of her turn-of-the-century childhood in rural western Massachusetts noted that her family "lived mostly in the big dining room and between meals the dining table was used for every purpose from my school work to dress making." Even though the family had another "sitting room," it was "used chiefly for writing letters and made a nice quiet place for the baby to sleep." The parlor was preserved unused, with shades "nearly always drawn except for Sunday afternoons when the minister or my sister's beau might call."[48]

The Howard Yearick family of Konnarock, Washington County, Virginia, were Pennsylvania-Germans who moved to southwestern Virginia with a lumbering company at the turn of the century; the Yearicks also used the dining room as a family sitting room. Yearick was a boss carpenter, and the company housing for skilled workers and foremen provided both a dining room and a parlor. The Yearicks included a lounge and rocking chairs with their dining room furniture and used that room as the sitting room on most evenings. The parlor, with its Brussels carpet, sofa, and lace curtains, was reserved for special occasions such as hosting women's club meetings and displaying the Christmas tree. Portieres separated the parlor and the dining/sitting room; they were usually kept open.[49]

For some families, a "library" was the family sitting room, as in the elegant house in Hartford, Connecticut, where Samuel Clemens lived with his family between 1874 and 1891. The first floor also contained a formal parlor called the "drawing room." The Spencer family of Pittsburgh had a "library," the family sitting room, across the hall from the parlor. It gained its name from the presence, in one corner, of "built-in bookcases with drawers below them in which games were kept."[50]

By the end of the nineteenth century, families who aspired to demonstrate some level of parlor gentility but who had very little room in their households—who were living in better tenement apartments or very small company houses—still often set aside some space for the purposes of what social worker Margaret Byington called the "front room," even though this meant that precious living space was decreased or that family members had to sleep in that room (Fig. 18).[51] Byington's contemporary Louise Bolard More also described a number of parlors in respectable working-class households in her 1907 study *Wage-Earners' Budgets:* "The typical home of the wage-earners in this district is quite well furnished and fairly neat and clean. The 'parlor' is usually gaudy with plush furniture (sometimes covered with washable covers), carpet on the floor, cheap lace-curtains at the windows, crayon portraits of the family on the walls, and usually religious pictures of the saints, the Virgin Mary, or 'Sacred Heart,' sometimes a couch, and the ubiquitous folding-bed."[52]

In such crowded living conditions, elements of the recognized vocabulary of parlor furnishings often had to be adapted to signal that such a space existed. For example, convertible lounges, or flat beds disguised through

**Figure 18.** "Where Some of the Surplus Goes," photograph by Lewis Hine in Margaret Frances Byington, *Homestead: The Households of a Mill Town* (1910). Courtesy, University of Utah Libraries.

the use of "Turkish couch covers" and piles of decorative pillows, indicated the presence of a parlor during waking hours. A trade card for the Boston firm of Sidney Squires and Co., of the Squires Automatic Sofa Bed, advised, "See before buying a Parlor Bed," and the term survived well into the twentieth century in the advertising of the Kindel Bed Company of Grand Rapids, Michigan.

Other elements of parlor decor were also used in these minimal parlors, particularly portieres (door curtains), draped center tables, lounges upholstered with carpet or plush, and decoratively upholstered "fancy chairs" or rockers (Fig. 19). One 1894 photograph of a college boardinghouse room in Norton, Massachusetts, suggests how such "parlors"—special spaces devoted particularly to social ceremonies such as visiting—carved from single-room living spaces might have looked (Fig. 20).

Variations from house to house, and the labeling difficulties that sometimes accompany these variations, complicate efforts to make general statements about how middle-class parlors were used and furnished. Yet the parlor's function in middle-class households—presenting through its appearance the social identity of a family and serving as the site for domes-

**Figure 19.** Family in parlor, Rockland County, New York, by unidentified photographer, about 1895. This New York State family used a center table, a rocking chair, and an upholstered lounge to say "parlor." The halo effect was caused by the photographer's flash powder. Author's collection.

**Figure 20.** Girls' room in boarding house, Wheaton College, Norton, Massachusetts, by unidentified photographer, 1894. Courtesy, The Society for the Preservation of New England Antiquities.

tic ceremony—is not called into question. The problem, for middle-class parlor makers, was how to accommodate comfortably the various functions of the parlor when there was only one room in which the family could congregate specifically for leisure. The domestic and the formally social functions of such a room could seem quite incompatible in their requirements, resulting in a tension that could be resolved with a variety of compromises. The parlor, however it was used, was still the focal point of furnishing expenditures, and furnishing solutions depended on the calculations of desire and necessity made by each family.

# CHAPTER THREE

# "Orthodox as the Hymn Book"

## The Rhetoric of Parlor Furnishing,
## 1850–1910

No matter how a family resolved the tensions between social ideals and actual means and use of household space, middle-class parlors between 1850 and 1910 relied on certain conventions of furnishing and arrangement in order to demonstrate and proclaim a family's understanding of what a parlor was and how it was ideally used (Fig. 21). In creating such a room, a family created a rhetorical representation of itself and a statement about the nature of its relationship to cultural values as well.

Between 1850 and 1880, the recognized and ideal vocabulary of modern parlor furnishing encompassed ornate matched sets of parlor seating furniture, which might be augmented by upholstered "reception" chairs, parlor rockers, and decorative upholstered footstools. Wall-to-wall carpets and the fanciest window drapery in the house were also fundamental, as were decorative lighting devices including fancy lamps and chandeliers, center tables that had marble tops or were elaborately covered, display shelves or cabinets, pianos, mantelpieces (with large mirrors above if possible), and wall decorations, including small wall-hung decorative shelves and objects in frames. Some women's handwork was displayed, while needlework in the form of pillows, throws, and tidies (pieces of fabric intended to protect upholstery from the oil of hands and hair) contributed to the decorative effect of the upholstery. When the Fulton family of Rockport, Texas, purchased furniture for the parlor of its new house in 1876, the choices reflected typical tastes of the time: a "Fine Parlor Suite," according to the invoice, as well as two parlor rocking chairs, two "Window Chairs" for

**Figure 21.** Parlor of Dr. H. A. Tucker's summer cottage, Oak Bluffs, Martha's Vineyard, Massachusetts, stereograph, photographed and published by C. H. Shute and Sons, Edgartown, Massachusetts, about 1875. Most of the "vocabulary" of middle-class parlor furnishing is visible in this image of Dr. Tucker's parlor: parlor suite, center table, folding reception chairs, wall-to-wall carpet, fancy window drapery, piano, carpet-covered footstools, and a fancy fireplace and mantel surmounted by an elaborately framed mirror. Courtesy, The Society for the Preservation of New England Antiquities.

the bay window, a marble-topped center table, several smaller tables, and a pedestal.[1]

After 1880 a number of additional elements, many of them embellishments on earlier furnishings, became common parts of the parlor vocabulary. Often these were textile furnishings: door curtains (called portieres); myriad additional forms of semipermanent drapery (piano covers, mantel lambrequins, and fabric coverings affixed to tables—forms of "scarf drapery"); and mountains of elaborately decorated sofa pillows. Parlor organs, which were less expensive than pianos, appeared as the newest bearer of parlor musical culture. Between 1880 and 1910, parlor suites were still common, but the number of pieces offered and their importance slowly declined. Some new forms of seating furniture, such as platform rocking chairs and a new range of unusual "fancy chairs" in wicker, faux bamboo, and even metal tubing, could be purchased separately or as part of parlor suites. The purchase of fancily upholstered lounges and backless couches, which had appeared occasionally in parlors between 1830 and 1880 as parts of large expensive sets of furniture, became an increasingly important way for families of lesser means to participate in parlor making.

Communicating through parlor furnishing was a two-sided affair. In selecting and manipulating furnishings, middle-class families demonstrated their fluency with the terms of this vocabulary, and their success could be measured by the degree to which the messages of parlor furnishings were intelligible to and approved by visitors. Along with the conventions of parlor furnishing listed above, a family could include more personal objects—family photograph albums, family Bibles or gift books, or homemade objects such as needlework pictures and wax flower arrangements—to inflect the messages of their decor. These familiar things, which were missing from the gala parlors of the early nineteenth century and from the public parlors that helped shape the broad outlines of middle-class taste, communicated details of a family's particular character within that setting. Finally, other small objects—natural specimens (such as the amethyst-colored quartz that Alice Hughes Neupert recalled), paintings or prints, ceramic figures or vessels, or bibelots from foreign places—communicated further details of the cultured facade of the parlor owners (Fig. 22).

Within the range of furnishings available after 1850 that signaled the presence of a parlor, even consumers of ordinary means could create a room that emphasized the tradition of the gala apartment, the parlor as a theater of culture. French-style furnishings and upholstery, which promoted the concept of planned unified decor, were purchased by some consumers as well-understood expressions of the gala parlor. Or, through the styles of decoration and the upholstery they chose, consumers could opt to create a less ostentatious space, a comfortable parlor that expressed the middle-class ideal of virtuous civility. After 1880 some changes and additions to parlor furnishing also reflected the influence of what has been called the "aesthetic movement" in America; advocates of aesthetic furnishing urged the abandonment of what they perceived as rigid formulas for matching furnishings, including the use of a single style and a single

**Figure 22.** "Our Home. / From Samp (?) and Abbie / To Fannie Rich / Minneapolis, Minn. / Oct 8th 1878," stereograph photographed and published by M.
Nowack, Minneapolis, Minnesota, 1878. The couple in this photograph took care
to have themselves photographed as cultured people with their art corner. The
side stand, or étagère, displayed their modest library, natural specimens and other
small treasures, and a large bust of Shakespeare perched precariously on the top
shelf. The photographs displayed the couple's network of friends and kin. The
needlework match-holder shaped as a slipper, the front of the wall pocket, and
Samp's fancy slippers were probably Abbie's own work. Courtesy, Smithsonian
Institution; private collection.

color in a room, and encouraged the use of "art needlework" in portieres and other drapery. However, even though ordinary consumers were certainly interested in the aesthetic taste, the movement affected popular choices in parlor furnishing only in a few specific ways. For example, portieres did become extremely popular although in the form of factory-woven chenille or "tapestry" rather than the labor-intensive, elaborately embroidered designs recommended by advocates of aesthetic furnishing (Fig. 23). The art needlework that middle-class women turned out in enormous quantity—wall pockets, mantel lambrequins, embroidered Japanese fans, and artistic piano drapes—was also probably not exactly what aesthetic reformers had in mind. Aesthetic taste in furnishing seems not to have influenced many consumers' belief that parlor suites (the pieces of which matched by definition) were the core of parlor furnishing, nor does it seem to have altered the common use of such elements as the center table.

The eclecticism encouraged by aesthetic taste, however, well suited many aspiring parlor makers. Often families had to make do with mixed lots of furniture: out-of-date parlor suites too good to throw away, favorite rocking chairs, recovered upholstered chairs, simple wooden chairs, and recycled or homemade window curtains, table covers, and cushions. Thus, what one inexpensive advice book called the "esthetic craze" dovetailed nicely with the financial necessities of most middle-class people, encouraging them to consider miscellaneous combinations of furnishings not as the pathetic result of financial necessity but as the ingenious expression of up-to-date furnishing taste (Fig. 24).[2] In 1888 one author of furnishing advice offered this counsel to amateur decorators:

> The most popular view of the parlor is as a shrine into which is placed all that is most precious. . . . this is really the most sensible view to take. Unless one has a very large establishment it is unwise to endeavor to give a distinct style—to make out of it Queen Anne, Louis Quinze, Marie Antoinette, a reminiscence of Pompeii, or a reflection of Japan. To indulge in a date, epoch, or national idiosyncrasy in surroundings implies a purse deep enough to gratify any passing caprice. Moreover, anything of this sort must be perfectly done. . . . The safe plan is to make of your parlor a cosmopolite, equally at home with all nations and all ages.[3]

Although domestic critics carped about the impracticality and nonsensical character of much parlor furniture, some understood that the parlor was

**Figure 23.** Unidentified parlor, photographed by J. J. Henry, Chapinville, New York, about 1900. This modest room contains a factory-woven chenille portiere, long sheer curtains, and the settee from a parlor suite. An older piece of furniture, the settee carried a message about proper parlor deportment in its formal lines, which were disguised with piles of soft cushions—a transitional moment in the gradual change to less-controlling forms of seating. Courtesy, The Strong Museum, Rochester, New York.

the most artificial—that is, the most cultural—space in houses and that its furnishings expressed in rhetorical fashion both aspects of sensibility and ideals of social relationships. Ada Cone, a contributor to *Decorator and Furnisher* in 1891, understood the power of parlor furnishing conventions even as she disapproved of many of them. In "Aesthetic Mistakes in Furnishing—The Parlor Centre Table," she wrote:

**Figure 24.** Parlor of the Osborne house, Victor, New York, about 1895. The parlor was decorated for the first time in around 1870. This photograph, of the room as it looked twenty-five years later, shows how one family updated good, but out-of-date, furniture by adding many small items of drapery and new accessories. Courtesy, The Strong Museum, Rochester, New York.

It cannot be contended that because a few persons of taste have disgarded it, it is therefore out of fashion, it is an institution, as orthodox as the hymn book. It is practically universal; in expensive as well as in humble houses [it is] still the objective point and the *pièce de résistance* of the room. . . . The fact that this piece of furniture holds so tenaciously its place, though contrary to convenience and taste points to an ideal in furnishing the parlor other than that of convenience and taste.[4]

Cone's comment indicates the degree to which parlor making was heavily burdened with conventions by the 1890s. Between 1830 and 1880, commercial parlors taught aspiring consumers something about modern parlor furnishing and "parlor gentility." Beginning in the 1870s, furnishing advice books, many with a didactic "household art" focus, proliferated. They were directed at those consumers who already had furnished their homes but were ready for a change in style, especially if that style carried connotations of particular sophistication on their part. However, just as these authors of sophisticated architectural and furnishing advice urged readers to abandon the parlor for the "living hall" or "living room," other titles—such as those published by Henry T. Williams in the late 1870s and Orange Judd and Co. in the 1880s—addressed a different audience, one still interested in learning the standard conventions. These advice books were written to teach brand-new consumers what they should wish for. Williams outlined the typical contents of a parlor for his readers:

> The regular suite of parlor furniture consisting of chairs, table and sofa is generally accompanied by piano with its stool and stand for music, *etageer* [*sic*], ottomans, and various knick-knacks or *bric-a-brac* as these are now termed; also pictures, brackets, tasteful wall-pockets perhaps, and the mantel which is now almost a piece of furniture, while the windows are draped as has been suggested, those who can procure them will find a charming natural adornment for simple muslin or lace curtains, in Ferns, Ivy-sprays, and other woodland productions.[5]

At the turn of the century, mail-order catalogs also introduced new consumers to the vocabulary of parlor furnishing, both through the typologies of merchandise they presented in their pages and through the concise statements of standard decorating advice they offered in their descriptions of curtains, carpets, and furniture. *Sears, Roebuck and Co. Catalogue No. 104, 1897* was filled with furnishing advice for its rural and small-town audiences, not only in the choices offered but also in tidbits that could be gleaned from the hours spent poring over the printed descriptions. At "Rattan Chairs," the aspiring parlor maker learned that rattan was suitable "for parlor or library at all seasons of the year" and that "odd pieces" (chairs, shelves, and small tables that did not match the rest of the room's furnishing) were "sought after more largely than ever." A caption under "Princely Parlor Furniture" informed readers that the "prevailing style in furniture" was "to have the various odd pieces upholstered in harmonizing colors of different shades," although the same text also offered to send matching sets.[6]

The conventional elements of parlor furnishing contributed in several ways to the rhetorical statements that the complete room setting was capable of making. For example, objects containing imagery or mottoes provided obvious clues to a family's values. Engravings of cultural heroes at critical moments in their lives or in typically instructive moments, such as the common prints showing George Washington, Abraham Lincoln, and other statesmen as good family men, made such statements. The parlor of Alice Hughes Neupert's German Catholic family contained an engraving of Charles I going to his execution (an appropriately pious and popular Catholic historical subject) and, over the piano, a scowling portrait of Beethoven, indicating both the family's interest in music and their Germanic identity.[7]

Some objects that had no narrative content were also quite readily understood as symbols because of their use (as well as their obvious expense in some cases). Pianos suggested hard-won, usually feminine accomplishments and the family's appreciation of music. Even unopened elaborate family albums suggested the owners' ties to a network of other like-minded individuals and documented the bonds of sentiment, and their plush covers and ornament signaled the value placed on those ties.

Other parlor furnishings operated as symbols even less directly because they worked at the level of sensibility, shaping sensory experience. Settees and the various types of chairs offered cues about seated posture and deportment, suggesting the appropriate character of parlor social life. Carpets hushed the sound of footfalls and helped to muffle other sounds (a quality that received special notice from authors describing commercial parlors), further distinguishing the room from the noisy bustle of everyday life. While the layers of draperies on parlor windows helped to preserve other furnishings from light damage, they also shaped the sensory experience of parlor life. Blocked and partly absorbed by draperies, light spread unevenly over objects and, broken into patches of light and dark, became the colored light of refined parlor sensibility. Lace curtains preserved privacy while admitting a filtered daylight appropriate to parlor people, who found it "unpleasant to have the full glare of sunlight streaming through the apartment."[8]

The center table, which Cone described as the pièce de résistance of typical parlors, is an example of the ways in which symbolic meanings are crafted from the conjunction of necessity and desire in furnishing practices.[9] In a world where artificial light was precious, and was provided for most families by kerosene lamps rather than municipal systems, parlor center tables were the location of the brightest pool of light in the room and the most decorative lamps. They were an obvious gathering place after dark for families whose budgets required thrift in the use of lamp fuel. However, the image of gathering around a table was also an old and powerful visual trope symbolizing the close ties and unity of purpose for voluntary associations, and tables in portraits were also associated with scholarly study. Tables draped with "Turkey work" carpets in portraits from the seventeenth and eighteenth centuries displayed wealth in the form of textiles. In the Christian context, draped tables also were related to the iconography of the Last Supper, representing here the ceremony as well as the unity of religious belief. Draped tables, located in the front of churches, were the location for the sacrament of communion. Center tables were shrines within the ritual space of the parlor; they were the site of carefully edited selections of familial possessions—family Bibles, other important books (including family albums, which both organized family pictures and made them historical by encapsulating them in a book), calling card baskets, and a miscellany of other items such as stereoscopes. Thus the image of the family gathered closely together around the closed circle of the center table symbolized the ideal of middle-class family life.

The cover of the center table elaborated the ceremonial character of the table for the parlor's important social rituals. A table cover could qualify any table for center table use, even one that was roughly made or damaged. By being voluminous and elaborate in its design, the cover emphasized the importance of the table. If handworked, the table cover both reflected a woman's accomplishments in the household and further emphasized the table as the focal point in the room. Just as the health and happiness of the domestic world required constant embellishment and attention to detail, so the presence of objects that represented hours of that attention, especially ornamental needlework, signaled the watchful care of family members, particularly women. Overtly religious artifacts, such as wax crosses under glass domes, in and around the center table cued the association of religion and home, an aspect of the middle-class conception of comfort. In time, this relocation of religion into the home evolved into a kind of secular equation in which the religion was of the family itself. In the vocabulary of parlor furnishing, the center table with its decorative drapery and its selection of valued objects expressed this most profoundly.

In the last quarter of the nineteenth century, some advice writers on domestic interiors were so familiar with the common equation of the parlor and the shrine that they could treat the formulation ironically, as Cone did in her discussion of the center table as a "mistake" of parlor furnishing. Shrine building continued in more than one location in the parlor, however. As Abbie and Samp's self-portrait (Fig. 22) suggests, "art corners," decorated mantels, draped shelves, and small tables could also become secular shrines dedicated to the values of cosmopolitan culture, the other axis of parlor values made manifest in furnishings. The displays of exotica, souvenirs, minerals, and books on the étagère of the Hughes parlor in Buffalo formed the family's own modest shrine to culture.

The "culture" pole of values reflected the best qualities of civilized living in the domestic world, a hierarchy of value that could be represented in microcosm by the parlor's refinement, its highly artificial quality, and paradoxically, its connection with (and control of, through consumption) the cultural goods of the world outside its walls. Here the parlor and its contents became a memory palace for the best aspects of the world outside. Étagères, hanging shelves, piano tops, and the art corners of the 1880s and 1890s were miniature museums. Textile furnishings reinforced the cosmopolitan, gala ideal in two ways. They contributed to the cultured facade of the room through historical revival styles, particularly French design. Second, they functioned as metaphors for popular understanding of civilization's action on human character. Textiles influenced the sensory character of the parlor, affecting vision and tactile sensation in particular and softening the world of sensation overall. They obliterated the edges of hard furniture surfaces and mediated, through structural padding, the contact of the body with seats. Heavy door and window curtains muffled sound, softened light, and enhanced domestic quiet. Thus textiles represented the softening benefits of civility, which was evidence of the progress of civilization.

Once aspiring parlor makers owned the appropriate trappings for a modern parlor, they faced another challenge. In order to be considered genteel, a parlor person was required to be comfortable with the manipulation of the furnishings of the room, to demonstrate the ability to pick up the cues offered by their appearance. Pianos, paintings, furnishings—in theory, all these offered opportunities to communicate in ways that other parlor people could appreciate. This shared self-display among appreciative peers was the essence of gentility in the parlor, but mastering the requirements for self-presentation was difficult enough that thousands of Americans seem to have turned to etiquette books for advice.

Although eighteenth-century English guides to conduct had suggested that gentility was not a closed stratum of society but a set of standards for living, the idea that gentility was a potentially inclusive standard found its fullest expression in American manners advice books.[10] Becoming genteel by dint of personal effort was a corollary to the American belief that individual economic progress was possible. The titles and opening pages of inexpensive etiquette books quickly suggested to browsing shoppers or casual readers that do-it-yourself gentility was possible. Arthur Martine's *Handbook of Etiquette, and Guide to True Politeness* (which sold in 1866 for fifty cents) billed itself as "A Complete Manual for Those Who Desire to Understand the Rules of Good Breeding, The Customs of Good Society, and to Avoid Incorrect and Vulgar Habits," whereas the first sentence of

*Decorum* (1881) promised, "High birth and good breeding are the privileges of the few; but the habits and forms of the gentleman may be acquired by all."[11]

Several serious, unresolved tensions are evident in the explanations of etiquette and parlor behavior promulgated by manners books published well into the 1870s. What historian Karen Halttunen has termed "sentimental culture"—middle-class culture in the first decades of what we call the Victorian era—valued sincere emotion and believed in the importance of mutual correspondence between feelings and behavior. But etiquette books argued that deep feelings were inappropriate to the parlor and required restraint in their expression. To succeed in the domestic theater of the parlor, parlor people had to be models of self-control, able to conduct their self-presentation with disciplined restraint of both feelings and body. A parlor person knew how to enter a room, how to sit gracefully, how to control the hands and feet, and how to modulate the voice. "Let your carriage be at once dignified and graceful," Florence Hartley wrote in *The Ladies' Book of Etiquette, and Manual of Politeness* (1860). "To sit with the knees or feet crossed or doubled up, is awkward or unlady-like. Carry your arms, in walking, easily; never crossing them stiffly or swinging them beside you. When seated, if you are not sewing or knitting, keep your hands perfectly quiet. . . . Never gesticulate when conversing; it looks theatrical, and is ill-bred; so are all contortions of the features."[12] Physical self-control was to be accompanied by control of the feelings. *Etiquette for Ladies*, a manners book that was plagiarized a number of times in the nineteenth century, warned: "Excessive gaiety, extravagant joy, great depression, anger, love, jealousy, avarice, and generally all the passions, are too often dangerous shoals to propriety of deportment. . . . It is to propriety, its justice and attractions, that we owe all the charm of sociality."[13] The restrained physical self was meant to be the harmonious expression of restrained parlor feelings.

The popular belief that anyone could learn perfect politeness created problems, however, because taken to its logical extreme, it suggested that the socially polished legions could contain multitudes of bad but very mannerly people.[14] Authors of etiquette books tried to circumvent this inconsistency by developing a "sentimental typology of conduct" that insisted that true manners were sincere, true intentions were always legible, and insincere manners could be detected.[15] They also took care to identify a second, negative pole of parlor etiquette. Authors of manners books warned their readers to avoid manners that were slavish in their adherence to fashion, hence ridiculous and "affected." "Looking, speaking, moving, or acting in any way different when in the presence of others," Florence Hartley wrote in *The Ladies' Book of Etiquette*, "especially those whose opinion we regard and whose approbation we desire . . . , is both unsuccessful and sinful." Not only was it hypocritical, and hence sinful, but affectation exposed its perpetrator to contempt because it was "the false assumption of what is not real."[16] Insincere manners were not heartfelt, nor were they consistent in their efforts at civility. "A well-bred gentleman or lady will sustain their characters as such at all times, and in all places—at home as well as abroad," one 1857 volume advised. "If you see a man behave in a rude and incivil manner to his father or mother, his brothers or sisters, his wife or children . . . you may at once set him down as a boor, whatever pretensions he may make to civility. Good manners should always begin at home."[17] In sum, middle-class manners were to be sincerely felt, moderate and controlled in their forms of expression, and representative of a consistent method and point of view for interacting with the world.

The nineteenth-century thinking that identified two poles in etiquette—the "sincere" manner as opposed to the empty forms of affected and insincere etiquette—had already appeared in discussions of manners in the eighteenth century, both in England and on the Continent. The dichotomy developed first as part of the European rhetoric of middle-class self-definition. Sociologist Norbert Elias has argued that *civilisation*—the process of improving standards of education, behavior, and economic growth by which human society progresses—emerged from the courtly ideal of the "civil man" or "man of honor," a term that members of the French courts used to describe and distinguish themselves from the rest of the rude, uncivil populace. The "courtly bourgeoisie," those members of the French middle classes involved with the administration of the regime during the second half of the eighteenth century, further developed the concept.[18] Members of these middle classes joined members of aristocratic classes in the social and intellectual life of the salons of Paris. To these bourgeois thinkers, the process of "true civilization" contained, in addition to increasing means and refinement in knowledge and behavior, one other component—"the ideal of virtue." Members of the courtly bourgeoisie claimed virtue was essential to a true understanding of the concept of civility. Virtue, they also argued, was a necessary attribute of character among members of their own class. Without virtue, all forms of civility were empty and false. To Elias, the concept of true civilization was the way in which the middle class could define itself in relation to an aristocratic society whose behavior and customs it did not necessarily respect but did not completely reject.

A similar process of middle-class self-definition was occurring in seven-teenth- and eighteenth-century England—and also in its Anglo-American colonies. The middle-class model of civilized behavior separated the forms of manners—etiquette—from a general code of behavior that could be developed in children through example and the cultivation of childhood proclivities. In "Good Manners" (1711), Jonathan Swift characterized the distinction: "I cannot so easily excuse the more refined critics of behaviour, who having professed no other study, are yet infinitely defective in the most natural parts of it. . . . On the other hand, a man of right sense has all the essentials of good breeding, though he may be wanting in the forms of it."[19] England's bourgeoisie was larger and its society more fluid; however, it still created a set of distinctions between the "fine gentleman of intellectual and social accomplishment," whom contemporaries identified as having strongly continental, especially French, origins, and its own version of true, virtuous civility—the "Christian gentleman."[20]

In America, etiquette books employed the distinction between fine and virtuous manners to somewhat different ends than in England. In the political culture of the United States between 1790 and 1850, this set of distinctions was a counterpart to debates about republican virtue, and it was used both to identify the desirable characteristics of republican citizens and to ferret out real or imagined threats. Controversy and debate centered on perceived connections between economic and political systems. Jeffersonians tried to establish a link between republican virtue and agrarian life and used the squalid conditions of the English industrial working class as evidence that industrialization was one more threat to the ability of Americans to govern themselves.[21] Followers of Alexander Hamilton, on the other hand, argued that only through manufacturing could the nation and its government become independent and wealthy enough to survive.

Sincere manners were appropriate to republican America and compatible with a number of other American characteristics, including political virtue, self-sufficiency, and virtuous, self-disciplined consumption. Empty and affected social forms were associated with servility and moral ruin, just as an unhealthy dependence on and infatuation with fashion, particularly European luxury, inevitably led to financial ruin. Thus, a family's life always contained, in microcosm, the risk of the larger cycle of rise and decline of an entire civilization. But like the American republic, virtue could enable both the individual and the nation to be free from what seemed an inevitable cycle. The unresolved tensions in parlor etiquette, between the demands of etiquette's forms and the desire to appear natural and sincere, resonated with an entire structure of thought about the nature of, and threats to, American virtue. This thinking dominated discussions of art and architecture in the first decades of the republic but also focused on the concept of "fashion."[22] The relationship among virtue, fashion, and luxury in the realm of manners and household consumption provided the stuff of debate in women's periodicals and manners books for decades. Manners that were merely fashionable were not republican manners. Consumption that was predicated only on fashion's dictates was equally suspect.

The discomfort that authors of middle-class etiquette books expressed about the relationship of manners and character was related to another rhetorical position in the popular literature of household consumption and furnishing, domestic economy, and sentimental fiction. Just as manners demanded sincerity in self-expression, "sentimental fashion"—the representation of middle-class sincerity in women's clothing—argued that "dress was an index of character" and identified "sincere" and "insincere" modes of dress.[23] However, the search for sincerity extended beyond dress because the possibilities of middle-class purchasing power increasingly included fashionable household furnishings. According to Lydia Sigourney, the author of *Letters to Mothers* (1838), "Simplicity of taste, extending both to dress, and manner of living, is peculiarly fitting in the daughters of the republic."[24] It was not simply fitting but absolutely essential, because "home and its virtues" were considered "the great conservative influence to which especially our country is to look for its security against anarchical disorder." Home provided the "best support" for the values on which a republic was particularly dependent.[25] Yet the parlor was a source of temptation located inside the household because, in its guise as a gala apartment, it was particularly vulnerable to fashion's unholy sway.

A debate about the appropriateness of middle-class and aristocratic forms of parlor making in America—their etiquette, their furnishings, and their corresponding degrees of comfort—grew out of both the "mixed ancestry" of the parlor that Edith Wharton and Ogden Codman Jr. acknowledged in their 1897 volume *The Decoration of Houses* and the rhetorical demands for "sincerity" in furnishing. The descendants of the eighteenth-century drawing rooms of the beau monde were the decorated spaces that middle-class domestic critics would later label "aristocratic." Unlike sitting rooms, these parlors were not homey, nor were they meant to be used in the family's moments of private leisure. Rather, their formal, matched furnishings—expensive, specialized accessories in sets such as mantel garniture and candelabra, large suites of furniture, elaborate upholstery, and examples of the fine arts—were symbolic of a more formal, even ceremonious, function and character. They were the theatrical settings for the fine gentleman and his feminine counterpart, the lady of fashion.

In American cities, cosmopolites who continued to model themselves on the eighteenth-century English and French beau monde participated in a genuine social "season," marked by a full round of balls or "routs," receptions, and card parties. In their parlors, as one late 1820s American reprint of an English etiquette book stated, "the graces of social intercourse" were "chiefly displayed," and the furnishing of such rooms was supposed to reflect the tone of the social life conducted there— "light and elegant."[26] Thus the gala parlor continued to be identified with aristocratic or courtly taste in parlor furnishing. The view of a "New York Merchant's Parlor" in an 1854 issue of *Gleason's Pictorial Drawing-Room Companion* (see Fig. 4) represents a typical "aristocratic" version of the parlor ideal at midcentury; its caption suggested that the room, owned by "one of the most eminent of our merchants, . . . looks like a fitting abode of a man of refinement—a drawing room where a lady of elegant manners and educated tastes might appropriately receive her guests."[27] (It is no accident that, from its carpet to the chandelier, the room was furnished in the most flamboyant expression of the "French taste," including both rococo revival and "French Renaissance" furnishings.)[28]

In the gala parlor, manners, humanistic education, and habits of consumption were united because the concept of civilized living contained, by implication, the ideal of enlightened consumption. Material possessions not only were props for the social life of gentility but became outward expressions of inner gentility. This equation first appeared in eighteenth-century France. As Rosalind Williams has noted:

> To many enlightened thinkers of the eighteenth century, it seemed
> self-evident that enlightened consumption—patronage of the arts,
> the vivacious conversation of the salons, collection of paintings and
> books—was a necessary means to the advancement of civilization.
> With a little mental effort the habitues of the salons could equate
> their concrete social pleasures with the highest and most abstract
> social goals. The nature of "the civilizing process" remained mixed
> and ambiguous, a blend of idealism and materialism. In the eigh-
> teenth century the idea of civilization referred both to a general
> social and political ideal and, more narrowly, to a comfortable way
> of life reserved for the upper classes.[29]

The same patterns of thought that associated consumption with quality in the eighteenth century could be applied to other groups entering the arena

of consumer culture in the nineteenth century. If possessions could be outward expressions of the civility of the courtly world, they could also become the outward mark of middle-class virtue—if middle-class people did
not succumb to the temptations of fashion. Fearing the dangers that social
ambition contained for middle-class people, advice writers promoted a
vision of parlor life that was in opposition to the parlor of gentility, that
instead stressed moderation and family closeness. The engraving of Abraham Lincoln's parlor published by *Frank Leslie's Illustrated Newspaper* in
1860 is an emblem of the middle-class model of parlor furnishing, modest
in ambition and appropriate for thrifty consumers with middling incomes
(Fig. 25). Its publication suggested that knowing the room was crucial to
knowing the man.

Since the ideal of virtue was an aspect of middle-class identity, any vision
of appropriate middle-class consumption had to stress virtue. The origin
of middle-class ideals of etiquette may lie in European society of the eighteenth century, but the vision of middle-class consumption seems, naturally enough, to have found its fullest expression in the middle-class century, the nineteenth century, and in the world's most middle-class nation,
the United States. It appeared among members of the middle classes who
did not have a permanent aristocracy of birth against which to react but
who still fretted over the possible attractions of aristocratic fashion and its
potentially debilitating effects on republican virtue. Middle-class ideals of
appropriate etiquette and consumption forced a redefinition of the character of the parlor in the mid-nineteenth century. For much of the American
middle class, parlor life emphasized modest consumption and self-control.
It took place too in a narrower social world—among members of a family
and its intimate friends rather than among the select company of social
peers.

This middle-class vision of the parlor as the location for a family-
centered social life grew not only from a distinctive view of consumption
but also from the intersection of a number of circumstances of daily living
in Anglo-America. Historian John Cornforth has suggested that in the second half of the eighteenth century, England experienced the rise of a more
home-centered culture among the well-to-do, both middle-class and gentry. In these years a new realm of domestic ritual developed among the
gentry—calling, family dining, and intimate musical evenings rather than
large-scale entertainments. Some English families of means displayed an
articulated preference for "homey" interiors at the end of the eighteenth
century.[30]

Cornforth has connected the informal style of domestic comfort that
came to characterize interiors in country houses during the first half of the

**Figure 25.** "Front Parlor in Abraham Lincoln's House, Springfield, Ill.—
Sketched by Our Special Artist," engraving in *Frank Leslie's Illustrated Newspaper*,
1860, reproduced in Peter Thornton, *Authentic Decor* (1984). In the article that
accompanied this engraving, a reporter for *Leslie's* observed: "The house in which
a man of mark dwells is, like his handwriting, interesting, as to a certain degree
indicating his character. The sitting-room and parlor of Abraham Lincoln, in his
house at Springfield, are . . . simply and plainly fitted up, but are not without indications of taste and refinement." Courtesy, Viking Penguin, a division of Penguin
Books USA Inc.

nineteenth century to the taste for country life among the well-to-do, for
whom family activities at home formed the center of social life as opposed
to the public socializing that took place in London during the social season. For those who could afford it, city houses provided the family's beau
monde facade while the country was where one was really at home. However, it would be erroneous to suggest that the homey parlor was a phenomenon simply of country living among the well-to-do. Such "homey"
parlors were already in existence among middle-class families with adequate but more limited incomes on the Continent as well as in England.[31]
Not having the resources for gala rooms, or the cosmopolitan social life
that required them, ordinary families had always experienced even their

most public rooms as multifunctional, family spaces. Such rooms were formal on one occasion, less formal and more familial day by day. The homey interiors of English country houses may simply have provided additional confirmation of the desirability of "hominess"; bourgeois necessity may have intersected with new genteel preferences.

However, in the American context, middle-class hominess took on a unique and highly charged character because of the association of middle-class virtue with the future of the republic. The rhetorical banner under which the debate about domestic virtue took place was the concept of "comfort." At midcentury, the champions of comfort were domestic advisers and critics, mostly women whose outlets were nationally circulated periodicals and books of household advice and sentimental fiction. Their discussions not only claimed that comfort was appropriate for middle-class people but also contended that only people unblinded by the demands of fashion could understand the concept. Caroline M. Kirkland, author of *A Book for the Home Circle* (1853), staked out a typical position on the topic:

> Comfort is one of those significant and precious words that are apt to be much abused. It is so comprehensive that people try to make it everything, just as "religion" has been stretched to cover the burning of heretics, and "justice" the gratification of vindictive feelings or the vices of envy. It is so good a word, in its true character, that none but honest and true people can use it with propriety. It is, by tacit consent, banished from the vocabulary of Fashion; and if Ambition should make a dictionary, Comfort would find no place in it. The French, who are lovers of *pleasure*, have been obliged to transplant our word *comfort* bodily into their language, as they had before naturalized a correlative word—*home*, after they had adopted the idea. Strange that we, proud as we are of our right to it, should ever misuse it.[32]

By contrasting "comfort" and "fashion," Mrs. Kirkland suggested that comfort was both permanent and rational, whereas fashion was transient and capricious. By opposing comfort to "Ambition," she suggested that comfort was the stable, modest, and true result of self-knowledge. The very concept of comfort also was Anglo-American. Comfort was not the unrestrained "pleasure" of the French, who were the epitome of fashion, who were unhomelike, and who were, therefore, uncomfortable.

In ordinary middle-class households, American advisers charged, parlors conceived along the lines of the merchant's parlor illustrated by *Gleason's* were inappropriate for middle-class living. Such parlors were too formal for daily use, wasted family resources better spent on books and other tools for family education, exhausted middle-class housekeepers with their maintenance requirements, and restricted normal family living to one or two downstairs rooms in houses. In their most extreme criticism, they argued that the parlor of fashion damaged the formation of youthful character.[33]

The negative effects of parlor making on domestic comfort were often explored in what may be termed "moral tales of furnishing" in popular books and magazines. In these stories, which were by turns wryly humorous or earnest and overwrought, domestic critics often attacked specifically the vocabulary of fashionable parlor furnishing as the public understood it and offered the middle-class "comfortable" parlor as an appropriate alternative. Harriet Beecher Stowe, the most famous of the sentimental domestic writers, drove home the message of middle-class comfort many times in the course of her long career. One of the most striking forums was a series of columns, *House and Home Papers*, published under the pseudonym and in the narrative voice of a man, "Christopher Crowfield." Throughout the text, Stowe critiqued certain parlor furnishings as symbols of fashion and suggested that even innocent ambition led to wasted money, energy, and family happiness.

In the humorous opening story, "The Ravages of a Carpet," the Crowfield family was introduced to the reader in its homey but well-worn parlor. The family spent comfortable evenings there reading, sewing, or talking with friends who casually dropped in; the children played games with each other and with their pets. These evenings were disrupted, however, by the purchase of a brand-new Brussels carpet in a vivid floral print. The new prize made the rest of the furnishings appear even more shabby, and a general redecoration, done with the aid of a fashionable upholsterer, ensued. The effects of this change were disastrous:

> In a year we had a parlor with two lounges in decorous recesses, a fashionable sofa, and six chairs and a looking-glass, and a grate always shut up, and a hole in the floor which kept the parlor warm, and great heavy curtains that kept out all the light that was not already excluded by the green shades.
>
> It was as proper and orderly a parlor as those of our most fashionable neighbors; and when our friends called, we took them stumbling into its darkened solitude, and opened a faint crack in one of the window shades, and came down in our best clothes, and

talked with them there. Our old friends rebelled at this, and asked what they had done to be treated so, and complained so bitterly that gradually we let them into the secret that it was the great south-room which I had taken for my study, where we all sat, where the old carpet was down, where the sun shown in the great window, where my wife's plants flourished and the canary-bird sang, and my wife had her sofa in the corner, and the old brass andirons glistened and the wood-fire crackled,—in short, a room to which all the household had emigrated.[34]

The Crowfield family's new parlor was shut up, an unused, unwanted room that served as a daily reminder to the family of the follies of fashion and social convention. As Stowe described it, middle-class comfort had no facade; middle-class people, because they were naturally sincere, did not need to present a different public face to society. Her contention that the contents of the homey middle-class parlor reflected the family in its true character articulated an alternate conception of room decor, one that contrasted the parlor as a material reflection of fashion and gentility with the room as a reflection of middle-class character, empty rhetoric versus sincere statement.

Other moral tales of furnishing were less good-natured, however, often conveying the message that consumption in the pursuit of fashion could and did lead to financial ruin, the tragic separation of families, and permanent damage to young, impressionable family members. In "Furnishing; or, Two Ways of Commencing Life," which appeared in *Godey's Lady's Book* in 1850, Alice B. Neal contrasted the parlor furnishing decisions of two young women to compare their moral characters. Neal's abbreviated descriptions of the two models of parlor furnishing suggested that her middle-class readers already knew something about the debate between the tendencies to create aristocratic versus domestic parlors and that they knew both models well enough to be able to picture for themselves the settings, completing in imagination what was only sketched in the text.

"Furnishing" contrasted the consumption habits of two cousins as they prepared to begin married life. The profligate and fashion-conscious city cousin, Adelaide, had an unlimited budget with which to purchase furnishings for her parlor. Without looking elsewhere, she selected its contents from the warerooms of George J. Henkels of Philadelphia, who we know was also supplying furniture for palace hotels. The country cousin, Anne, who was soon to marry a poor young doctor, had only six hundred dollars (still a tidy sum) to purchase the entire contents of her house. She shopped carefully, comparing the prices at Henkels's (the site of her first expedition, undertaken with Adelaide) with the more reasonable prices for furnishings offered at smaller, less fashionable establishments.

Adelaide, whose taste followed the aristocratic ideal, chose a rosewood parlor suite with black and crimson silk damask covers, tables with Siena marble tops, an étagère, and a velvet carpet. Anne, whose tastes represented solid middle-class comforts, opted for a three-ply tapestry carpet, a single sofa instead of a suite, an "octagon center table" (emblem of her soon-to-expand family circle), and "mahogany chairs with cane seats" which were expected to wear well. Needless to say, Adelaide and her new husband, George, began their marriage on a standard of living that they could not maintain; George was eventually forced to sell the house and its contents and leave for California to begin life anew. Anne took in the bereft Adelaide, who, seated at her cousin's side on one of the mahogany chairs at the octagonal parlor table, before George sent for her to join him, gradually learned to appreciate the true meaning of domestic life.[35]

On occasion, Stowe could be equally hyperbolic in her condemnation of the parlor of fashion. In another of the *House and Home Papers*, titled "Home-Keeping vs. House-keeping," Christopher Crowfield described how the family of an old friend was destroyed by the burden of caring for possessions, especially a fashionable parlor containing furniture covered in "garnet-colored satin" and "heavy, thick, lined damask curtains, which look quite down to the floor." Since they had been a gift, these furnishings did not strain the couple's finances; still, the marriage was ruined and the dispositions of the couple's children became embittered because "social freedom" had been "crushed under a weight of upholstery."[36]

The prescription for avoiding the moral and social disasters of fashionable furnishing was the necessary symmetry of economic resources and desire. In her *Domestic Receipt Book*, written for "young and inexperienced housekeepers," Catharine Beecher advised that good taste, "that nice perception of fitness and propriety which leads a person to say and do whatever is *suitable* and *appropriate* in all possible circumstances . . . leads a woman to wish to have her house, furniture, and style of living, in all its parts, exactly conformed to *her means*, and *her situation*."[37]

Symmetry also required the consistent, orderly application of means to situation along rational principles. A woman with "good sense and good taste," Beecher noted, "will not, while all that is *in sight* to visitors, or to out-door observers, is in complete order, and in expensive style, have her underclothing, her bedroom, her kitchen, and her nursery ill-furnished, and all in disorder. She will not attempt to show that she is genteel, and belongs to the aristocracy, by a display of profusion, by talking as if she was indifferent to the cost of things, of by seeming ashamed to economise." Like the inconsistent man, cited by etiquette writers, who treated his family badly while displaying fine manners to outsiders, the woman who attended only to a family's public face showed herself to be a "vulgar, unrefined person."[38]

The authors of midcentury architectural advice books oriented to middle-class families made a point of concurring with the conceptual symmetry of means and situation. In *Village and Farm Cottages* (1856), Henry William Cleaveland and William and Samuel D. Backus urged the housewife to avoid the "folly of imitation." They wrote, "Good sense, good taste and good morals alike repudiate the paltry vanity which furnished a house not for its constant occupants to use and enjoy, but for occasional visitors to look at and admire."[39]

Keeping up with fashion reduced homeowners to being "only exhibitors" in their homes. Worse yet, the financial strain destroyed the carefully prescribed boundaries between the domestic realm and the heartless world of commerce. Almira Seymour noted, "Volumes might be written on the moral effects upon character of the home of assured comforts held in unquestionable possession, however simple in its details, compared with palatial show-rooms held by a more-or-less uncertain tenure, in the midst of which the husband knows no rest from pecuniary anxieties, and is constantly tempted into the business-gaming risks of the present; where the wife is overburdened with cares in which the heart has no place."[40] As Emma Wellmont warned her audience, consumption that, by offering employment to artisans, was "commendable in a millionaire" was imprudent for those who had "only a comfortable competence." She noted, "We regret to add, the definition of this distinction often introduces imitators into a labyrinth of trouble, from which it is hard to become extricated."[41]

Finally, attaining true comfort required more than avoiding the allurements of "the absurd demands of ever-changing fashion."[42] Those who would seek true comfort also had to avoid the misapprehension that comfort was simply a physical state, the "consolation" of the "mortal frame." Mrs. Kirkland and other conservative middle-class domestic critics questioned the evidently popular preoccupation with bodily comfort, demonstrated at least in part by the efforts of thousands of aspiring inventors of furniture, heating and lighting devices, and other ingenious domestic improvements.[43] The critics alleged that increasing affluence, invention, and acquisition threatened the necessary and fundamental opposition between comfort and fashion, and they tried to guide women toward a middle way, toward appropriate levels of domestic consumption and domestic comfort. This middle way had to be carefully monitored. Kirkland suggested that "making present gratification [of sensory desires]" one's most important concern had a "hardening effect" on character.[44]

To these advisers, comfort was a moral condition with requirements like those of sincere etiquette. Seymour made the connection explicit when she argued that making a home truly comfortable demanded "that sublimest and most saving of all heroism,—*perfect sincerity*."[45] Unfortunately, knowing how much physical comfort was too much was very much like walking the fine line between natural and affected manners. As Kirkland warned her readers, "We are all more or less disposed to self-indulgence, and as some amount of it is proper enough, it is not always easy to determine where right ends and the wrong begins."[46] Middle-class people in the world of increased creature comforts were not expected to abjure all its facets but to select carefully and not neglect the inner person.

If parlors were the rooms in a home most apt to mirror fashion, upholstery in that room was particularly prone to manifest this capriciousness. Among domestic critics, upholstery became a critical benchmark in the effort to define the material limits of middle-class comfort. The fashionable upholsterer interpreted new, usually foreign fashions in room decor and supplied these expensive conceits to frivolous consumers. He was to "dressed" rooms as the fancy dressmaker was to women, pandering to their most fickle impulses.[47] Moreover, although upholstery was the most important element in setting the tone of a room, its expense and comparative impermanence also disturbed advocates of thrift. In their attribution of moral content to furnishing, Cleaveland, Backus, and Backus charged upholstery with "dishonesty," especially in the innovation of spring seating (Fig. 26): "Even the hardest and homeliest bench that was ever made of oak plank, is a more comfortable and more respectable article of furniture than many of the spring-seat and hair-cloth sofas and rocking-chairs, which we have met with,—soft plump and elastic to all appearance, but which when we, in good faith, accept their invitations, let us down with a sudden jerk, and make us painfully acquainted with their internal mechanism."[48]

Not only was parlor upholstery dishonest, but its transitory character broke the chain of domestic associations that made household furniture truly comfortable. In "The Quaker Settlement," chapter 13 of *Uncle Tom's Cabin*, Stowe compressed both of these criticisms into a brief passage describing a pair of rocking chairs: "a small flag-bottomed rocking chair, with a patchwork cushion in it, neatly contrived out of small patches of different

**Figure 26.** "Solid Comfort. No. 25," illustration in Clarence Cook, *The House Beautiful* (1878). As Cook's caption suggests, the equation of fashionable uphol-stered furniture with dishonesty continued in design reform or "aesthetic" advice literature in the 1870s. Courtesy, The Strong Museum, Rochester, New York.

colored woollen goods, and a larger sized one, motherly and old, whose wide arms breathed hospitable invitation, seconded by the solicitation of its feather cushions,—a real comfortable, persuasive old chair, and worth, in the way of honest, homely enjoyment, a dozen of your plush or broca-telle drawing-room gentry."[49] Some authors argued that a transient existence in constantly changing fashionable "theaters" such as hotels damaged "that strongest bond of society, the power of association."[50] By extension, the fashionable furnishings of hotel interiors and elite parlors could have a negative impact on individual morals and, ultimately, on the national character.

Even though parlor making was not just a phenomenon of big cities (because it was a middle-class activity), the authors of moral tales of fur-nishing repeatedly suggested that rural people were the bastion of true comfort, just as they were the source of republican political virtue (Fig. 27). Some authors simply compared city and rural people, as Neal did in

**Figure 27.** "A New England Fireside," engraving in *Ballou's Pictorial Drawing-Room Companion*, March 10, 1855. The anonymous author of the article accompanying this illustration described this scene as the "interior of a good old-fashioned New England homestead, many of which yet exist, remote from cities and large towns, in all their primitive purity and attractiveness." The author added: "We do not look with jaundiced eyes upon a brilliant ball-room, crowded with graceful forms . . . —but it is a relief sometimes to turn away from the contemplation of the highest social refinement and splendor, and see how comfortable and happy people may be with a few wants and no luxuries. From such firesides great and noble men and women have gone forth into the world." Courtesy, The Winterthur Library: Printed Book and Periodical Collection.

"Furnishing." Other "comfort theorists" used the plot device of rural people lured by city fashion as a way to demonstrate the folly of fashion and the solidity of rural comfort.

An example of this formulation of "city fashion, rural comfort" may be found in *The Widow Bedott Papers*, a series of comic "letters," dialogues, and stories in the popular literary genre known as "Yankee papers," published serially in the mid-1840s.[51] The Widow Bedott, a simple but ambitious woman who had always lived on farms, snared a second husband in the form of a Baptist preacher, the Reverend Sniffles. The reverend resided in a distinctly unfashionable parsonage. After their triumphant honeymoon tour through various rural outposts in upstate New York, the new Mrs. Sniffles began a campaign to update the house, declaring, "'Tain't fit for ginteel folks to live in." When the reverend protested that he had always found the house "very comfortable," Mrs. Sniffles displayed her understanding of the material signs of respectable parlor life, information gained by visiting parlors made by neighbors who had New York City contacts. The widow's misguided preference for gentility over comfort, for novelty and fashion over the sturdy antique, provided a humorous lesson for middle-class readers.

> Comfortable! who cares for comfort where gintility's consarned! *I* don't. I say if you're determined to stay in it, you'd ought to make some alterations in't. You'd ought to higher the ruff and put on some wings, and build a piazzer in front with four great pillars to't, and knock out that are petition betwixt the square room and kitchen, and put foldin' doors instid on't, and then build on a kitchen behind, and have it all painted white, with green winder blinds. *That* would look something *like*, and then I shouldent feel ashamed to have ginteel company come to see me, as I dew now. . . . I say we'd ought to have new furnitur—sofys and fashionable cheers, and curtains, and mantletry ornaments, and so forth. That old settee looks like a sight. And them cheers, tew, they must a come over in the ark. And then ther ain't a picter in the house, only jest that everlastin' old likeness o' Bonyparte. I'll bet forty great apples it's five hundred years old. I was raly ashamed on't when I see Miss Curnel Billins look at it so scornful when they called here. I s'pose she was a counterastin' it with their beautiful new picters they're jest ben a gittin up from New York, all in gilt frames.[52]

Through such fiction and essays, domestic critics argued that the courtly parlor, a public facade contained within a family's dwelling, was inappropriate for middle-class people, whereas the homey parlor of comfort, the parlor without a facade, reflected the best qualities of family life. They encouraged simplicity and sincerity in both parlor furnishing and parlor social life and the judicious, moderate acquisition of material goods rather than the heedless pursuit of fashion. They also argued that parlor display did not create true parlor people, an argument that the presence of parlors in commercial spaces everywhere contradicted by inviting participation. Critics' arguments disregarded a set of cultural priorities that gave birth to these models, among them the perceived need to set aside a space for social ceremony. For consumers with the means and space, the way to give both social ritual and family life their due was to have both kinds of rooms, a "best parlor" or "drawing room" where they could express their hard-earned, hard-learned parlor selves, and a sitting room for their more private, familial selves.

# CHAPTER FOUR

# Bodily Comfort and Spring-Seat Upholstery

In the decades when domestic advisers were claiming comfort as a middle-class state of mind, a condition of internal and external harmony created through the symmetry of modest economic means and modest desires, the public at large was experimenting happily with a number of inventions designed to increase bodily comfort, inventions that these same critics considered of dubious value on moral and symbolic grounds. For example, architectural and domestic advice books voiced a common litany against parlor stoves, which made rooms considerably warmer and less drafty than did open fireplaces. The authors disliked parlor stoves at least partly because of the symbolic meanings attached to the open hearth. Lewis F. Allen, author of *Rural Architecture* (1852), described an airtight stove in a farmhouse as "looking black and solemn as a Turkish eunuch upon us, and giving out about the same degree of genial warmth as the said eunuch would have expressed had he been there." Allen added, "A farmer's house should *look* hospitable as well as *be* hospitable, both outside and in, and the broadest, most cheerful look of hospitality within doors, in cold weather, is an *open* fire in the chimney fireplace."[1] The fireplace was "intimately con-nected with our ideas of domestic comfort," a symbol of family togeth-erness (literally so, when the hearth was packed with individuals struggling to keep warm).[2] Its replacement by the parlor stove seemed to signal a devaluation of family life.

As we have seen in the debate over the definition of comfort, these same critical voices found current fashions in furniture, particularly in the parlor, too "prinked up," to use Allen's words, too "gingerly," and "fatal to domestic enjoyment." Some singled out modern upholstery for special abuse. Concurring with the authors of *Village and Farm Cottages*, who considered "the hardest and homeliest bench" as "more comfortable and more respectable" than modern haircloth-upholstered furniture, Allen found "positive comfort" in a seat "by the wide old fireplace, in the common living room, comfortably ensconced in a good old easy, high-backed, splint-bottomed chair" (see Fig. 26).[3]

At the same time that Allen offered his opinions on true comfort in seating furniture, American inventors patented a number of improvements in the physical support offered by both beds and seats through the use of resilient structures that incorporated coil springs or metal strips held in tension. Simultaneously, American upholsterers adopted new European techniques for building and fastening together increasingly deep layers of traditional stuffing materials. Even when resilient spring structures were applied to chairs that were in no way designed for seated comfort as we know it today, popular understanding seems to have been that these innovations were the newest and therefore best way of making comfortable seating furniture.

At first, spring-seat upholstery was expensive to produce because of the materials and skilled labor it required, but it became so desirable that a market for cheap versions seemed guaranteed. In the second half of the nineteenth century, particularly after 1870, large upholstery shops and manufactories explored a variety of production alternatives to reduce the cost of spring-seat upholstery, efforts that will receive further analysis in chapter 6.

However, much upholstered seating furniture made between 1850 and 1910 does not fit modern ideas about comfortable seating. Today, seating furniture that fulfills the definition of a comfortable chair for home (as opposed to a comfortable chair for the office, for example) typically has one or more of the following characteristics. It is upholstered, especially where it is in contact with the hips, the thighs, and the back. It has a resilient structure, which now often consists of foam (introduced as early as the 1930s but uncommon for several decades) but which, until the 1950s, almost always consisted of an internal structure of springs and layers of stuffing held in tension. An analysis of the human body has affected the structure of the chair frame itself in some cases, whereas other specialized chairs, called "loungers," are adjustable, allowing reclining as well as upright postures. However, the most popular "comfortable" furniture allows users to adjust their postures without changing its form. It permits sitting with feet curled underneath the body, sitting slumped, and lying down. In fact, some pieces of furniture are so large and soft that it is difficult to sit up straight in them with one's feet on the floor.

Broadly, the trend in popular upholstered furniture between 1850 and 1930 was toward types of seating that we might consider comfortable today, although such furniture did not commonly enter the ordinary parlor until the 1920s. This evolution can be traced in the illustrations in this chapter and chapter 6, which offers an account of the development and decline of the parlor suite and the upholstered lounge. Overstuffed chairs with spring seats, and perhaps spring backs or wire frames, were still expensive and unusual in the 1850s and 1860s. Such chairs represented tours de force of American upholstery skills and were exhibition pieces, such as the "Turkish faulteuil [*sic*]" covered in "white brocade silk" displayed at the New York Crystal Palace in 1853.[4] Over the next three decades, similar chairs were introduced in factory upholstery catalogs, often as single reading chairs, and "Turkish" overstuffed suites were one middle-class alternative, albeit a rarely used one, for parlor furniture by the late 1870s. By the 1890s, much upholstered seating furniture was less posture controlling and larger in scale than typical parlor chairs made twenty years earlier. However, this trend was slow and uneven, and changes in consumption are difficult to chart. Individual households seem to have placed types of upholstered furniture in specific settings, with more "comfortable" chairs and sofas placed in libraries or sitting rooms and the furniture we now consider stiff and uncomfortable in parlors. Just as families used parlors in different ways and varied the standard vocabulary of parlor furnishing to reflect personal preference, so too attitudes about what constituted comfortable seating and where it properly belonged differed. With the introduction of popularly priced "davenport" sofas in the 1910s, seats we now consider comfortable were included in the middle-class parlor, contributing to its transformation into the modern "living room."

This changing preference in upholstered seating also was influenced by a range of social and cultural customs and constraints that varied by room, by the demands of etiquette on social ritual, by the restraints on posture and movement imposed by dress, and by the impact of gender roles on furniture use. In these contexts, furniture that seemed to invite relaxation was not always relaxing. Observing structure and form to deduce how furniture was used may not provide accurate indications of how it was actually used. Like the parlor itself, upholstered parlor furniture had a mixed ancestry. Its functions were not defined by utility alone but expressed long-standing notions about the symbolic functions of seats. Some chairs, such as parlor reception chairs, were never meant to be comfortable; instead they were props for social ceremony—rhetorical devices. They signaled a family's knowledge of social conventions and represented the absent, but expected, guest. Parlor seating furniture also communicated the ability to consume and the status associated with this ability, whether "genuine" or merely claimed.

The decorative covers of chairs were one way to make these rhetorical statements. Historically, richly decorated chairs, which had embroidered seats and fabric-covered legs and arms or were draped with "chair cloths" or padded with elaborate cushions, were concrete symbols of wealth and indicators of power in Europe.[5] Between 1100 and 1500, when most furniture was rough and when fine possessions were necessarily portable, such chairs were "seats of authority," emblems of power and precedence in households. Seats of authority were signaled by their raised position on a dais, by the presence of backs and arms, and by the use of ornamentation, particularly textile coverings that were either part of the permanent construction or were a type of temporary drapery that might even include a canopy. Originally, chairs that were permanently upholstered with fabric were padded no more than were saddles; the upholstery trade originated with saddle-making (Fig. 28). Cushions might have been added to such chairs as a concession to physical comfort, but they were not critical to the symbolic status of the chair as an adjunct of state.

By the seventeenth century, upholstered chairs had evolved into a variety of forms, and well-to-do households might have had many chairs with upholstered seats and backs, particularly the type known now as "farthingale chairs." Still, the symbolic roots of these chairs lay in the idea that textile-covered chairs were emblems of status. Ownership of many such chairs was a new expression of wealth made possible both by economic and commercial development leading to the growth of cities and by the end of the political necessity for large households to move and transport valuable possessions frequently.[6]

The "reception chairs" commonly found in nineteenth-century parlors seem to recall the old symbolic function of chairs with decorative upholstery. Ostensibly reserved for formal social occasions, reception chairs did not match other parlor chairs. Their elaborate frames and covers often combined more than one fabric, multicolored trims, and decorative needlework including beading and tufted Berlin work that would have been destroyed if the chairs had seen much use (Fig. 29). Reception chairs were Victorian adjuncts of state; their intricate appearance and accepted function embodied one more metaphor for the cultural function of the gala parlor.

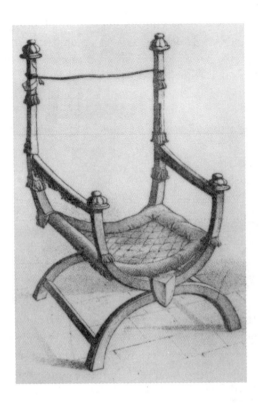

**Figure 28.** Armchair at York Minster, illustration in George Ayliffe Poole and J. W. Hugall, *York Cathedral* (1850), reproduced in *Furniture History* 7 (1981). Courtesy, The Furniture History Society, London.

Thus upholstered chairs were always props for symbolic behavior, whether political or, by the eighteenth century, social ideals. In the eighteenth century, beautifully carved chairs with seats upholstered in haircloth, moreen, or damask served as symbols of another kind of power, the social power of the beau monde of gentility. Their forms and decoration made manifest ideas about the character of cultivated social life in the salon and signaled the presence not only of money but also of new forms of cultivated taste. All the furnishings of salons—writing tables, cabinets for display of small treasures, bookcases—represented in their forms and ornament a vision of graceful social interaction based on personal cultivation and on manners and deportment that were polished yet effortless.

This "easy manner" was part of the behavioral typology of gentility. According to the *Oxford English Dictionary*, the word *ease* may mean the "absence of pain or trouble" and a condition of rest that is "comfortable, luxurious, quiet." However, being "easy" is not a condition of unself-conscious relaxation; rather, the "easy manner" was characterized by freedom from "constraint or stiffness; chiefly of or in reference to bodily posture or

**Figure 29.** Reception chair, walnut, wool rep and Berlin work, United States, 1865–75. Courtesy, The Strong Museum, Rochester, New York.

movements. Also *transf.* of manners and behavior; Free from embarrassment or awkwardness."[7] Thus the easy manner of gentility was one in which genteel behavior was second nature, in which deportment was characterized by effortless self-control. Its ideal was embodied in the social interactions of the salon, where cultivated minds, graceful deportment, refined manners, and beautiful settings and furnishings were in perfect correspondence. When we study eighteenth-century "conversation pieces" or portraits of gentlepeople, the postures depicted are upright and dignified but not stiff (Fig. 30).[8] The "easy" posture was not unconstrained; in fact, the heavy shaping of garments aided proper deportment. Women's corsets kept their postures straight, and the vests and coats of gentlemen were tai-

**Figure 30.** *The Samels Family,* oil on canvas by Johann Eckstein (1736–1817), United States, 1788. Erect posture, with the sitter's back held straight and away from the chair's back, was an important expression of genteel deportment reinforced by the structures of ladies' corsets and skirts and men's tightly fitting formal waistcoats. Courtesy, Museum of Fine Arts, Boston; Ellen Kelleran Gardner Fund.

lored so tightly that they helped shape their wearers' postures into a characteristic "S" curve. In their portraits, these epitomes of gentility often sit away from the backs of chairs, yet they seem comfortable and in harmony with their settings. The carved chair backs seem to be a decorative element in a composition of the seated person and the chair.[9]

Whatever they symbolize when unoccupied, chairs are most expressive in a context of use, where they are part of a communicative unit including the culturally shaped body and deportment of the sitter and his or her dress. Any examination of physical comfort in seating furniture must take into consideration this social and cultural dimension, not necessarily clear in even a close scrutiny of the form of the chair apart from its context of use. For example, posture had long been considered one indicator of rank and character. In medieval Europe, posture and bearing, as well as clothing, helped distinguish a person of rank. The world of gentility in the eighteenth century continued to employ a version of the historical connection between deportment and social rank, but deportment now signaled personal cultivation and was a critically important component of education.[10]

As we have seen in the advice on deportment published after 1850, the Victorian ideal of bodily self-control in the parlor still relied on the older conception of the "easy manner" of gentility, even though advice offered to middle-class people was given a different cast, and made more confusing for would-be parlor people, by the demand that their behavior be sincere. The sheer number of rules articulated by advice authors suggests that enterprising, self-improving individuals in quest of proper deportment faced a daunting task in their effort to appear both sincere and cultivated. Authors of etiquette books still argued that the correct use of chairs, props in the theater of the parlor, should display both graceful, easy, and genteel deportment and, by extension, the character of the sitter.

Florence Hartley, author of *The Ladies' Book of Etiquette, and Manual of Politeness* (1860), urged her readers to "let the movements be easy and flexible, and accord with the style of a lady."[11] This ease, however, required extraordinary control of the voice, feet, hands, arms, and posture. Hartley did not automatically equate such labored composure with artificial manners. The goal was self-mastery so flawless that it became second nature. In the interim, as would-be gentlepeople learned etiquette, they had both to act naturally and to guard constantly against displaying ill-breeding, a painful exercise at best (Figs. 31 and 32).[12]

The structure of parlor furniture could play an important role in advancing or sabotaging the efforts of parlor people to communicate their gentility through their deportment. Miss Eliza Leslie advised her readers to avoid purchasing sofas and chairs with "high and narrow" seats and backs that "incline forward," for "they allow little more than their edge to the sitter, who is also obliged to keep bolt upright, and remain stiffly in the same position."[13] A preference for chairs with slanted backs was not meant to imply that complete relaxation was permissible: Leslie also urged caution in sitting in rocking chairs. "Swaying backwards and forwards in a parlour rocking chair," she wrote, "is a most ungraceful recreation, particularly for a lady . . . and very annoying to spectators, who may happen to be a little nervous."[14]

Other advice authors also warned readers against the temptation to relax completely in the parlor, even if the room was provided with furniture that seemed to invite repose. Men were cautioned, "Lounging on sofas or easy

**Figures 31 and 32.** "Ungraceful Positions" and "Gentility in the Parlor," engravings in Thomas E. Hill, *Hill's Manual of Social and Business Forms* (1885). Author's collection.

chairs, tipping your chair back on two legs, throwing your leg over your knee, or sitting in any unnatural position—these habits are always considered indecorous, and when ladies are present are deemed extremely vulgar."[15] Hartley advised: "Avoid lounging attitudes, they are indelicate, except in your own private apartment. Nothing but ill-health will excuse them before company, and a lady had better keep [to] her room if she is too feeble to sit up in the drawing-room."[16] Popular fiction sometimes used the deportment of characters as a clue to their personal strengths or failings. In *High Life in New York, by Jonathan Slick, Esq.* (1854), Slick's parvenu cousin, Mrs. Beebe, exposed herself as a fraud not only by her "puckered up" appearance (she was adorned with ruffles, false hair, and a corset so tight that her waist "warn't any bigger round than a pint cup") but also by the affected, romantically languid way in which she sat in a parlor rocker: "She sot down in one of the rocking-chairs and stuck her elbow on her arm and let her head drop into her hand as if she warn't more than half live."[17] Finally, along with the ability to imply genteel ease, erect posture was sometimes claimed to be essential to proper health. "Lounging, which a large number of persons indulge," and sitting "with the body leaning forward on the stomach, or to one side, with the heels elevated to a level with the head" was not only exemplary of bad manners but "exceedingly detrimental to health."[18]

Parlor etiquette tamed human behavior by binding it within certain boundaries. As parlor furnishing evolved, the forms of some upholstered furniture—lounges, couches, and parlor rockers in particular—created potential new sources of confusion about parlor deportment. In the 1880s and 1890s, new fashions for "Turkish" furniture, particularly low couches, apparently presented parlor people with unanticipated deportment difficulties that some periodicals tried to assuage with advice such as "How to Sit on a Divan."[19]

The requirements of deportment aside, even with the gradual trend between 1850 and 1910 toward seating furniture that modern eyes can recognize as comfortable, another set of constraints on posture and seated comfort existed that affected women alone. Products of the centuries-old practice of corseting and using padding and frames for skirts in undergarments, these strictures were designed to create fashionable body shapes and to aid deportment. Throughout the nineteenth century, the elaborate structure of undergarments compelled middle-class women in full dress (that is, in the clothing they would have worn for social occasions and in public) to limit their range of movement, constrained their ability to interact with furnishings, and harnessed their experience of their bodies in social settings.[20] The presence of corseted women in social situations served not only as a statement about fashion but also as a bodily metaphor for the larger setting of parlor social ritual. Women, the conservators of culture, experienced bodily constraints that were analogous to the restraining morals and manners of civilized living.[21] At least one nineteenth-century commentator noted a direct and necessary connection between corseting and morals: "It is an ever present monitor indirectly bidding its wearer to exercise self-restraint; it is evidence of a well-disciplined mind and well-regulated feelings."[22]

The degree and kind of encumbrance offered by women's underclothes varied as fashions changed. In the 1850s and 1860s, wide skirts with stiff crinolines and hoops made contact with chair backs and sitting in chairs with full arms difficult. From this problem arose the parlor suite convention of the "ladies' chair." Although their legs were freed and their corsets were relatively short, women would have found it difficult to assume a relaxed posture in a full crinoline or "cage" (a petticoat stiffened by metal or whalebone hoops). Drawers, loose-fitting underpants with a split in the middle, were still not a universal element of women's dress in 1850. Crinolines contributed to their acceptance.

Wide hoops disappeared by the mid-1860s, but cages for skirts continued to be used through the 1880s, for evening wear in particular. They were augmented by another form of encumbrance, the bustle, which survived in one form or another into the 1890s. Although ladies' chairs in parlor suites appeared through the 1870s, there seems to have been little real correspondence between the forms of upholstered parlor furniture and the advent of the bustle in women's clothing. Bustles first appeared as simple tie-on pads stuffed with horsehair or down or made from several ruffled layers of horsehair fabric. As the draping of women's derrieres became more elaborate, large bustle structures, with a metal framework, were necessary. Like hoops, large bustles made sitting back in chairs difficult at best, inspiring a number of inventors to patent folding bustles. An advertisement for Taylor's Patent Folding Bustle, a contraption of tensile steel bands, included a telling "before-and-after": "Once she had to sit down this way" (showing a woman teetering on the edge of a chair because the large stiff bustle under her dress prevented her from moving back in the seat) "but now she wears Taylor's Patent Folding Bustle" (showing the same woman, now resting her back against the chair).[23]

Unlike the full skirts of midcentury, the longer, narrow lines of dresses that appeared in the 1870s and again at the turn of the century required the use of very long corsets. Fashion advisers never discussed the simple logistical problems of negotiating one's way through the world laced tightly from sternum to pubic bone, but advertisements for corsets sometimes indicate that the simple act of sitting, bending, or lounging could result in broken corset boning (and certainly abdominal bruises) (Fig. 33). Thus women were offered products such as the "Pearl Corset Shield," which the Montgomery Ward and Co. catalog for the fall and winter of 1894–95 noted "prevents corsets breaking at the waist and hips. . . . Will protect the body from the ends of broken stays."[24] Between 1870 and 1910, the "relaxed" pose of a fully dressed, corseted woman was one in which she rested her stiffened torso sideways against the corner of a sofa or propped her upper back (at the shoulder blades) against the back of a chair. "Turkish" overstuffed furniture, especially large, deep "pillow-back" chairs, must have presented particular challenges. And, as clothing historian Cecil Saint-Laurent has observed, just as overstuffed lounges and davenports became truly popular between 1900 and 1914, corsets reached their greatest length and "strangled" women "from the shoulder to the thighs."[25]

**Figure 33.** Advertisement for "Flexible Hip Corset," engraving in *Edward Ridley and Sons' Catalog and Price List Fall and Winter 1882–1883* (New York). The caption guaranteed that a purchaser's money would be refunded if the corset "breaks over the hips"—that is, if the boning of the corset snapped when the wearer sat down or bent over. Courtesy, The Strong Museum, Rochester, New York.

The limits a fully dressed woman experienced in her ability to sit in a relaxed manner suggest that certain kinds of upholstered chairs, particularly the various forms of reclining and adjustable chairs, were sex-specific in their use, whether they appeared in parlors or in other rooms. Advertisements for the Marx Patent Folding Chair, a popular and well-publicized recliner of the 1880s, show only men enjoying the chair's "Solid Comfort." Of course, women were not always fully dressed in their layers of chemise, drawers, corset, crinolines or bustle, and petticoats. Those who did their own housework or outdoor chores were less encumbered by necessity, and women who had servants also wore morning dresses that permitted "half-corsets" and no bustles. Parlor social life required full dress, however, a process of adornment onerous enough that etiquette books urged women to set aside one morning each week for receiving callers if "home duties make it inconvenient to dress every morning to receive visitors."[26]

Reconstructing patterns of use and meaning associated with upholstered parlor furniture is made more complex by technical and technological developments in the craft of seat upholstery during the second half of the nineteenth century. By 1850, parlor seating furniture was almost always made with layered seat structures containing stuffings of horsehair and plant materials (tow from the waste of flax, dried Spanish moss and "sea moss," wood shavings, and cotton batting) underpinned by a layer of metal coil springs held in tension by tying them together and to the chair frame. Spring-seat upholstery changed the design of chairs because of the depth needed for the upholstered structure and the tension it put on frames. It required new skills on the part of upholsterers, set off a spate of new patents for furniture, and created a new sector of the furniture trade in spring manufacture. Spring seats also appear to have had an impact on popular thought about how bodily comfort in seating furniture might best be achieved. The seats were not an inevitable result of efforts to attain greater bodily comfort in furniture but represent a particular culture (European and Euro-American) and its singular technological solution to a perceived need. How that need was articulated and where spring-seat structures first appeared in ordinary furniture also provide some clues to changing popular thought about individual entitlement to certain kinds of comfort and about how such comfort might best be achieved.

Upholstered furniture provides bodily comfort through its resilient padding. Until the advent of foam upholstery, this padding was a "sandwich" of layers of stuffing and fabric held together and on the chair frame with stitching, ties, and tacks or staples. The history of chair upholstery techniques can be described briefly as the story of craftspeople's efforts to stuff more, thicker, and more resilient fillings into the upholstery sandwich contained within and wrapped around the frames of seating furniture. Until the advent of spring-seat structures, all upholstered furniture had "dead seats," seats that did not have the elasticity of interior springs.[27] Any resiliency that dead seats provided was the result of the natural elasticity in materials, as in the "give" of wadded or curled animal hair or the woven webbing attached to the underside of the seat frame. The stuffing material was stitched into place, and an undercover of cotton or linen was generally fastened to the seat frame. The decorative fabric selected for the chair was then cut and sewed and tacked into place (Fig. 34).

Although the layers of padding in upholstered chairs certainly mediated the contact of the sitter with the chair frame and provided more warmth than wood alone, most structural upholstery (as opposed to cushion seats) was stuffed to be quite firm rather than luxuriously soft. This was even the case with most pleated tufting in America until the end of the nineteenth century. Because stuffing in the arms and backs of chairs tended to get lumpy, upholsterers used tied stitches like those in simple unquilted comforters to hold the layers in place. Sometimes the stitches were passed through the cover as well and became a decorative element in the chair; thus they were forerunners of decorative button tufts.[28] The other type of early padded upholstery, the loose or cushion seat (also called a "squab"), sat on top of the chair seat and was a type often used by amateur upholsterers in the nineteenth century.

By 1830, upholsterers in Europe and America began to offer their customers the innovation that had the single greatest impact on the construction of upholstered furniture in the nineteenth century—the use of coil springs in seat structures. An 1822 patent taken out by Viennese upholsterer George Junigl stated that his "improvement on contemporary methods of furniture upholstery . . . by means of a special preparation of hemp, with the assistance of iron springs" resulted in a structure "so elastic" that it was "not inferior to horsehair upholstery," which set the standards for resiliency.[29] Coiled springs had appeared in a piece of furniture more than seventy years earlier: the "Chamber-Horse," an exercise apparatus, had been advertised by Henry Marsh in the *London Daily Post and Advertiser* in 1739 and 1740.[30] This early use was isolated, however, and seems to have had no real impact on the upholsterer's craft at the time.

Construction of upholstered furniture became more complex and difficult to master as a craft with the adoption of springs, which changed the structure of the upholstery sandwich dramatically. Spring tying was a tricky proposition, as it is still, and early efforts probably failed frequently, with

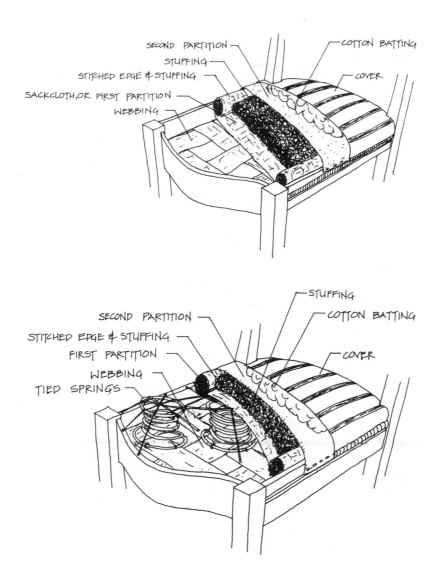

SECOND PARTITION

STUFFING

STITCHED EDGE & STUFFING

SACKCLOTH, OR FIRST PARTITION

WEBBING

COTTON BATTING

COVER

SECOND PARTITION

STITCHED EDGE & STUFFING

FIRST PARTITION

WEBBING

TIED SPRINGS

STUFFING

COTTON BATTING

COVER

**Figure 34.** Cross sections of a dead seat and a spring seat. A typical dead seat is composed of several layers: a platform of interwoven strips of linen or jute webbing, nailed to the underside of the chair frame; a piece of closely woven cotton or linen that keeps the stuffing from falling through the webbing; an edge roll, stitched in place to keep the seat edge from breaking down; a stuffing layer, called a "cake," of curled horsehair or less-expensive plant material; and a cotton undercover. In spring seats of good quality, the spiral springs first were sewed to the webbing; they then were lashed in place in a state of tension with twines. Fabric was fastened over the tied springs. Drawings by Cory Jensen.

the springs exploding out of the seat frame or even cracking it. The first chair springs were made from copper, but that metal did not retain its resiliency long enough. Tempered steel eventually supplanted copper, but it also created problems. Apart from rust, which could eventually damage the twines, the first steel springs had an alarming tendency to break from brittleness caused by improper tempering. These difficulties contributed to the suspicion among critics that spring-seat upholstery was "insincere." In 1877 the authors of *Suggestions for House Decoration in Painting, Woodwork, and Furniture* still protested against the "'grins and grimaces' of modern upholstery," praising the softness of "honest horsehair and feathers" over "iron springs," which, they argued, were "always out of order"; "their anatomy" could not be "readjusted without the intervention of the manufacturer, by whom alone the complexity of their internal structure is understood."[31]

Coil springs applied to furniture were introduced to Anglo-America in the late 1820s and early 1830s. John Claudius Loudon, author of the influential *Encyclopedia of Cottage, Farmhouse and Villa Architecture and Furniture* (first published in England in 1833), illustrated a spiral spring and explained its use in carriages and seats, but he devoted most of his discussion to its benefits in mattresses.[32] Indeed, before 1850, most American furniture patents that incorporated springs in furniture focused on the eternal human quest for a good night's sleep. Bedsprings were efforts to replace rope-bottom beds, which required frequent adjustments to prevent mattresses from sagging in the middle; tying the ropes required so much strength that advice books such as *The Workwoman's Guide* recommended that women not tackle this chore without masculine help. Some early bedspring patents offered woven-wire bed bottoms or variations much like the structure of trampolines, which used small coil springs to hold fabric tautly in bed frames.[33] Bedsprings were expected to provide even bodily support and to require little maintenance. At a time when bedbugs were difficult to control, such bed bottoms also were easier to keep clean.

Like their English counterparts, many of the first American patents exploring the use of springs in chairs described the benefits to invalids. Springs were expected to support bodies more evenly, and the inventors' specifications also recalled the provision for exercise that had been incorporated in the eighteenth-century chamber horse. Daniel Harrington's 1831 rocking chair patent incorporated springs to provide a "rocking and rolling motion," an "improvement for giving motion or exercise to invalids in their room of confinement."[34]

In their attention to the needs of the sick, these early chairs incorporating springs also reflected another of the historical circumstances that traditionally fostered upholstered seating furniture before the nineteenth century. In the houses of prosperous Americans in the seventeenth and eighteenth centuries, completely upholstered chairs such as wing chairs were typically reserved for the comfort of ill or aged members of a household. Such chairs featured both padding and particularly supportive framing that not only blocked drafts but also allowed weak sitters to lean to one side. On occasion, these invalid chairs were adjustable and sometimes seem to have served as chamber potty chairs. Peter Thornton has noted that the earliest adjustable chairs "seem to have been those derived for some illustrious invalid." Upholstered chairs with reclining backs also were used in the chambers of pregnant women by the middle to late seventeenth century.[35]

Providing the most physically accommodating and warmest seat in the house for people with special physical needs remained one of the motivations for owning certain kinds of upholstered chairs throughout the nineteenth century. Loudon equated the provision of certain "comfortable easy chairs" with the care of the aged and infirm. He even suggested that families of limited means might provide an easy chair by tying homemade back and seat cushions to ladderback arm chairs.[36] Upholstered chairs that were adjustable continued to signal the presence of illness as much as the desire for relaxed comfort. In the 1880s the manufacturers of the Marx adjustable chair still advertised the product both as a chair for invalids and as a dandy reclining chair. In early twentieth-century Pittsburgh, the Spencer family's reclining chair was known to the children as the "sick chair."[37]

In the 1830s, advertisements for American upholsterers called specific attention to the spring-seat chairs they offered. The first form widely and specifically advertised as such was the "spring-seat rocking chair," which appeared in upholsterers' notices as early as 1829.[38] At first, such "spring seats" appear to have consisted of a spring-filled, stuffed, and covered wooden frame that could rest on a board seat in a Boston-type rocking chair. Several of these early rocking chairs that survive bear the labels of the Boston upholsterer and furniture merchant William Hancock. Advertisements for upholsterers in the Boston and Philadelphia city directories as early as 1831 called particular attention to "Patent Spring Seat Rocking Chairs" and "Boston Spring Seat Rocking Chairs."[39] Incorporating spring structures into rocking chairs was a natural development from the early interest in spring structures as aids for invalids; rocking chairs too were associated with the ill or aged members of households in the eighteenth and the first half of the nineteenth centuries and were an inexpensive alternative to fully upholstered wing chairs. Later in the century, rocking chairs still served as invalid chairs in special circumstances. In a memoir of growing up in the 1870s near Corning, New York, Jane Williams Insley recalled days spent at a sanatorium called "The Pinewoods" as a guest of the doctor's children. The dining room was furnished with "Boston rockers, instead of straight chairs" for the accommodation of the patients. "When the patients ambled in, they sat down in the rocking chairs and then utterly relaxed, their heads hanging down from limp necks."[40]

At around the same time that these early spring-upholstered rockers appeared, springs were incorporated into special, personal chairs, such as the singular painted Windsor-type armchair now in the collection of the Metropolitan Museum of Art (Figs. 35 and 36). Dating from around 1830, it has a drawer under the seat, a writing arm, and a box-framed, spring-filled cushion seat that rests on top of the board seat. "Spring seat sofas," which were sold separately as special seats that could double as beds in emergencies, were another type of such upholstery specifically mentioned in advertisements in the 1830s.[41]

By the mid-1830s, upholstered sofas and chairs containing springs did not always signal illness or age. In the 1840s, upholsterers dropped specific mentions of spring-seat upholstery from their advertisements, probably because the technique was becoming commonplace for some types of seats. Thus, spring-seat upholstery, like upholstered chairs in general, gradually became a middle-class decency. To this end, an anonymous contributor to Edwin T. Freedley's *Philadelphia and Its Manufactures: A Hand-Book* (1858) singled out spring-seat upholstery as a particular sign of change and progress in ordinary furniture: "The Cabinet-making business has very much progressed, both in point of taste and extent of production, the last few years. In 1840 there were but few Furniture stores in Philadelphia, and they mostly small ones. . . . A Spring-Seat Sofa was then a luxury—almost a novelty."[42]

There is no single explanation for the change in the sense of entitlement on the part of ordinary people to certain kinds of bodily comfort, a change signaled by the rapid acceptance of spring-seat furniture in the second quarter of the nineteenth century. We know very little about what ordinary people thought about the matter. However, Loudon's 1833 *Encyclopedia* may serve as one early benchmark of a new attitude toward bodily comfort. Upholstered furniture, both with and without springs, played a key role in Loudon's discussion of cottage interiors for workers. He devoted considerable space to describing inexpensive sofa beds that could serve for both sitting and sleeping in cottage parlors. Loudon deemed ownership of a sofa in particular "a great source of comfort" and argued, "The cottager ought to have one as well as the rich man."[43] Advertisements and advice

**Figure 35.** Armchair, mahogany, wooden inlay and painted decoration, embossed wool plush, probably by Boston, Massachusetts, manufacturer, after 1828. The board seat on this chair is low, suggesting that it was initially designed to have a box-spring seat. Several rocking chairs with similar boxed-spring construction from the shop of William Hancock of Boston, Massachusetts, survive in collections at Old Sturbridge Village and the Essex Institute. Courtesy, Metropolitan Museum of Art, Sansbury-Mills fund, 1976 (1976.50).

literature of the 1830s and 1840s seem to evince a general increased interest in upholstered furniture, particularly with spring seats as an improvement in comfort, even when these furnishings were relatively costly and beyond the reach of many consumers. This interest in the mediation of physical sensation in chairs coincides with other changes in sensory life, such as the possibility of improved domestic heating with the parlor stove and the gradual improvement in domestic lighting culminating in the development of kerosene in the 1850s. Thus upholstery springs may be one more expression of the sensibility of "softening," the mediation of contact with the physical world, which reached its fullest popular expression decades later.

**Figure 36.** Detail of Figure 35's box structure during conservation in 1981.
Courtesy, Metropolitan Museum of Art, Sansbury-Mills fund, 1976 (1976.50).

Yet the presence of spring structures in many chairs produced after 1840 is puzzling because it seems unnecessary in relation to the typical uses of those chairs and sometimes even detrimental to the structure of the chair itself. This is particularly so with the more formal seats of parlors—reception chairs, small parlor side chairs, and taborets (upholstered stools). Because these seats were used less frequently than other household chairs and in circumstances requiring strict decorum, certainly sitters had less need for the absorption and distribution of force that springs could provide. If we try to link springs in beds and springs in chairs conceptually, the underlying message of springs is that comfort is linked to relaxation. In this sense, using springs in reading chairs or furniture for private rooms seems appropriate.

Perhaps in different contexts, springs in chairs bore other kinds of meanings. In their first decades of use, springs were probably a fashionable novelty as well as another way of putting money "into" chairs, because they increased the cost of upholstery. Stiff little armless parlor chairs, for example, once had dead "slip seats" that could be removed for easy recovering. They were intended for formal, short-term, social use anyway, and thus the addition of springs may have been more a function of the place of the chair in a set that "matched" in all respects, including identity of structure, than a significant improvement in their comfort.

Although adjustable furniture was the object of much patent interest, ordinary people seem to have felt that the best chairs were not those that

GUSTAV E. SPARMANN,

Successor to CHAS. RAYHER,

MANUFACTURER OF

# IRON BACK FRAMES

For Sofas, Lounges & Chairs,

## 93 Orchard Street,

NEAR BROOME STREET,   **NEW YORK.**

**Figure 37.** Advertisement for Gustav E. Sparmann, "Manufacturer of Iron Back Frames," in *Improved Commercial Directory and Mercantile Report Combined, of the Furniture, Carpet, and Upholstery Trades of the U.S., 1874–5*. Although the finished chairs were expensive, demand for wire or "iron back" chairs was large enough that frame production was a specialty in the furniture trade in a few places such as New York. The spring edge, an innovation of the 1860s, consisted of a row of upholstery springs with a wire or piece of bamboo fastened across the front of an upholstered seat, replacing a rigid "edge roll" of stuffing materials. Both innovations allowed the creation of deep seats that were even more resilient; in fact, wire frames transformed the entire chair into an "elastic" structure. Because of the amount of workmanship involved in constructing a stable seat with so little frame as an anchor, wire frame upholstery and spring-edge seats were more expensive than those with traditional wooden frames. Courtesy, The Strong Museum, Rochester, New York.

were adjustable but rather those whose structures were increasingly elastic. Chairs with springs in their backs as well as seats had been introduced by the 1850s, and by the 1860s, the "spring edge" and the wire-frame chair appeared; the entire seat and back structure was, in essence, a large tensile spring (Figs. 37 and 38).

Elasticity may also have served aesthetic functions. Spring seats returned to their original shape when a sitter rose, so chairs maintained a smooth appearance. Further, the inclusion of springs in traditional types of chairs allowed such "improved" seats to be at once modern and traditional, to be stylish at the same time that they expressed their historical origins, which had little to do with bodily comfort but everything to do with serving as long-standing symbols of economic and social power.

Why should increased elasticity, rather than adjustability or scientific design, have set the standard for desirable seating? One possible answer may lie in the conjunction of traditional expectations about the appearance and aesthetic function of chairs, particularly upholstered chairs, with the

**Figure 38.** Iron-frame overstuffed armchair, walnut legs and seat rail, wire frame covered with burlap, cotton undercover, springs and horsehair stuffing, traces of red or maroon rep cover, probably United States, 1855–75. The iron frame of this *crapaud*-type "Turkish" chair is visible below the arm. The wells at the front of the seat and around the arm and back were filled with a roll of cotton batting covered with rep that was loosely pleated or "ruffled." Courtesy, The Society for the Preservation of New England Antiquities; photograph by J. David Bohl.

popular interest in new technology as a herald of progress. "Elastic" springs were the objects of deep interest among inventors in several fields of technology, most particularly transportation, where they not only lessened the amount of jouncing that passengers experienced in both carriages and railroad cars but also helped preserve the equipment from damage. *Scientific American* paid particular attention to inventions of this stripe; one article in the issue of July 31, 1847, "New Wagon Springs," praised a new design for "a wagon hung upon invisible spiral springs" which promised "improvement in comfort and economy." "It is said to be easy and graceful in motion, especially in crossing gullies or rough ground—it having more the motion of a light boat in gliding over the waves, than a vehicle upon wheels." Another praised Thomas Warren's patent spring, meant for use in vehicles and furniture, as a "perfect invention."[44]

The forces harnessed in springs seemed mysterious and exciting to mechanics and inventors in the first half of the nineteenth century, perhaps all the more so for their practical usefulness. Two articles in the ongoing series "Science of Mechanics" published in *Scientific American* discussed the "Elasticity of Bodies," including metal springs, and suggested that elasticity was particularly interesting because it transferred momentum without "perceptible loss of power." "The cause of elasticity, or the philosophical principles of the elasticity of metallic bodies, has never been clearly explained," the magazine pointed out. "It is in fact, difficult to comprehend that the particles composing the distended surface of a tempered steel spring, do not remain in actual contact with each other. Yet there is abundant evidence that such is the fact; that the attraction of cohesion is not sensibly diminished." The elasticity of springs could be turned to the most mundane of uses, from an improved carriage ride to "Improved Blind-Fastenings" for windows and spring doorstops.[45]

Thus, springs in seats were one of the few ways in which technological progress could be harnessed inside a particularly traditional artifact, the chair. For someone unacquainted with woodworking, the use of machines for making chair frames was not necessarily apparent. However, springs could be perceived through the act of sitting, even if they were invisible on the surface. And a practiced eye could discern their presence by the depth and shape of chair seats. Thus spring seats made technological progress manifest in furniture.

Further, we may conjecture that elastic structures in seats were congenial to the broad sensibility of refinement because of their responsiveness to the human body as well as their mediation of physical sensation as the chair seat "gave" whenever someone sat down. Adjustability also made chairs responsive, but resilient upholstery was more subtle in its working and, again, maintained the appearance of the traditional chair while avoiding the connotations of illness or total relaxation connoted by adjustability.

Increased padding in chairs, particularly pleated tufting, was another innovation of the nineteenth century. Padded upholstery presents subtle problems of understanding and interpretation similar to those of springs in seats. It softened bodily contact with chair frames; it also made chairs and couches warmer, mediating the sensations of heat and cold. However, although padding is resilient, it is not necessarily soft, as pleated tufting in most nineteenth-century American furniture demonstrates.

Before tufting developed into a pleated, sewn-in method of anchoring stuffing and of elaborating chair surfaces, it consisted of a simple form of stitching through layers of seat or mattress stuffing (Fig. 39). The large single stitches were spaced evenly through the upholstery and at first did not appear through the cover of a piece of furniture, although later in the nineteenth century these stitches were frequently marked with decorative buttons. In the late nineteenth century, catalogs applied the term "tufting" both to buttoning and to pleated tufting. At the level of popular taste, simple buttoning was an acceptable paraphrase for more labor- and material-intensive techniques of pleated tufting (see chapter 6 for a fuller discussion of the use of this technique).

**Figure 39.** Parlor suite with horsehair covers showing simple buttoning, photograph in Rand and McSherry, *Descriptive Catalogue of Sofas, Lounges, Tetes, Chairs, and Parlor Suits* (Baltimore, 1872). Courtesy, Smithsonian Institution.

During the first half of the nineteenth century, French upholsterers developed additional methods for building up the padded surfaces of chairs, particularly the vertical ones of seat backs and arms, through the use of sewn-in channel and pleated tufting. Pleated tufting (see Fig. 50) contained one final layer of stuffing material—usually cotton—creased, buttoned, and in the early years of the practice, sometimes sewn in place in muslin over the stuffing layers above the layer of springs. The varied forms of pleated tufting broke upholstered surfaces into facets, stuffed and held in place by folding the fabric and buttoning the points of each tuft. Early pleated tufting on seat backs is sometimes fully stitched in place in the undercover, an unnecessary step (see Fig. 38).

Contrary to its appearance, most pleated tufting was usually not soft, although it contributed to the overall elasticity of a piece of furniture. In America, particularly in the ordinary products of upholstering manufactories, pleated tufting seems to have been stuffed rigidly full, especially on the vertical surfaces inside chair backs and arms. Thus pleated tufting on many pieces of furniture was as much a contribution to the aesthetic standards that favored complexity as it was a contribution to the physical comfort of a piece of furniture. As late as 1954 the author of one how-to book devoted exclusively to tufted upholstery noted this fact. "Tufting has a natural tendency to be hard," he wrote, "in spite of the soft appearance it gives."[46] Soft, "sloppy" stuffing appeared for the first time in more expensive upholstered chairs of the 1880s and 1890s and was considered a particularly "French" upholstery characteristic.[47] Unfortunately, it is often difficult to tell just how soft or rigid nineteenth-century upholstery was because the stuffing breaks down over time, some springs lose resiliency, and the webbing and ties break away.

Judging from the surviving objects and trade catalogs, we can see that attitudes about what constituted acceptable parlor seating furniture did change, gradually and unevenly, in the direction of chair types that were traditionally considered informal and comfortable. Parlor rocking chairs became standard components of middle-class parlor suites, and larger-scale, completely upholstered, and less posture-specific furniture, such as the common lounge, became popular. Critics regarded spring-seat furniture, particularly overstuffed "Turkish" pieces, as "dishonest"; the anonymous author of the decorating advice chapters in *How to Build, Furnish and Decorate* (1889), for example, excoriated "luxuriously debilitating puffy sofas and chairs which our ancestors would have scorned." The same author, however, also disliked "stiff, high chairs" and was trying to define some middle ground in furnishing, as had the commentators of the previous generation.[48] But the middle ground itself seems to have shifted toward more informal furniture. It is fascinating that this change occurred while the conventions of parlor furnishing and popular thought about the formal social character of parlors, as well as customs of the room's use, seem to have remained unchanged.

In the 1880s other authors applauded this move toward greater informality and poked fun at traditional standards of deportment. "How to Sit on a Divan" not only offered advice on how to use this new form of household furniture properly but also showed, as an object lesson, a proper young woman who attempted to sit perched on the edge of that piece of furniture, as her upbringing had suggested she do (and as her clothing probably demanded).[49] In 1883 one commentator even turned the middle-class critique of appropriate domestic comfort on its head by suggesting that furniture, even the beloved rocking chair, had made unfeeling barbarians of our nation's colonial founders:

> The popularity of comfortable furniture, such as this lounge, goes a great deal toward civilizing the people generally. It seems to us impossible for the human race to be good-natured and good tempered if forced to sit in a "bolt upright" position in the extreme corner of a horse-hair covered sofa, with arms and back built on the very straightest and most perpendicular principle. . . . It is not surprising that our forefathers were given to atrocities and cruelties when they were brought up to endure such tortures as could be inflicted by the furniture of even twenty years ago; it served to deaden the sensibilities.[50]

Throughout the last half of the nineteenth century, the forms of upholstered parlor furniture continued to reflect their jumble of origins: upholstery as a symbol of social and economic power, upholstery as a source of bodily comfort, and the new spring seat as a manifestation of the progressive impact of technology on traditional furnishings. Many parlor seats were "elastic," yet their forms did not invite repose. Additionally, some forms of upholstered seating furniture, such as lounges, seemed to invite behavior and deportment that was not acceptable in formal social settings. Even as a slow change in favor of less-posture-controlling, larger-scale, and completely upholstered seating furniture occurred, the social restraints of etiquette and the physical restraints of women's full formal dress made "getting comfortable" a complicated proposition.

# CHAPTER FIVE

# The Quest for Refinement

## Reconstructing the Aesthetics of Upholstery, 1850–1910

Our desire is to give some specimens of plain, simple, but substantial furniture, which, by proper and tasteful enrichment of painting, staining or carving, or the addition of hangings, trimmings and embroidery, may be made so rich and elegant in appearance as to stand the test of critical observation and not offend the eye of correct taste.

Henry T. Williams and Mrs. C. S. Jones,
*Beautiful Homes* (1878)

Victorian consumers valued parlor furnishings for their associations with the ideals of culture and comfort; they also located important cultural principles in the formal visual and tactile qualities of these objects.[1] The preference for such qualities as intricacy, an attribute that even moderately priced upholstery available to middle-class consumers embodied, was linked to real changes in the sensory lives of ordinary people, including a new popular appreciation of the act of looking that was itself connected to new technologies of image-making. A mutually reinforcing process of applying meaning to appearances, which in turn strengthened popular preferences for those appearances, took place. This process of meaning-making was self-conscious, time-linked, and cultural, and it can be described and analyzed. It created a constellation of objects, aesthetic preferences, and symbolic meanings centered on the concepts of "refinement" and "cultivation" and reinforced the parlor's role as a ceremonial space.

**Figure 40.** Bracket shelf with lambrequin, painted wood, Berlin work with glass-bead fringe, United States, about 1870. A decorative shelf lambrequin could disguise and embellish a plain or poorly made bracket shelf like this one, making it suitably ornamental for the parlor. Courtesy, The Strong Museum, Rochester, New York.

Even minor elements of parlor upholstery illustrate what Victorian culture thought was beautiful and why. Certain kinds of room decorations seem alien—fussy, dirty, and useless—to contemporary eyes, yet they were common, were clearly prized, were considered suitable for parlor display, and finally, were thought to be beautiful. Just as some of the large, important pieces of upholstery typically found in parlors were designed with levels of visual elaboration, these small pieces also are characterized by a high degree of careful detail. For example, shelf lambrequins, a minor form of drapery with many surviving examples in museum collections, were labor intensive and characterized by remarkable visual complexity (Fig. 40). They were introduced to American home needleworkers in the early 1850s. Directions pubiished in women's periodicals of the 1850s and 1860s repeatedly introduced such decorated brackets as a European fashion and a popular novelty in Philadelphia and New York; the September 1877 issue of *Peterson's Magazine* informed readers that plain bracket shelves could be "made ornamental" by the application of shelf drapery.[2]

Shelf lambrequins typically have complex outlines, repeating scallops or small shield shapes.[3] These shapes are like those of window valances (also called lambrequins or pelmets), so shelf drapery was related conceptually to popular forms of window upholstery. Needlepoint (Berlin work) examples often used many colors, which, in combination, created shading and the illusion of three dimensions in some designs. The visual and tactile texture of shelf lambrequins also can be complex, thanks to the combinations of materials and stitching. One example of an apparently

**Figure 41.** Shelf lambrequin, Berlin work with silk tassels, cotton backing, United States, 1870–80. This lambrequin is embroidered with the "double Leviathon stitch," which was used to create emphatic texture in a geometric grid rather than to follow delicate representational patterns. Courtesy, The Strong Museum, Rochester, New York.

crude-looking lambrequin was actually made with a particularly complicated stitch called the "double Leviathon," which created small textured blocks (Fig. 41). The beads and the wool and silk yarns in other surviving examples—and there are many—react to light in different ways. Trims finished the edges, added additional contrasting materials, and created complex outlines; fringes of beads or tassels also created interest through movement, creating variations in light and shadow. Lambrequins made with other popular needlework techniques such as crochet or macramé also offered complex textures and variations of light and shade rendered in one or a few colors.

Close examination of surviving shelf lambrequins makes it possible to appreciate the amount of detail in a single small lambrequin that appears in a stereograph of an upstate New York parlor (Fig. 42). In the corner above the piano hangs a bracket shelf with a needlework lambrequin, itself only one small component of an extremely complex decorative scheme. A ceramic figure stands on the shelf, and a collection of what appear to be bird feathers and dried plant materials is tucked into the space between the shelf and the wall. This small assemblage in "Mrs. L. H. Owen's Room" is an intricate composition in itself, its juxtaposition of elements and materials carefully thought out. In every part, the room displays what can be called equivalent levels of detail; the eye of an onlooker can take in only a finite amount of the detail in the entire room and perceives an equivalent

**Figure 42.** "Mrs. L. H. Owen's Room," at Trembley House, Trumansburg, New York, about 1870. Even though the levels of detail visible in this stereograph are remarkable, imagine the additional stimulation of color that is missing in all such views. Courtesy, Smithsonian Institution; private collection.

amount of visual information when focusing on a smaller section of the room. Single objects such as the bracket with lambrequin, the rococo revival chair with needlework upholstery in the lower left-hand corner, and the "Sleepy Hollow" chair with highly dimensional "bun" tufting visible in the mirror's reflection all offer complex visual experiences for the careful looker. The objects are arranged in a number of many small, complicated constellations; these are, in turn, orchestrated into one large scheme.

What did the makers and consumers of such visually complex parlor furnishings think about the aesthetic experience such assemblages provided? How did they describe upholstery, and what did their descriptions signify? What did they *see* when they looked at and selected furnishings for their parlors? Repeatedly, writers of advice books and articles in ladies' magazines, books on the displays at international expositions, and mail-order catalogs used a particular vocabulary for admired examples of "decorative art," including both the large and the minor elements of upholstery. Such objects were described as "rich" in appearance, "elaborated," well "finished," "elegant," and "ornamental"; they were praised for their detail, for their "softened" or "softening" effect, and finally for their contribution to the "refinement" of a room.

Both the large and the small elements of room upholstery were described with the same vocabulary; a few examples here represent myriad similar observations. An 1854 description of the upholstery in the La Pierre House in Philadelphia praised the bridal suite draperies, "a *rose* red, be it understood, of the most delicate shade, softened still more by the pure transparencies of the lace embroideries falling from the rich canopies above the bed."[4] In 1878 a rustic drapery cornice made from spruce branches and "ornamented with the delicate little spruce twigs" was praised for being "complicated in form, and rich in color as some wonderful mosaic" with "the richness and variety of the brown color."[5] The same descriptive vocabulary was still in popular use after 1900, when the 1908 Sears, Roebuck and Company catalog offered a "Rich Persian Striped Couch Cover" guaranteed "an ornament in any room" for $2.59. Another cover, available for $3.50, was touted as "one of the heaviest and richest Oriental couch covers ever put on the market."[6]

Even when this specific vocabulary did not appear, a particular technique of description was often used to imply these qualities. Here each element used in making an object, or each object serving in the composition of a room, was described in careful, realistic detail capable of satisfying the mind's eye of the reader. In such descriptions, the aesthetic standards by which such furnishings were judged are implicit in the levels of detail noted and praised. Such observations occasionally refer to more than one sensory experience, as did the descriptions of hotels and photographers' parlors; both the softening of sound by thick carpets and the visual detail of gorgeous upholstery and gilded wood were recounted.

By the 1880s this kind of description reached its apex of elaboration, coincident with the proliferation of upholstery in parlors. The author of

"The Best Room: Its Arrangement and Decoration at Moderate Cost," winner of second prize in an 1888 essay competition for amateur decorators who were readers of *Decorator and Furnisher*, devoted more than fifteen hundred words to a tour of a single room, "a combination of parlor and drawing-room." She offered her readers vivid detail and concluded by using some of the signal terms applied to prized aesthetic features:

> Diagonally across from the fireplace, the upright piano can stand, pulled out from the wall and covered with a scarf of dark terra-cotta plush. . . . this scarf would be much improved by a design of conventionalized pomegranites and leaves, worked in shades of pink and greens and outlined with gold thread. . . . two small odd-shaped chairs of different designs, one gilded, with a cushion of pale blue plush, the other, with a back of dark wood the cushioned seat in shades of brocaded copper. . . . The windows in the recess should be draped with filmy sash curtains, while from the square frame around them depend heavy rich hangings of dull blue, with a dado of conventionalized flowers and leaves on a ground of old pink. . . . I think now that we have a room which can be fitted up at moderate cost, which is full of soft rich color, and which is pervaded by a general air of comfort, culture and refinement.[7]

Even catalog descriptions and images of parlor furniture sold by mail-order firms such as Sears, Roebuck and Company at the turn of the century demonstrate well the popular connection of particular kinds of descriptive language and specific formal qualities in upholstery. Such descriptions frequently noted decorative elements in a formulaic, repetitive fashion. Illustrations of every item allow a comparison of descriptions with the visual characteristics of pieces in a way that cannot be done using contemporary wholesale catalogs directed "to the trade" alone; furniture men knew what they were looking at and needed little more than factual information on price lines and decorative options. The loaded vocabulary used to sell "refined" furniture to a new group of consumers—newly prosperous rural and small-town Americans—indicates the process of what may be called "educating to ascribe" (teaching people which consumer goods are expressions of desired social and cultural characteristics). It also demonstrates how design economics interacted with both the preferences of consumers of limited incomes for visual intricacy and their understanding of how "refinement" was manifested in choices about design and materials.[8]

In the 1897 catalog section headed "Princely Parlor Furniture," Sears offered its customers "parlor suits" of from three to six pieces, ranging in price from $18.50 to $47.00, as well as a range of couches, lounges, and "Fancy Stylish Pieces." The cover options were all machine-woven versions of once rare and expensive fabrics: cotton or silk tapestry, pile fabrics (either "Wilton rug," "crushed plush," or corduroy) or brocaded or damask silks, which represented the top of the line (Fig. 43). Most of the suites were free-ranging interpretations of some "Louis" style; several over-stuffed "Turkish" sets represented the design cutting edge of the Sears line. All depended, for their aesthetic effect, on the elaborate cut-out and machine-carved outlines of their frames, the contrast between the upholstery and the wood profiles, the color and texture of the fabric, and the ways in which the fabric surfaces were broken up with banding, colorful cords, or tufting. The chair backs of "No. 9505" featured a fantastic design of scrolls, floral ornaments, and a carved crest shaped like a crown. The back and the seat were upholstered "plain," but their shapes were defined by cording and elaborated by the design of the fabric pattern. The description vowed that the set was "not only perfect in detail and handsome in outline" but "one of the richest and most stylish appearing parlor suits . . . of 1897." "No. 9500," a five-piece suit for $11.35, was guaranteed to be "an ornament to any parlor" with its carved back and plain-seat upholstery of tapestry or plush, outlined and broken visually into bands by cording.[9]

Visual intricacy (attention to detail, ornament, and decoration) signaled cultivation and refinement so much that it supported whole categories of furniture that functioned mostly as visual embellishments to the appearance of the parlor. Take, for example, the "Fancy Chair" (the descendant of the reception chairs discussed previously) described in the *Sears, Roebuck and Co. Catalogue No. 111, 1902* as "a dainty, odd chair, with neat, graceful lines, made of curly birch, finished a rich mahogany color; back is finely carved and is handsomely covered in silk tapestry, damask or brocatelle. A beautiful parlor decoration."[10] The caption advertising a five-piece parlor suite (proclaimed to be a $30.00 value available to customers for $15.45) in the same catalog guaranteed: "In every point of appearance attention has been given that no detail shall be overlooked whereby the suite shall be less finished and artistic than it should be. . . . Neither time nor money has been spared in elaborating on the pattern to make it tasty and desirable in every respect." Another suite, "Our Big Five-Piece $20.75 Leader," featured frames that were "beautifully carved, decorated, and ornamented . . . very highly polished and finished." Guiding the tastes of new consumers,

# $23.00 BUYS A $45.00 PARLOR SUIT

**OUR SPECIAL OFFER:** SEND US $5.00 as a guarantee of good faith and we will send you the suit by freight. C. O. D., subject to examination; you can examine it at your freight depot, and if found perfectly satisfactory pay the freight agent the balance, $18.00 and freight. Three per cent. discount allowed if cash in full accompanies your order, when $22.31 pays for the suit.

No. 9503 This elegant Turkish parlor suit consists of 1 Tete-a-Tete, 1 Rocker, 1 Gents' Easy Chair, 1 Parlor or Reception Chair. All these pieces are made in extra large size, high backs and large comfortable seats, and are very latest design. The upholstering or cover of this suit is in the latest design and pattern of imported goods; each piece is covered in a different color. We will be pleased to mail you samples of six different colors to select from, or if left to us to make selection in colors our upholsterer will in all cases give your colors on this suit that will please you in every respect. The suit is finely upholstered, with plush band and rolls on top and sides of back and trimmed with a heavy worsted fringe. This suit is made with good steel spring seats and spring edges and every piece is made with spring backs. This is without a doubt one of the best parlor suits ever put on the market at the price we ask for it and will be an ornament in any home. We can furnish this same parlor suit upholstered in good grade of crushed plush, assorted colors, and other styles of covering.

| | |
|---|---|
| 4 piece Parlor Suit, price in cotton tapestry | $23.00 |
| 4 piece Parlor Suit, price in crushed plush | $35.50 |
| 4 piece Parlor Suit, price in silk brocatelle | $39.50 |
| 4 piece Parlor Suit, price in silk damask | $45.00 |

## A $35.00 PARLOR SUIT FOR $24.00.

In offering this Parlor Suit of six pieces for $24.00 we fully believe that no such suit can be secured at less than $35, and if bought at retail at that price you would consider it a great bargain.

Made with a solid oak or a solid birch frame If furnished In solid birch it is finished In imitation mahogany, a most desirable and attractive finish.

No. 9504 The backs of this suit are upholstered in the same quality of material as the seat, and the decorations in the way of hand carving are decidedly unique and attractive. Easy spring seat and edges corded with handsome cord with silk plush banded front. The suit is furnished complete with a full set of casters, and weights, when packed for shipment, about 250 lbs. We show in illustrations only pictures of the large sofa, large rocker and large parlor chair. The six piece parlor suit complete consists in addition to the three shown of a divan, same as the sofa only smaller; an extra Parlor Chair and a large Arm Chair of same size as rocker shown. Bear in mind that our C. O. D. terms of shipment are very liberal, also that we allow a discount of 3 per cent when full cash accompanies order. Most of our customers send full cash with order, knowing the goods are guaranteed and may be returned if not satisfactory and money refunded.

Upholstered as follows:
Our special price for 6 piece suit in an excellent grade of cotton tapestry ........................ $24.00
Our special price for same upholstered in a very excellent quality of imported corduroy .................... 26.50
Our special price for same upholstered in a fine grade of brocaline crushed plush or silk tapestry ................ 30.00
Our special price for same upholstered in very fine brocatelle or choice silk damask ........................ 33.00

Be sure to advise us when ordering, what special combinations of colors are desired. We can furnish you with a suit which for harmony of colors as well as durability and elegance will delight you more than you could possibly expect.

## A $50.00 PARLOR SUIT FOR $33.00.

No. 9505 It is difficult to imagine a more beautiful and artistic suit than the one which we show in the illustration. Our artist has endeavored to draw the different pieces so that you can get an idea of the handsome design. It is one of the richest and most stylish appearing parlor suits made for the season of 1897. It is after a design executed by expert artists in this line, and the manufacturers are taking particular pains that the suit shall be not only perfect in detail and handsome in outline, but thoroughly substantial and durable in every respect. It is a suit that will last a lifetime and a suit that you will never become tired of. It is made with a solid oak frame or a frame made of curly birch with imitation mahogany finish. Either wood is decidedly handsome and thoroughly substantial. The frames are beautifully carved after the most stylish pattern, and the suit as a whole has the appearance of one which would retail frequently at from $75.00 to $80.00. It consists of 6 pieces, a large divan, large easy rocker, large arm chair and two parlor chairs. We upholster this suit in five different styles of upholstering. D. E. F. G and H. D is a very fine biocaline crush plush; E is an elegant silk tapestry; F a superb Wilton rug; G a choice grade of silk brocatell and H a very handsome and durable satin damask. You have your choice of upholstering. In all grades the patterns are the very latest designs, and in coloring you will have your choice of all the popular shades. We recommend, however, that you leave the matter of coloring in general to our designer, as we make these parlor suits specially to order and will upholster the various pieces in the latest popular shades, all harmonizing perfectly. The weight of this suit when packed very carefully for shipment is 300 lbs. We pack each of these pieces with the utmost care, covering all parts with burlap so that they will reach you in perfect condition. Casters free.

Our special price for above 6 piece Parlor Suit, upholstered in grade D or E ............................ $33.00
Same Suit, upholstered in grade F, our special price ............... $37.00
Same Suit, upholstered in grade G or H, our special price .......... $38.00

**Figure 43.** "Parlor Suites," engraving in *Sears, Roebuck and Co. Catalogue No. 104, 1897* (New York). Courtesy, Chelsea House Publishers, Philadelphia and Broomall, Pennsylvania.

the catalog noted: "The backs of this suite are diamond tufted, as shown in the illustration. This can only be found in the highest grade furniture such as this suite represents."[11]

Underlying these formulaic descriptions of individual pieces of upholstery and of entire parlors are mental constructs resonant in more than one realm of Victorian culture, constructs that are referenced in shorthand through this extremely compressed descriptive vocabulary. Some of the terms used in evaluating the appearance of things—"refined," "finished," "polished"—are also common to other genres of Victorian popular literature (etiquette and popular technology, popular histories, and didactic sentimental fiction) advising readers on other facets of their lives and teaching them how to judge the quality of experience. Along with the specific terminology, the minuteness of these descriptions is a clue to a set of assumptions about the world—an operating sensibility that valued fine, carefully rendered detail and elaboration of shapes and surfaces. This sensibility also valued formal characteristics of artifacts that operated on the senses of hearing and touch (we have seen, in chapter 1, the appreciation for wall-to-wall carpet, which softened sound), but it particularly emphasized the dominant sense of sight. Perceiving these qualities as material expressions of a set of cultural ideals, this sensibility construed the sensory experiences offered by parlor furnishings as having analogues in other realms of human action—social behavior and technological change, for example—and therefore applauded their expression, wherever it was found.

This nineteenth-century "aesthetic of refinement" (*aesthetic* being here defined as the set of guiding constructs for appreciating the world perceived by the senses, rather than the criticism of taste), as it was made manifest in parlors and in upholstery and, it seems likely, in other types of Victorian material culture, was not wholly new. Rather, just as the commercialization of symbols in Victorian culture built on historical precedent, particularly the commercialization of gentility, the valued formal qualities of things also emerged from historical traditions. Types of textiles that had once been extremely expensive and rare continued to be prized for upholstery, for example, even though they could now be woven by machine. However, the aesthetic of refinement also ascribed additional meanings to fine-looking things, and it insisted that whole new categories of furnishings, including the modest goods promoted by Sears, also could be made to demonstrate refinement.

The Victorian aesthetic of refinement employed sets of sophisticated analogies between realms of human activity. The "softening of the world" of refined behavior could be symbolically rendered through upholstery and drapery in the parlor. "Refinement" could be rendered visually as attention to and appreciation of detail. Social "polish" was manifested through competence in the use of specialized artifacts and also through ownership of objects that displayed high "finish." "Finish" incorporated the characteristics of smoothness, shine, and ornament, which were expressive of increasing control over materials, just as "finished" or "polished" manners indicated perfect self-control. Finally, all these valued characteristics in the material world and in social behavior were demonstrations of artifice, the techniques of improving natural materials with human skill; thus refinement also implied the treasured and enlightened ideal of progress.

The sensibility that linked these varied aspects of human activity can be reconstructed by analyzing its "semantic taxonomy," a code that cut across categories of culture and society not usually directly compared—technology and art, for example, or etiquette and technology.[12] Some anthropologists have examined the relationship of aesthetics to other components of culture, providing models for looking at the Victorian aesthetic in this way. The work of Robert Farris Thompson among the Yoruba tribe of western Africa, for example, shows how connections are made between appearances of artifacts and cultural ideals for all kinds of human action. Yoruba carvers and their audiences consider a precise, clean line the foremost aesthetic quality and use a "vocabulary of linear qualities . . . colloquially and across a range of concerns far broader than sculpture."

> It is not just their statues, pots, and so on that Yoruba incise with lines, they do the same with their faces. Line, of varying depth, direction, and length, sliced into their cheeks and left to scar over, serves as a means of lineage identification, personal allure, and status expression; and the terminology of the sculptor and of the cicatrix specialist . . . parallel one another in exact precision. But there is more to it than this. The Yoruba associate line with civilization: "This country has become civilized," literally means, in Yoruba, "this earth has lines upon its face."[13]

The research of Daniel P. Biebuyck into the arts and rituals of the Lega people of central Africa also links visual aesthetics and broader sensibility. Biebuyck deciphers the connections among Lega artistic standards, notions of value in relation to the natural world, conceptions of moral development and ethical value for individuals and whole villages, and a remarkable semantic taxonomy through which the Lega people express the relatedness of these aspects of their culture.[14] Biebuyck's observations center on the importance to Lega culture of *bwami*, a large, multilevel organization that is a means of teaching the "theory and praxis of a moral philosophy that must produce harmony in social relationships and individual happiness and beatitude."[15]

One fundamental set of concepts that the Lega incorporate in their system of value is the opposition of darkness, ruggedness, and the absence of order to light, smoothness, and the presence of order and harmony. For example, ivory carvings with a smooth and glossy patina represent the highest level of aesthetic appeal; ceremonial stools are polished to a high gloss. The highest level of *bwami* initiates is also said to be "smooth." Light-colored and smooth natural objects—white birds, white mushrooms—serve as natural analogues of ivory carving and other such beautiful and pleasing things. New initiates rub themselves with the same oils that are used to polish ivory carvings and thereby express their own developing "smoothness." The semantic taxonomy organizes both significant objects and people in these terms, which refer also to the ideas of unison or harmony in singing, *kukonga;* the related term *kubongia*, which describes all special objects such as carvings or stools, implies the creation of harmony and unison. Moral, artistic, and natural qualities are thus folded together and expressed in terms that every Lega can "speak" with some degree of competence; *bwami* initiates become more adept than the average Lega over time.

These scholars have enjoyed the advantages of working with living people, but the work of art historian Michael Baxandall suggests that a similar methodology, albeit one that relies on traditional historical sources of evidence rather than participant observation, can be used to partially reconstruct long-dead sensibilities and sensory preferences. He argues that the cognitive style that Renaissance Florentines brought to bear in their judgments of pictures can be found by comparing the practical or social skills that people used when they viewed pictures, contemporaneous descriptions of both artistic techniques and the characteristics of the work of specific artists, and the surviving works from those artists. For example, Renaissance orators, popular preachers, and dancers all used a highly developed grammar of pious and secular movement and gesture to make their points clear to large crowds. Painters employed this same code as a means of expressing the mental and spiritual condition of painted figures in a way that was intelligible to the public.[16]

Baxandall also demonstrates that judgments of quality in pictures were connected to judgments of quality in other areas of life. Authors writing about pictures drew on the descriptive language used to evaluate other arts of living considered worthy of critical judgment: literature, etiquette, musical and dance performance, hunting, and painting. For example, the term *sprezzatura* (difficult to translate but roughly analogous to the ideal of the "easy manner" or "ease") was used to praise successful performance in all these arenas; laborious displays of skill were to be avoided at all times.[17] *Sprezzatura* was part of a Renaissance "semantic taxonomy," and painting displaying this quality revealed a kind of easy virtuosity.

All this work suggests that the rules and words applied to the appearance of Victorian artifacts may similarly have had the capacity to express ideas about centrally important cultural issues such as the appropriate relationship of the civilized person to the world of the senses and the construction and perception of standards of excellence. It suggests that, as expressions of sensibility, decorative arts objects may also serve that process of self-measurement and comparison in which people engage more or less consciously, and more or less constantly, as members of a culture.

We have seen that Victorian culture transformed ordinary domestic artifacts into symbols by means of a theory of associations, where a chain of thoughts linked an object, such as a rocking chair, to larger cultural concerns or ideals, such as motherly women and the proper character of family life. The particular semantic taxonomy under examination here organized another level of associations along particular lines. Whereas the rhetoric of middle-class comfort emphasized homey, familial symbolism as appropriate to the formation of character, parlor furnishings were more than simply domestic—they were also worldly. Even though lambrequins, portieres, layers of draperies, and fabric-swaddled chairs, tables, mantels, and pianos seemed "cozy," their formal qualities of finish, complexity, and softening could be understood as expressions of the progress of civilization (Fig. 44). Thus they also referred to the world of culture.[18] As the fundamental cultural concept underlying a set of related terms—"cultivation," "elegance," "richness," "finish" or "polish," "ornaments" or "ornamental"—refinement cut across the boundaries of nineteenth-century thought about individual behavior, the nature of technological and social progress, and the advancement of civilization, which was often viewed in terms of progress inside the middle-class home. The concept of "refinement" influenced popular aesthetic preferences in household furnishings because it could be associated with specific visual and tactile characteristics.

### DEFINING REFINEMENT

The *Oxford English Dictionary* devotes considerable space to definitions of *refine* and *refinement*. Some encompass technological uses such as metallurgy, as in "to free from imperfections or defects; to bring to a more per-

**Figure 44.** "From Savagery to Civilization," frontispiece of William DeHertburn Washington, *Progress and Prosperity* (1911). Washington's book-length exercise in American boosterism included this ingenious, concise set of visual comparisons, which use the concept of progressive refinement as their fundamental assumption. In the images of modern life, people were more physically comfortable, more expressive, more secure, and capable of a higher degree of control over their surroundings. "Progress" also assumed a highly specific kind of greater "refinement," particularly visible in the images of the complex, intricate interiors of the modern home and the modern place of worship. Courtesy, The Strong Museum, Rochester, New York.

fect or purer state"; an obsolete French usage of *refin* referred to "fine wool or cloth." Both these uses express the idea of application of technique and labor to the practical arts. By the eighteenth century, the ideas behind *refine* and *refinement* included the concept of progress—"an instance of improvement or advance toward something more refined or perfect," both in the realm of technology and science and in the world of the humanities, as in "to polish or improve (a language, composition, etc.); to make more elegant and cultivated." This concept of improvement and advancement not only encompassed scholarly learning but also included a broader notion of personal cultivation—"fineness of feeling, taste, or thought; elegance of manners, culture, polish" (the *Oxford English Dictionary* defines *polish* as being "free from roughness, rudeness, or coarseness"). This grouping of definitions is significant for its conflation of material and social qualities; it also contains the possibility of expressing ideas about moral character in terms of progress. The concept of "refinement" is strikingly like the association of shine and smoothness in objects and moral perfection in human character that the Lega language and culture, analyzed by Biebuyck, express. Thus we can think of "refinement" as suitable for expressing certain qualities in human social behavior: technical skill; control of time for the purposes of improvement; attention to detail; and development of "fineness of feeling," self-control, and mastery of social forms.

The terms related to *refine* and *refinement* also fold together qualities associated with scientific or technological activities, progress in modes of living, and the physical characteristics of objects. The words *cultivation* and *elegant*, or *elegance*, are particularly interesting. *Elegant*, which is derived etymologically from the Latin word for "choosing carefully or skillfully," refers to both people and artifacts in "refined grace of form; tastefully ornamental," to the broader notion of "modes of life, dwellings and their appointments, refined luxury," and to expressions of ingenious technological or scientific problem solving (as in the "elegant solution"). The origin of *cultivate* and *cultivation* is in the Latin *cultivare*, the verb meaning "to till (the ground)." Its primary meanings developed from this Latin source; all refer to the bestowing of "labor and attention" to the land, plants, and animals, with the implied sense of constancy and care in this employment. When "cultivation" was first applied to the notion of "developing, fostering, or improving (of the mind, faculties, etc.) by education and training . . . refinement," the implication of careful, steady attention to detail remained. Conceptually, although not etymologically, other culturally related terms include *polish*, *finish*, and *ornament*.

For ordinary people living in the second half of the nineteenth century, "refinement" was not a matter of reduction to a pure essence but rather a process associated with progress and proliferation. "Refinement" in etiquette was popularly conceived as attention to social detail and the increasing nuances of polite behavior, including the competent use of highly specialized domestic artifacts. "Refinement" in the realm of science and the industrial arts was perceived at the popular level as a certain form of progress, the process of perfecting and proliferating the technology and productive activities that increased human comforts and embellished basic needs, especially in the context of the private household (a sort of Victorian version of the General Electric appliance advertisements that once trumpeted, "Progress is our most important product"). Architecture plan books and "household arts" books of the 1870s and later also expressed the idea that popular interest in the embellishments of domestic interiors generally represented a form of progress. The "Publisher's Preface" to *Our Homes: How to Beautify Them* (1887) noted, "It is not alone the mansions of wealth and luxury which have experienced the results of this decorative advancement, but the humble homes everywhere through the land reveal the beautifying touch of taste and skill."[19]

The question of self-mastery—the personally willed refinement of the individual—is the crux of the conceptions of etiquette and civility over which the Victorians spilled so much ink. No matter how often the authors of etiquette books protested that manners were as much a matter of proper feeling as proper form, the message of the medium was that codifiable form was everything.[20] Well into the twentieth century, the real message of most manners books was found in the hundreds of pages of text devoted to renditions of minutely described formal calling rituals, table manners course by course, and the ins and outs of introductions on the street. One author of an inexpensive and popular manual summed up the message of all manners books in this passage, titled "Attention to Small Matters":

> There is nothing, however minute in manners, however insignificant in appearance that does not demand some portion of attention from a well-bred and highly-polished young man or women. An author of no small literary renown, has observed, that several of the minutest habits or acts of some individuals may give sufficient reasons to guess at their temper. The choice of a dress, or even the folding and sealing of a letter, will bespeak the shrew and the scold, the careless and the negligent.[21]

The importance of manners was not simply a question of self-control in the world for the purposes of self-defense and self-presentation. Interest in social "polish" and the increasing complexity of social relations reflected the nineteenth-century sense that, as one contemporary adviser wrote, "each successive age, since former periods of barbarity in the dark and feudal times[,] has tended to produce an increased refinement and civilization in this respect."[22]

Complicated manners were an expressive form for individuals to master. They represented, in their increasing polish and refinement, the progress of human civilization, which also was expressed through the increasing complexity and refinement of the material world. In the terms of the prevalent, commonsense belief that the physical environment of the home shaped moral character, refinements both in the appearance of the objects used in the home and in the realm of human social interaction were also necessarily linked. For example, an author calling for the use of more upholstery in rooms could plausibly describe drapery in the same language that was applied to etiquette; center table covers were "a most elegant mode of adornment, giving a sort of grace to what would otherwise appear stiff and awkward."[23]

An enthusiastic sense of American civilization's unstoppable advance through invention, improvement in production methods, and the blessings of economic plenty also supported the equation of more, and more complicated, things with refinement in civilization. This belief guided the pen of the anonymous author of *Eighty Years' Progress* (published in Hartford, Connecticut, by "L. Stebbins" in 1867), a two-volume compendium and overview of settlement, business, technology, education, art, and "social and domestic life" in the United States between the birth of the republic and 1860. The chapter "Social and Domestic Life" began by documenting the "somewhat uncommonly low average of comfort at the end of the Revolution" and then documented "the general progress of the nation" in the categories of "Domestic Architecture, Furniture, Food, Dress, and Mental Culture, Intercourse, etc." The general thesis of the chapter was that both the number and ingenuity of new inventions and the proliferation of inexpensive domestic comforts—glass and china, wooden furniture, pianos, less expensive food, and kerosene lighting—demonstrated "steadfast, and essential, and solid improvement" in the lives of most Americans. The blessings of mechanized weaving technology (the author praised domestic carpet production and the weaving and printing of cotton as a "beautiful" process) were signaled out as improving the quality of life, in terms of both comfort and aesthetic standards.[24]

At about the same time, the author ("An Antiquarian") of a series of eight "lectures" published in the *Household Journal* under the general title "Our Home: Its History and Progress, with Notices of the Introduction of Domestic Inventions," carried the argument of *Eighty Years' Progress* to its logical extreme. After charting the increasing complexity of and improvements in household architecture, heating and lighting, sanitation, and furnishings, the author declared: "Our American home . . . is the valued result of years of conquest in the realms of commerce and science. It is curious to observe how, in each advancing step, fresh wants were created, which, in their turn, encouraged and accelerated the efforts of science and art as applied to the convenience and embellishments of home."[25] To this author, the progress of civilization led inevitably and suitably to the proliferation and refinement of *things*, especially the objects dedicated to perfecting, through both "convenience and embellishments," the bulwark of republican civilization, the home.

An important marker of refinement in the Victorian world of things was a peculiar form of specialization, which had reference both to the world of technology and to the realm of etiquette. Popular understanding of refinement in artifacts was always progressive and was equated with increasing complexity in the appearance of each object and with increasing specialization of forms within categories of objects. This specialization consisted of creating endless variations of common domestic objects and narrowly defining their appropriate use. The proliferation of special-use silver flatware and the numerous types of domestic chairs for specific locations and functions (as in "window chairs," "reception chairs," "nursing rockers," "porch rockers," and so on) are only two examples of attempts at analyzing and separating out ("refining") categories of human behavior and providing them with their own supporting artifacts.

This set of assumptions figured largely in *The Growth of Industrial Art* (1892), a large government-financed publication arranged and compiled by Benjamin Butterworth, U.S. commissioner of patents. "Plate 80," "Chairs and Stools," was typical of the book's two hundred full-page plates (Fig. 45). The twelve images were arranged chronologically and progressively, from "No. 1," the "Primitive Seat," to the latest patented forms of folding chairs. The plate caption, which noted that 2,596 patents had been granted in the United States for chairs and stools, was also a concise statement of the intellectual assumption that "refinement" was a process naturally associated with all civilizations, even dead ones.

The Egyptians were among the first to make chairs. On the tombs at Thebes are found representations of almost all the kinds of chairs which modern ingenuity has devised. Thrones, couches, sociables, folding, reclining, lazy back, leather seated, cane seated, split

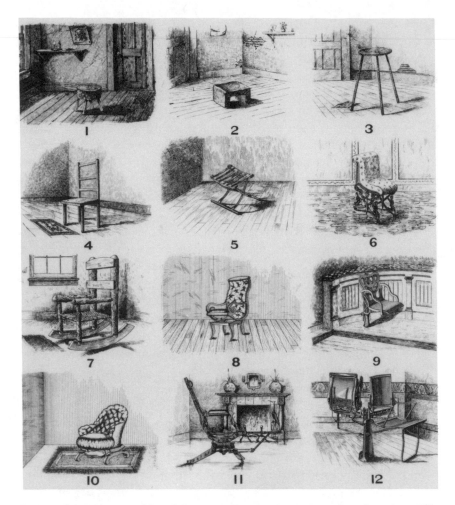

**Figure 45.** "Chairs and Stools," engraving in Benjamin Butterworth, comp., *The Growth of Industrial Art* (1892). Courtesy, The Strong Museum, Rochester, New York.

bottomed chairs, with curved backs, sides and legs with claw feet and foot pads, and upholstered with gorgeous coverings.

The Egyptians, being an Asiatic race, it is presumable from the squatting posture in their paintings and bas reliefs, that the introduction of the chair came in the progress of refinement."[26]

In upholstery, some of the characteristics associated with refinement had roots in the valuable furnishing textiles of the sixteenth, seventeenth, and eighteenth centuries.[27] Along with the simple expense of obtaining raw materials such as silk, the skill and amount of labor involved in spinning, dying, and weaving determined the cost of fine furnishing fabrics. Tapestry, for example, used readily available woolen yarns, but weaving was extremely time-consuming. Fine silk damask was more difficult to weave than its woolen counterpart, and the thread cost more. Weaving plain or patterned velvets of woolen and silk was also a highly skilled process; the fabric had an extra warp that was raised by means of wires and sheared by hand. Expensive textiles for upholstering included one or more of these characteristics: rare materials, close weaving of fine threads, complex surfaces (as in brocaded or voided pile fabrics) or very smooth ones (as in silk velvets or satins), elaborate patterns, and additional handwork applied after the weaving process (as in embroidery and other needlework).

However, in the late eighteenth and the nineteenth centuries, factory-produced textiles became available that paraphrased the characteristics of what were still expensive, hand-loomed fabrics. For example, nineteenth-century factory-woven mohair pile fabrics such as "Utrecht velvet" or voided cotton velveteens, or "velours," offered a version of the patterns and pile textures of expensive hand-woven velvets. Factory-made textiles with complicated figures or a high degree of surface texture were still considered as "rich" as their earlier counterparts, but the connection between appearance and cost had been altered. The results of this changing formula can be seen in chapter 6, figs. 55, 56, and 57.

The volume of fabrics used in upholstery was another aesthetic preference with historical roots. The idea of abundance in the use of textiles—the simple ownership and employment of large amounts of yardage—also originated in the historical scarcity of textiles and the connection of wealth with ownership and display. Both Victorian women's clothing (where dresses might use as much as fifteen yards of fabric) and upholstery, particularly window drapery, demonstrate continuing pleasure in extravagant-looking waterfalls of fabric. Abundance in drapery also meant covering hard surfaces for the purposes of social ceremony and display. In the aesthetic of refinement, abundance and draping developed a new association with "softening," a characteristic connected with the progress of civilization.

The best upholstery also could be expensive because of the labor-intensiveness of its production and its high degree of workmanship. Workmanship was most visible in the cut of materials, their ornamentation, and their elaborate manipulation—the artifice of fine craftsmanship. Many of the new technologies associated with making consumer goods, such as upholstery in the nineteenth century, partly—but only partly—broke the linkage between elaboration and cost (as when the tufting machine made buttoned surfaces common on cheap furniture, a development discussed in chapter 6). The traditional understanding that elaboration denoted cost was transformed, at the level of popular thought, into an equation between such artifice and expressive value, despite several generations of domestic and design reformers who carped that cheap artifice was dishonest. Thus, the prized qualities of upholstery were tied into historical traditions, but these historical associations were elaborated further in ways that reflected the particular preoccupations of Victorian culture, especially its search for evidence of progress in the form of increasing refinement in objects. The more artifice (or elaboration) that existed everywhere in the world, the more progress was manifest.

### SOFTENING

Covering rough or hard surfaces in association with social ceremony is a furnishing practice with a long history. The noble household of medieval Europe was necessarily mobile, since the lord kept tabs on large holdings in highly changeable political circumstances. Nobility invested in easily portable forms of furnishing that were also concrete displays of wealth: "plate" (silver and gold vessels and dishes) and other small precious objects, personal garb, and elaborate textiles such as tapestries. This last group included portable decor used to make canopies, cover walls, form platforms and seats or beds of estate, and cover the rough wood of "stepped buffets," shelves that were used to display plate.[28]

The practice of using valuable textiles as loose and temporary furniture covers survived in middle-class households of the seventeenth and eighteenth centuries when "turkey work" carpets were used as table covers rather than as floor covering. Even in the nineteenth century, before popular acceptance of the "Turkish taste" in the 1870s, with its use of loose textile covers over couches and other seats, the practice of making rough seats temporarily more ceremonial and refined by covering them with textiles on special occasions may have survived in modest households. In Mrs. C. M. Kirkland's short story "Fashionable and Unfashionable," the rural and untutored (but virtuous) Plummer family prepared its "new frame house" for a homecoming party in honor of the daughter Susan, who had spent the winter with city cousins. The family filled spare pitchers with flowers and placed green boughs "here and there"; in addition, "temporary seats had been formed, the rough material of which was carefully hidden by calico spreads and curtains."[29] Instructions for homemade upholstered furniture that consisted of padded and fully covered wooden boxes and barrels were common in architectural advice books, domestic economy manuals, and instruction guides for household arts beginning in the 1830s.[30]

In their made-up forms, furnishing textiles mediated and softened the sensory relationship of the human body to the parlor through the sense of touch, the most fundamental of the "proximate senses."[31] They improved physical comfort when they covered and padded seating surfaces and limited drafts and cold by covering doors, windows, and floors (in the form of carpets). Textiles also appealed to the sense of sight and controlled light in the rooms. As *How to Build, Furnish and Decorate* advised in 1889, "All that tends to soften too hard and prominent outlines; all that lends distance to effects that would otherwise be harshly and painfully near; all that gives variety and an indescribable charm to the mind and sense, should be cultivated in the fitting up of a drawing-room."[32] Upholstery changed the sensation of space in a room by rounding and blurring the forms of pieces of furniture and by providing contrast to the hard forms of ceramics, metals, glass, and wood. Thus, upholstery became a metaphor for the softening of civility.

Softness was often more visual than tactile in seating furniture. Upholstery did pad seats, but we have seen that its softening function was a relative characteristic, especially when the furniture of the 1850s through 1870s is compared with the overstuffed forms of the late nineteenth and early twentieth centuries. The author of *The Practical Upholsterer* (1891) noted that the introduction of "French Work" had led to "a decided revolution . . . during the past few years," in which parlor furniture was "upholstered very soft" with "very soft 8-inch springs" as well as other stuffing.[33] Never meant to be physically "comfortable," much parlor furniture was instead the highly "controlled" furniture of self-controlled parlor people, people who understood the refinement of etiquette. Horsehair seating (which could be woven in attractive patterns or dyed in colors and was valued for its sheen, as bright as silk) was hard, springy, and stiff. Mohair plush, one form of "poor man's velvet" of the 1880s and 1890s, had deep pile and held color beautifully, but the pile was quite stiff and could be hot and scratchy.

Drapery that controlled appearances on both sides of windows, table and mantel covers that swaddled and softened furniture outlines that were tactilely and visually harder, and fabrics that softened highly controlling seating furniture by means of patterns, shine, pile, and rounded profiles or forms of tufting—all these could be interpreted as material analogues to the refinement of civilization (Fig. 46). Modern civilization controlled the world by softening the rough, unrestrained relationships of people through etiquette, especially in the ceremonial realm of the parlor, and by the influences of high culture. One character in William Dean Howells's 1885 novel *The Rise of Silas Lapham* mused about the civilizing process, using the coded vocabulary of refinement: "Once we were softened, if not polished, by religion; but I suspect that the pulpit counts for much less now in civilizing." Its place had been taken by the secular realm of manners.[34]

### RICHNESS AND ORNAMENT

As a quality associated with furnishing textiles, "richness" described both visual and tactile qualities that sometimes, but not always, implied costliness. The term could be used to describe buildings. "The style of street architecture should be rich [varied, intricate] rather than classical," declared the editor of *Harper's New Monthly Magazine* in 1854; fifty years later, the term was used to describe the qualities of more ephemeral objects such as the "Rich Persian Striped Couch Cover" offered by Sears, Roebuck and Company.[35] In textiles, the typical characteristics of being "rich"— physical weight, luxurious surfaces, and deep color—could be reproduced through less expensive means that paraphrased the coded appearance. *Our Homes: How to Beautify Them* informed its readers that although portieres could be made from "rich silks, satins, and damasks, . . . a very rich yet cheap material is found in wool blankets dyed any desired color."[36] "Richness" also described visual intricacy created by workmanship (cutting, sewing, and embellishing with fine details), no matter how inexpensive the material, as when Fanny N. Copeland informed the readership of *Peterson's Magazine* that the "effect" of window valances was "made much richer by a fringe, which may be attached to almost every kind of piped valance with a certainty of improvement."[37] The Victor Manufacturing Company of Chicago advertised its "Parlor Suite No. 336" in terms of its richness: "You will observe the rich upholsterings, the back being arranged with bisquit tufting and the front ruffled and buttoned."[38] Appreciative observers enjoyed the interplay of folds and shapes and the juxtaposition of drapery with other surfaces below. Even a rapid survey of other decorative uses of textiles—clothing and building draping, for example—indicates an in-

**Figure 46.** Woman sewing in her "softened" parlor, frontispiece of *Needlecraft: Artistic and Practical* (1889). Because the softening effects of upholstery were gentle influences, rather than demanding and overtly didactic, they also could be read as a particularly "feminine" sensory experience. Household textiles had always been associated with women, even if they were the products of professional upholsterers. Courtesy, The Winterthur Library: Printed Book and Periodical Collection.

creasing interest in artifice in the use of fabrics, especially after 1870, and an overarching style of fabric use that cut across artifact categories.

Like specialized form, properly finished ornament, evidence of the progress of craft, was a metaphor for higher levels of civilization. One 1850 *Godey's* article, "A Visit to Henkels' Warerooms," suggested how even a visit to a furniture manufactory could encapsulate the progress of refinement. The author regarded "more florid and ornate" furniture styles "where the *carver* is to decorate and embellish" as "rising higher" than "simple styles of construction." Further developing the connection of "finish" to progress, the anonymous visitor to Henkels's manufactory and warerooms proceeded through the establishment in a sequence that made furniture-making a clear metaphor for the progress and refinement of civilization. The visitor passed "hundreds of respectable and temperate artisans, fashioning sumptuous and splendid articles, from their rudest commencement up to the most elaborate decoration and finish." The tour culminated in the arrival at "the saloons, where is displayed the perfected furniture in all its variety of graceful forms, beauty of execution, and delicacy of finish." Having arrived at the "present" in these furniture displays, the author then stopped to admire the fine details of carving in particular, "the hanging foliage, budding flowers and waving scrolls."[39] He showed evidence of his own refinement in his attention to these small niceties.

Increasing accuracy in the rendering of illusionistic, three-dimensional detail on the surfaces of textiles, including carpets, printed fabrics, and needlework, also signaled progressive refinement in the realm of popular taste. The author of an article on the "Mosaic Hearth Rug" in *Frank Leslie's Ladies' Gazette of Paris, London, and New York Fashions* remarked: "It is wonderful to what perfection the manufacture of carpets has arrived. First, checks, stripes, and stars were considered wonderful inventions of the loom. Then came flowers trailing over a ground of some positive color . . . and clusters of fruits were beautifully interwoven in the loom; now we have whole pictures rendered, as with the hand of an artist, perspective foreground, all preserved until one shrinks from treading on anything so perfect."[40] The trellises, clinging vines, and flower bunches of Victorian wallpapers and printed fabrics probably provided similar pleasures.

Fiction sometimes parodied the taste for naturalistic depiction in carpets and on furniture by making these objects the focus of admiration among characters who were depicted as rubes. *High Life in New York* parodied this presumed affectation when Slick encountered such furnishings as "little square benches, . . . all kivered over with lambs and rabbits a sleeping among lots of flowers, as nat'ral as life." Slick also admired naturalism in painting. He commented on a rooster on a coat of arms: "Nat'ral, it seems to me, as if I could hear it cockadoodledoo right out."[41]

Design reformers debated whether accurate naturalistic rendering or "conventionalized" (flattened and somewhat abstracted) depiction of design motifs was more advanced and refined. Yet even with the animosity that proponents of the two points of view displayed toward each other, they were debating simply the terms of progress and refinement, not the desirability of increasing progress in design or the desirability of intricacy itself. Charles Locke Eastlake acknowledged as much when he complained about exactly the kind of popular eye we have been describing. He loved detail as much as any of his peers, but he approved of only certain kinds and believed that the characteristics of "elegance" and "richness" were being falsely ascribed to other kinds of details:

> The taste of the public and of the manufacturers has become vitiated from a false notion of what constitutes beauty of form. Every article of upholstery which has a curved outline, no matter of what kind the curve may be, or where it may be applied, is considered "elegant." Complexity of detail, whether in a good or bad style of ornament, is approved as "rich," and with these two conditions of so-styled elegance and richness, the uneducated eye is satisfied.[42]

We have seen that visual complexity was an integral component both of whole rooms and of single objects furnishing those rooms. "Turkish cushions for settees and sofas" were praised for their "rich appearance" in an 1891 issue of *Decorator and Furnisher* because "the details of ornament" were "very minute."[43] Complex compositions could vary in scale from the entire arrangement of artifacts in a room setting to the juxtapositions of materials, techniques, patterns, and textures within a single artifact. This suggests a general interest in long, careful looking. Consider the exercise of viewing photographs of interiors, from the last quarter of the nineteenth century in particular, as if through a lens of increasing magnification. The same interest in detail and elaboration is expressed in the whole decorative scheme, on the display of a single tabletop, and finally in a single object on that tabletop. "Mrs. L. H. Owen's Room" in Trumansburg, New York, demonstrates such an interest (see fig. 42). Furniture and drapery trimmings and hardware exemplify the level of visual detail given to small components of decorative designs (Fig. 47).

# Curtain Poles.

We give below a number of specimens of Curtain Poles, each pole showing with two different styles of ends, thus giving in a comparatively small space thirty-two distinct patterns to select from. The cost of the pole varies according to the style of trimmings, as will be seen from the price opposite each end.

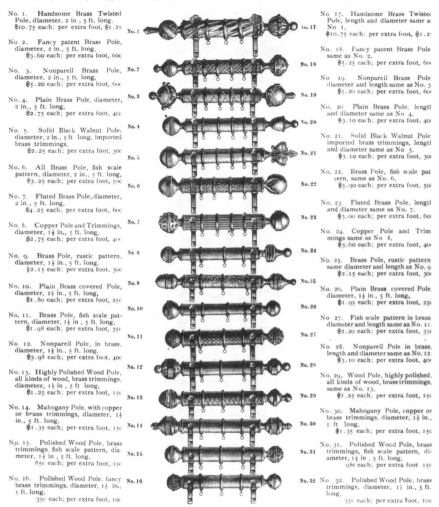

No. 1. Handsome Brass Twisted Pole, diameter, 2 in., 5 ft. long. $10.75 each; per extra foot, $1.25

No. 2. Fancy patent Brass Pole, diameter, 2 in., 5 ft. long, $3.60 each; per extra foot, 60c

No. 3. Nonpareil Brass Pole, diameter, 2 in., 5 ft. long, $5.20 each; per extra foot, 60c

No. 4. Plain Brass Pole, diameter, 2 in., 5 ft. long, $2.75 each; per extra foot, 40c

No. 5. Solid Black Walnut Pole, diameter, 2 in., 5 ft. long, imported brass trimmings, $2.25 each; per extra foot, 30c

No. 6. All Brass Pole, fish scale pattern, diameter, 2 in., 5 ft. long, $3.25 each; per extra foot, 50c

No. 7. Fluted Brass Pole, diameter, 2 in., 5 ft. long, $4.25 each; per extra foot, 60c

No. 8. Copper Pole and Trimmings, diameter, 1½ in., 5 ft. long, $2.75 each; per extra foot, 40c

No. 9. Brass Pole, rustic pattern, diameter, 1½ in., 5 ft. long, $2.15 each; per extra foot, 30c

No. 10. Plain Brass covered Pole, diameter, 1½ in., 5 ft. long, $1.80 each; per extra foot, 25c

No. 11. Brass Pole, fish scale pattern, diameter, 1½ in., 5 ft. long, $1.98 each; per extra foot, 35c

No. 12. Nonpareil Pole, in brass, diameter, 1½ in., 5 ft. long, $3.98 each; per extra foot, 40c

No. 13. Highly Polished Wood Pole, all kinds of wood, brass trimmings, diameter, 1½ in., 5 ft. long, $1.25 each; per extra foot, 15c

No. 14. Mahogany Pole, with copper or brass trimmings, diameter, 1½ in., 5 ft. long, $1.35 each; per extra foot, 15c

No. 15. Polished Wood Pole, brass trimmings, fish scale pattern, diameter, 1½ in., 5 ft. long, 85c each; per extra foot, 15c

No. 16. Polished Wood Pole, fancy brass trimmings, diameter, 1½ in., 5 ft. long, 35c each; per extra foot, 10c

No. 17. Handsome Brass Twisted Pole, length and diameter same as No. 1, $10.75 each; per extra foot, $1.25

No. 18. Fancy patent Brass Pole same as No. 2, $5.25 each; per extra foot, 60c

No. 19. Nonpareil Brass Pole diameter and length same as No. 3 $5.20 each; per extra foot, 60c

No. 20. Plain Brass Pole, length and diameter same as No. 4, $3.10 each; per extra foot, 40c

No. 21. Solid Black Walnut Pole, imported brass trimmings, length and diameter same as No. 5, $3.10 each; per extra foot, 30c

No. 22. Brass Pole, fish scale pattern, same as No. 6, $5.90 each; per extra foot, 50c

No. 23. Fluted Brass Pole, length and diameter same as No. 7. $3.00 each; per extra foot, 60c

No. 24. Copper Pole and Trimmings same as No. 8, $3.60 each; per extra foot, 40c

No. 25. Brass Pole, rustic pattern, same diameter and length as No. 9, $2.15 each; per extra foot, 30c

No. 26. Plain Brass covered Pole, diameter, 1½ in., 5 ft. long, $1.95 each; per extra foot, 25c

No. 27. Fish scale pattern in brass, diameter and length same as No. 11, $2.20 each; per extra foot, 35c

No. 28. Nonpareil Pole in brass, length and diameter same as No. 12, $3.10 each; per extra foot, 40c

No. 29. Wood Pole, highly polished, all kinds of wood, brass trimmings, same as No. 13, $1.25 each; per extra foot, 15c

No. 30. Mahogany Pole, copper or brass trimmings, diameter, 1½ in., 5 ft. long, $1.35 each; per extra foot, 15c

No. 31. Polished Wood Pole, brass trimmings, fish scale pattern, diameter, 1½ in., 5 ft. long, 98c each; per extra foot 15c

No. 32. Polished Wood Pole, brass trimmings, diameter, 1½ in., 5 ft. long, 35c each; per extra foot, 10c

**When ordering, mention number of article desired and number of page. Do not cut the book.**

**Figure 47.** "Curtain Poles," wood engraving in Daniell & Sons, *Catalogue, Spring and Summer 1885* (New York). Courtesy, The Strong Museum, Rochester, New York.

REFINEMENT AND VISION

The tenets of the popular aesthetic of refinement implied that not only the ability to make but also the ability to see and appreciate intricate detail were natural outgrowths of the civilizing process. If, as the historian Carroll L. V. Meeks has suggested, Victorian picturesque taste laid "consistent emphasis on visual qualities," why might this be so? The character of this set of aesthetic preferences was not, Meeks observed, a simple regurgitation of earlier styles. Through an analysis of the century of American railroad architecture between 1815 and 1914, he argued instead that nineteenth-century art and architecture combined a formal vocabulary of "picturesqueness" with a selective restatement of the ornamental vocabulary of past historical styles. The formal qualities of the "special mode of vision" that he christened "picturesque eclecticism" were variations in silhouette and surface treatment, a sense of movement in masses and outline ("movement" often took the form of asymmetry), visual intricacy, and rough or emphatic texture. These preferences stood in opposition to the classical preferences of the century before and, to Meeks's mind, were the outgrowth of a larger cultural shift "from reason to sensibility"—that is, the growth of romanticism among intellectuals and artists. At the same time, however, Meeks argued that picturesque eclecticism was so dominant that there was no separate vernacular stream of architecture. "The picturesque point of view," he asserted, "dominated all strata of taste and was so universal as to constitute a broadly inclusive system."[44] Meeks's list of the basic characteristics of picturesque eclecticism in architecture can also be applied to an analysis of decorative arts objects; even the small shelf lambrequins noted at the opening of this chapter seem to display some of these characteristics. (Some, asymmetry in particular, can have only a limited application to objects that require balance in order to function, such as a chair or a teapot. Such qualities will instead turn up in the ornament on the teapot, in the ornament of a chair or lounge back, or in asymmetrical groupings of symmetrical objects.)

Although Meeks confined his analysis to buildings, popular enthusiasm for visual detail actually reflected important changes in the sensory life of ordinary people in the nineteenth century. Innovations in the technology of image-making in the nineteenth century introduced people to a new realm of visual detail. Photography showed Victorians how the world "really looked" by rendering fine detail with apparent impartiality. So did engraving, particularly wood engraving, the inexpensive medium used by newspapers, periodicals, and trade and mail-order catalogs until the turn of the century.

Mid-nineteenth-century commentators were highly conscious of the proliferation that had occurred in published images, especially in illustrated books and popular periodicals. Calling engravers "wonder workers," "A Chapter on Book Illustrations" published in *Ladies' Repository and Home Magazine* for October 1869 stressed the wonder of this change, which also was a result of the availability of cheaper wood-pulp paper for printing: "Among the wonders of the day we number the rapidity with which we are favored by the publishers of our own and foreign lands with illustrated works in prose and verse. . . . What trophies of the genius, taste, and skill of the nineteenth century—the culmination of ages of patient thought and persevering labor!"[45]

A decade earlier, the lead article in the August issue of *Godey's*, describing the technology of engraving for readers, suggested that the proliferation of images was "the best [method] for diffusing knowledge amongst mankind . . . the rapidity and cheapness with which an object now can be sketched, engraved, and printed, suggests the possibility of obtaining an instrument for forwarding the improvement of mankind more powerful than the press for printing words."

> Pictures have a great advantage over words, as they convey immediately knowledge to the mind; they are equivalent, in proportion as they approach perfection, to seeing the objects themselves, and are universally comprehended. . . . Not only have the facilities for multiplying designs by means of engraving been instrumental in conveying knowledge through the medium of the eye, but the arts and sciences, in all their varied branches, have been highly indebted thereto.[46]

Wood engraving was the process of choice for most popular periodicals and less expensive books because it was easier to execute (and therefore cheaper) than steel engraving, and the cut boxwood blocks could easily be added to pages of set type. The vivid depictions of news events, sentimental or comic illustrations in fiction, and renderings of consumer goods also encouraged the pleasure of looking at detail. Because it is a linear medium, produced by cutting away from a block of boxwood on the end of the grain, wood engraving cannot render tonal variation (as lithography can) except by means of built-up surfaces of lines. Outlines and textures represented by such linear means seem to suggest that the objects depicted are almost "hyper-real," and they invite a certain kind of deep looking. "A Chapter on Book Illustrations" suggested that these qualities were "valuable peculiarities" and that the "brilliancy of effect, a richness and crispness of touch, with gracefulness and freedom of handling [line]," made wood engravings an excellent means of translating the artist's hand into a mass medium, of creating a revolution in art for ordinary people.[47]

The second, and ultimately most profound, revolution in seeing in the nineteenth century was the development of photography.[48] Indeed, nineteenth-century photographic images are often astonishing in the amount of detail they render. Daguerreotypes presented what seemed an almost infinite amount of detail, thanks to the slowness of the exposure time, the mirrorlike quality of the sensitized plate that received the image, and the fact that the image was not enlarged in developing (in other words, it lost none of its resolution). Stereographic views, especially those from the first few decades of the process, were also cherished for the minuteness of their detail, the worlds contained in their images. Oliver Wendell Holmes's 1859 essay "The Stereoscope and the Stereograph" articulated the delights of long, thoughtful looking through a stereopticon, a visual form of loitering:

> This is one infinite charm of the photographic delineation. Theoretically, a perfect photograph is absolutely inexhaustible. In a picture you can find nothing which the artist has not seen before you; but in a perfect photograph there will be as many beauties lurking, unobserved, as there are flowers that blush unseen in forest and meadows. It is a mistake to suppose one knows a stereoscopic picture when he has studied it a hundred times by the aid of the best of our common instruments.[49]

Where might other evidence be found to support these speculations on increasing visual acuity among common people in the nineteenth century? We have seen that decorating advice literature sometimes offers not only thick descriptions of the contents of successful rooms but also clues to the ideal experience of looking at those rooms. *How to Build, Furnish and Decorate* described the parlor, the room most devoted to culture and the room richest in the possibilities it offered for refined looking:

> And now let the reader take a rapid survey of the drawing room here theoretically furnished. The door is flung open, and he crosses the cool Chinese matting, and steps upon the velvety pile or Persian carpet. . . . The walls, mirrors, seats and pictures seem to form one continuous, harmonious, though varied, panorama of pleasing

forms and colors, mingling and contrasting. The pieces of furniture
are not instantly received on the retina of the eye as so many inky
blotches on a white wall; but slowly, and as the eye becomes accus-
tomed to the room, one by one the different parts are unfolded. Bits
of color, unobserved at first, starlike appear. . . . the room [is] the
more enjoyed the more occupied.[50]

However, the records of individual experience—the diaries and letters of
ordinary people living in the nineteenth century—say little about their
aesthetic preferences and experiences, and this is not surprising. Artifacts
typically provide what Baxandall has described as "complex non-verbal
stimulations" that are rarely articulated, much less preserved in letters
and journals.[51] Many official accounts of the various expositions provide
lengthy descriptions of decorative arts objects, but their authors, like those
of decorating advice books, tend to be highly trained observers with a distinct aesthetic point of view. Other kinds of descriptions of visual phenom-
ena, those written by popular journalists and even the anonymous authors
of mail-order catalog text used throughout this chapter, are more useful
in an effort to reconstruct popular seeing. For example, an anonymously
authored history of the Brooklyn and Long Island Fair, held to aid the U.S.
Sanitary Commission in February 1864, offered descriptions of some of
the textile displays, which found favor because of their great variety and
their abundance of visual stimulation. Of the Berlin work (the "worsted
department"), the author noted: "This was one of the most interesting, as
it was naturally one of the most brilliant departments of the fair. . . . The
richness, vividness, and variety of the articles which heaped the tables,
fluttered from the pillars, or glowed from the walls, gave one the impression of a bevy of rainbows playing hide and seek in the room."[52] A hanging
display of throws and bedspreads, seen from below, "presented a spectacle
of wonderful brilliancy, completely tapestried as it was with afghans, quilts,
and spreads, of the most vivid colors."[53]

Deciphering the aesthetic of refinement as it applied to upholstery suggests that the consideration of formal aesthetic content is retained properly
within broader discussions about how people create meaning. In the case
of Victorian culture, we can, through such means as the study of popular
texts, find broad areas of cultural concern that shape the forms of association and meaning that people bring to those objects they consider important.[54] If the modes in which the ideals of refinement were expressed
seem redundant, that is because cultures never communicate important
messages only once. Whatever important messages Victorian furnishings
carry are repeated many times elsewhere, through many vehicles.[55]

All analyses of material culture are plagued to some degree by one question: How are we to know the extent to which makers and users of artifacts understood the levels of meaning that historical analysis now ascribes to what remains of their material culture? How, for example, can we know that a parlor maker who chose to drape every flat surface or opening into a room with elaborately cut, patterned, and embellished textiles *knew*, even if only tacitly, that these furnishing choices were metaphors of parlor etiquette? In truth, we often cannot know such a thing with any certainty, but what we can do is map the terrain of plausible meanings, chart what a motivated individual who is not a specialist could know, and speculate how participation in the sensibility of his or her culture was possible. Thus the concept of taste in any facet of cultural expression itself is largely a product of a matching process. Whereas one individual may be able to appreciate a visual experience in certain ways, another, having a different degree of formal and informal training, will "see things another way," so to speak.[56] Both individuals are operating within the range of visual cognition of their culture. Not every participant in Victorian culture was equally fluent in, or personally comfortable with the use of, the full range of visual discriminations and their cultural analogues from other spheres of activity. Clearly, popular literature in many forms made a concerted effort to educate its readership in these connections. Such variation among people constitutes levels of competence in making aesthetic discriminations. It is in part a demonstration of artifactual competence, one's ability to employ artifacts for the purposes of communication and to appreciate the levels of information contained in their appearance and use. Some Victorian consumers found rich, nuanced levels of meaning in their possessions; others brought less to the experience of owning and using goods.

Objects that present a particular form of play on visual qualities—visual punning—support the notion that the public's visual sophistication was increasing (Fig. 48). The assumption behind such plays on visual qualities, such as trompe l'oeil effects on painted "curtain papers" (painted shades popular in the mid-nineteenth century), is that the observer understands the relationship the visual pun has to the object on which it is modeled. It is doubtful that anyone who purchased a set of window shades painted with a landscape or a design of cornice, draperies, and lace curtains believed that those shades were the real thing. Rather, the shades constituted a visual pun on that "real thing," an expression of possibilities and participation in the refined aesthetic.[57]

Elaborately decorated domestic objects made of atypical materials— tours de force or "plays" on technological skill—had been popular exhibition items at all the expositions beginning with the Crystal Palace:

**Figure 48.** "Just Out—Our New Curtain Back Suit," broadside for Cleveland Upholstering Company, Cleveland, Ohio, about 1895. Courtesy, The Strong Museum, Rochester, New York.

bedsteads of papier-mâché, tables of glass, and the like.[58] Some visual play originated with elite taste; the decorators of the French Empire particularly delighted in rooms that were hung as tents and in drapery that appeared to be supported by spears. Illustrations of generic household goods that contain sophisticated visual play were common by the second half of the nineteenth century and seem to have been appreciated by ordinary people. An article that was published both in *Godey's Lady's Book* and in *Peterson's Magazine* around 1860 introduced one such pun, a "novel and pleasing effect" in which "the drapery appears to be supported by a rope instead of a cornice."[59] Cushions with life-size representations of lap dogs or cats were popular Berlin-work projects in the middle decades of the century. Sometimes artifact puns were almost mundane. A suggestion for a single aesthetic sofa cushion intended to look like a rumpled loose cover concealing a more precious fabric beneath appeared in the March 1888 issue of *Decorator and Furnisher:* "a Sofa Cushion covered with wine-colored plush, one side of cover turned back, revealing a gorgeous bit of striped embroidery in gold and silk."[60]

Thus the popular aesthetic of refinement received some of its most sophisticated manifestations in artifacts in which the visual message referred to other ordinary objects in the form of visual punning or play. These kinds of upholstery rarely survived. Perhaps they seemed too extreme in their artificiality and inexplicable to the simplified, "modern" popular eye of post-Victorian America and so found their way to the local dump. Understanding the puns behind such objects affirmed the sophistication of adherents of the hyper-visual aesthetic of refinement and afforded them a pleasure that is difficult to reconstitute and understand now. Perhaps Marcel Duchamp's statement about the life span of his own art is pertinent in trying to comprehend the aesthetics of even mundane artifacts made in eras other than our own: "No painting has an active life of more than thirty or forty years. . . . After thirty or forty years the painting dies, loses its aura, its emanation, whatever you want to call it. And then it is either forgotten, or else it enters into the purgatory of art history."[61] The Victorian aesthetic of refinement can never be experienced again as a living idea, but explorations into the language associated with the formal qualities of decorative objects such as upholstery can at least partially reconstruct its dimensions and meaning and give us some sense of its power.

# CHAPTER SIX

# Parlor Suites and Lounges

## Culture and Comfort
## in Factory-Made Seating Furniture

Purchasing a parlor suite (or "suit," both terms were in use throughout the period) was probably the single easiest way to create a modern, gala parlor in the second half of the nineteenth century. A parlor was established, if somewhat bare, when its furnishings included a suite and a center table, placed in a front room containing some kind of floor covering and simple decorative window draperies (see Fig. 21). This compressed vocabulary of parlor furnishing was actually used in some public spaces, such as in the large "parlors" at family resort hotels where a suite, grouped around a center table, represented a separate "parlor" for a single family or a party of visitors.[1]

Custom-made sets of "drawing-room" furniture, which included sofas, chairs, tables, and other cabinetwork, had been available for sale in the United States in the first half of the nineteenth century for well-to-do clients, but no particular formula existed for the number and kind of pieces of furniture included or ordered in these sets. In 1857 the decorating firm of Ringuet-LePrince and Marcotte invoiced Samuel Colt, the inventor of the revolver, for a matching set of furniture of eleven pieces for the drawing room of his new house, Armsmear, in Hartford, Connecticut. The invoice listed two "Stuffed front sofas, arms & legs in carved Rosewood," one "Stuffed Corner Divan," four "Rosewood Medaillon [*sic*] Armchairs," and four side chairs to match, all of which were provided with yellow-and-white satin damask upholstery. The set also included two elaborate rosewood center tables and two matching card tables. The number of chairs in the set may have been selected for the two card tables purchased for the room. The seating furniture alone cost the substantial sum of $822, which included some discounts to Colt from the firm.[2]

At around this time, more modest yet still up-to-date households sometimes contained surprisingly large sets of matching parlor furniture. A catalog for a New York City house auction in 1853 described the furniture in the front parlor as being "EN SUITE"; it included a "Sofa" and a "Tete-a-Tete," a "Sewing Chair," an "Arm Chair," and four "Parlor chairs," all of rosewood and "crimson plush." A marble-topped étagère, "mirror back and doors," and a sofa table completed the set.[3]

Before about 1860, matching sets of seating furniture were commonly incorporated into the parlors of ordinary houses in the form of sets of decoratively painted "fancy chairs." The 1856 inventory for the house of George Clinton Latta (1795–1891), an entrepreneur living in Charlotte, New York (a village on Lake Ontario near Rochester), listed "sets" among the contents of a pair of parlors; these were two groups of six painted wooden "fancy chairs" valued together at eighteen dollars. Latta's parlors represent a transitional type of furnishing between the older, multipurpose parlor and the parlor as modern, gala reception room. They were carpeted, had "damask and lace window curtains and strings [*sic*]" (valued at thirty dollars), and contained two center tables, a piano, a bureau, a bookcase, twelve paintings (family portraits), and a "tete tete" valued at twenty dollars.[4]

By 1856 Latta was an older man, and his family's parlors probably represented a mixture of old and new furnishings. At around the same time, prosperous middle-class families with money to spend and the opportunity to furnish from scratch could purchase sets of parlor furniture whose size and character anticipated a trend toward the seven-piece set, the "parlor suite," that became a furnishing formula in the 1860s.[5] Captain Richard H. Tucker, who operated a shipping line out of Wiscasset, Maine, and owned his own vessels, sailed to Boston to purchase furniture for his new house in 1857. Mrs. Tucker was indisposed, recovering from the birth of their first child, but Captain Tucker knew exactly what to purchase to create a respectable parlor. From A. G. Manning, a furniture dealer located conveniently near Boston's Maine Depot, he bought an eight-piece "parlor sett" for $165 consisting of a sofa, two armchairs, four side chairs, and a matching lounge (see Fig. 17 for a view of this furniture in the 1890s, with Captain Tucker as an old man).[6]

The relatively scarce trade catalogs published between 1855 and 1870 also suggest the gradual development of a standard formula for sets of parlor seating furniture (Fig. 49). Dating from about 1855, the catalog from

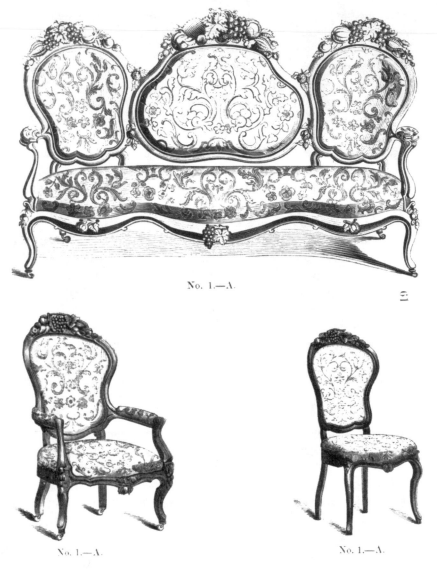

No. 1.—A.

No. 1.—A.

No. 1.—A.

**Figure 49.** Engraving in catalog of Foster and Lee (New York, 1858). This company illustrated most of its seating furniture by type, grouping sofas, armchairs, and other parlor seats on separate pages. However, six pages contained groupings of matched furniture pieces—sofa, armchair, and side chair—that are plainly meant to be sets. Unusual because it is completely illustrated (most furniture trade catalogs remained unillustrated for another decade), the Foster and Lee catalog is missing its price list; whether a standard number of pieces was offered as a set cannot be ascertained. Courtesy, The Winterthur Library: Printed Book and Periodical Collection.

the firm of George J. Henkels of Philadelphia offered a range of pieces in a variety of styles and prices but indicated no standard formula for the number of pieces or the types of chairs. Henkels priced out the options for sofas and chairs individually; advertisements and accounts of the appearance of his warerooms do suggest that he also kept groupings of parlor furniture on the shop floor, ready to be purchased on the spot. Henkels was locally famous for his imported French furniture. In 1855 a well-to-do customer who chose to make up a seven-piece set (a sofa or tete, one lady's and one gentleman's chair, and four armless side chairs) of French-made rosewood "Style Antique Drawing Room Furniture" would have spent $760 for the privilege. A less-expensive seven-piece group of carved rosewood in the "Style of Louis XIV" (probably of Henkels's own make) would have cost from $141 to $214 with plush upholstery and from $124 to $192 with haircloth (the cheapest and least fashionable furniture cover).[7]

## THE EVOLUTION OF THE PARLOR SUITE FORMULA

By the early 1870s, the seven-piece suite formula had become a staple of furniture manufacture (see Fig. 39). Almost all such suites included a tete (sofa), an upholstered armchair (a gentleman's chair), an upholstered armless chair (a lady's chair), and four small chairs having "brace" backs (small brackets support and connect the back to the seat) or "stuffed" backs and upholstered seats. Some catalogs of the 1870s offered consumers as many as fifty choices in wooden frames; wholesale prices typically ranged between $48 and $200.[8]

That so many trade catalogs offered seven-piece suites in the 1870s suggests the presence of a large audience for new parlor furniture; it also implies that these consumers recognized how the ownership of a parlor suite would "make" a modern parlor. However, none of these suites, even those wholesaling for as little as fifty dollars, were easily accessible to the families of farmers, skilled workers, lower-level clerks, or other daily wage earners in the middle decades of the nineteenth century. Two things had to happen before the suite, the consummate emblem of the parlor of culture as ordinary people understood it, could become truly popular: Still-lower price lines had to become available, and consumer credit had to be offered to aspiring parlor makers.

Trade and mail-order catalogs do suggest a steady production trend toward lower price lines between 1880 and 1910. Furniture manufacturers became increasingly adept at making compromises in the structure and embellishment of frames and in the structure and covers of spring seats. In the 1880s, manufacturers offered expanded lines of parlor suites that would retail for less than one hundred dollars in a range of attractive fabrics. The 1880 catalog of Baxter C. Swan of Philadelphia, a manufacturer who specialized in cheap parlor furniture "For The Trade," offered seven-piece suites in haircloth, printed raw silk, and raw silk embellished with velvet or silk plush bands across the seat fronts and backs. Assuming a 100 percent markup, Swan's parlor suites ranged between $72 and $225; sixteen of them would have cost $100 or less.[9] The 1883 catalog of Jordan and Moriarty, a New York City furniture store that targeted its advertising to a clientele with middling incomes, offered "an extensive stock of parlor suites in Hair Cloth, Reps, Brocatelle, Satin, Satin Delaine, Damask, Raw Silk, &c, &c." It illustrated a simple rococo revival grouping with unornamented seats and backs for twenty-five dollars in "haircloth or reps," which were no longer particularly popular or fashionable upholstery fabrics; this suite may, in fact, have been leftover stock from another failed firm. Still, it must have tempted customers with small furnishing budgets. The firm also offered cheap suites with more fashionable covers: raw silk upholstery for fifty dollars and higher and with plush covers for seventy-five dollars. To encourage new consumers, Jordan and Moriarty also offered the innovation of "whatever terms of Installment purchasers may find to be most convenient," an early example of the use of consumer credit in the furniture business.[10]

Price lines that were even cheaper developed in the 1890s. In 1895 Montgomery Ward and Co. offered six different five- and six-piece suites costing between $24.70 and $57.79, the price a function of fewer pieces and lower-quality upholstery. The catalog captions indicated particular pride in a five-piece offering, "the greatest bargain ever offered in a parlor suit at $17.50." Although the overall quality of such inexpensive suites was undoubtedly low, they still paraphrased the popularly desired qualities for parlor furniture: They had spring seats, decorative wooden frames, and showy upholstery in pile or woven figured fabrics, embellished with strips of furry plush.[11] The cheapness of such catalog suites also was a function of lower markups in the mail-order business.

Figuring out just who purchased parlor suites between 1850 and 1910, an era before scientific marketing surveys, is necessarily a speculative exercise. Secure and prosperous members of the professions, independent merchants, small entrepreneurs, managers and factory supervisors, and successful freeholding farmers could easily have purchased suites between 1850 and 1880. At the turn of the century, elaborate suites remained an important furnishing convention for upper-middle-class and middle-class people whose tastes were conservative, who decorated their homes themselves with the help of local merchants, and whose ideas of appropriate furnishing practices were traditional—at least by the standards of 1910.

The other expanding market for suites, especially after 1895, included new consumers such as the modestly prosperous small farmers who enjoyed a period of relative prosperity and had cash to spend after the tough years of the 1890s. Mail-order catalogs, U.S. Rural Free Delivery (1896), and U.S. Parcel Post (1912) offered these rural and small-town residents opportunities to spend their money on city-made furniture. Also among the new consumers were urban, working-class families who had relatively steady, adequate incomes.[12] According to Louise Bolard More's sample in *Wage-Earners' Budgets* (1907), the purchase of decorative furniture became possible when annual incomes ranged between $800 and $1,200; because her sample was from New York City, one assumes the income level and distribution of expenditures reflect the higher cost of living there.[13] Farm families who produced much of their own food probably required less cash to achieve comparable standards of living, as did working-class families in smaller communities.

Installment buying allowed working-class families in cities and towns to participate in parlor making. More noted that the "installment system" was "almost universal among the working-class" and that pianos, sewing machines, and parlor furniture were the most popular large items purchased in that manner. "The most extravagant tendency is to buy elaborate parlor furniture 'on time,'" she observed, "which is far out of keeping with the family's income." From $75 to $125 was the typical cost for parlor furniture, which generally included a "parlor set" and carpet. By the turn of the century, parlor suites may no longer have been fashionable in some middle-class eyes, but they had become truly popular. It is impossible to know how much of the vision of parlor gentility that suites had once engendered had been transmitted to working-class clientele; perhaps the vision had been muted to a general connotation of middle-class respectability. Even as she dubbed it an extravagance, More noted that the purchase of parlor furnishings did indicate "ambition and a higher standard."[14]

The seven-piece parlor suites of the 1870s were, for the most part, of French influence in design, as their predecessor upholstered sets of the 1850s and 1860s had been (see Fig. 49). Stylistically, many were versions of nineteenth-century French interpretations of eighteenth-century styles. This was true not only in the case of the furnishings of the "rococo revival," which were produced steadily at least until the end of the 1870s, but also in the case of suites with more restrained, classical oval (called "medallion") and shield-shaped backs, which were derived from Louis XVI chairs of the 1770s and later.

In addition to French stylistic influences, the range of forms offered in parlor suites of the 1870s also followed a typology, first developed by the French, about the levels of social intercourse and the kinds of seating furniture necessary for socializing in the *appartement de société*. This typological order (visible in the modest suite illustrated in Fig. 39) remained intact even when parlor suites in the late 1870s bore the rectilinear designs of "reform" furniture, which had been offered by Eastlake and other English designers as an alternative to what they considered bad French taste. Use of the term "tete" to indicate a sofa, for example, derives from the French term *tête-à-tête* ("conversation"; literally, "head-to-head"). In the eighteenth century, the French used *tête* to indicate a small-scale sofa that was really just an armchair doubled in width. The *tête* was also called a *confident*. Its name and scale imply that the eighteenth-century *tête* was meant for conversation and perhaps also for genteel flirtation.[15]

The forms of the two large chairs in a suite were derived from French *fauteuils en cabriolet*, armchairs whose curved backs were considered an innovation in seated comfort. (The archetypal "French" chair, the *fauteuil en cabriolet* has had many variations of form and use since the eighteenth century and is still in production.) One of the chairs was an armchair, sometimes termed a "gentleman's chair," with an upholstered seat and back and upholstered armrests. The arms were usually open at the sides. The second large chair was often called, in the 1870s catalogs, a "lady's chair." It had an upholstered seat and back and either recessed arms or none at all. Not an arbitrary feature, this design reflected adaptations undertaken to accommodate the encumbrances of women's full formal dress in the eighteenth century. The set-back, small arms of an eighteenth-century *fauteuil* took into account that women wore panniers (introduced in 1717), large padded frames that made formal dresses stand out on either side. (In less formal circumstances, and as panniers passed from fashion, women sometimes folded full skirts up over the arms of chairs.)[16] Parlor chairs of the 1850s and 1860s had to accommodate another form of exaggerated feminine skirts, the ever-expanding crinolines and hoops that required space to spread out around the chair in a large half-circle. Thus the original eighteenth-century chair design could be justifiably recycled. The disappearance of the crinoline by 1870 made the lower design of the arms of lady's chairs unnecessary, but this form survived in parlor suites until the 1880s. This survival may have been partly associated with doing needlework, because low arms accommodated this kind of sewing posture more easily. And as we have seen in the previous discussion of comfort, the disappearance of crinolines did not mean that women were any less encumbered by their formal dress. The form of the obstacles to sitting simply changed—into the bustle and the skirt cage (called the *tournure*).

The rest of the pieces in most parlor suites were small, armless chairs; trade catalogs often referred to them simply as "parlor chairs." They always had an upholstered spring seat, but the chair back sometimes had no upholstered pad. They also were of a smaller scale than the gentleman's and lady's chairs, which meant that they could be moved easily. Small light-weight chairs had been an important element in furnishing both gala and private rooms in the eighteenth century, whether to allow individuals to move closer to the fireplace or to form groupings for conversation or card playing, and this assumption continued in the modern suite. The four small chairs actually formed a set of their own. The 1883 price list of Mackie and Hilton, Philadelphia makers of cheap parlor furniture, lounges, and mattresses, suggested the traditional placement and function of these four armless chairs when it labeled them "Wall Chairs."[17] The view of Abraham Lincoln's Springfield parlor (Fig. 25) shows the typical placement of small armless chairs through the 1870s, when "aesthetic" ideas encouraged home decorators to scatter groupings of seating furniture throughout rooms.

Thus the seven-piece parlor suite was a concise catalog of the major types of social seating used in eighteenth-century French rooms for social-izing. The tete suggested relaxed social intimacy, the armchairs promoted the "middle ground" of social conversation with peers, and the movable side chairs (which one author acknowledged were "generally uncomfort-able") were meant for short-term sitting at receptions or during social calls.[18] The only notable exception to the French typology was the absence of the taboret or ottoman, an upholstered backless seat that descended from the upholstered stools used in the court of Louis XIV as part of its elaborate system of seating etiquette. Such ottomans occasionally appeared in large, elegant parlors after 1850 and were a graceful seat for women with full skirts. However, they were not incorporated into factory-made suites, perhaps because they echoed the old associations of backless seats with low status.[19]

The range of sizes in parlor seats and the presence or absence of arms, which made long-term sitting more comfortable by providing a natural place for people to rest their arms and hands, also recalled the ancient etiquette of precedence in seating. For hundreds of years, precedence—the set of formal rules for expressing relative social status—had been expressed through the use of a hierarchy of seating furniture. In an early modern European household in which all forms of seating furniture existed, the armchair would stand at the apex of this hierarchy, then the armless chair ("back stool"), the high stool, and the low stool, in descending order. The most honored person in a household would be given the armchair; in fact, the term "chairman" emerged from rules of precedence in seating.[20]

In the etiquette books of the nineteenth century, precedence survived in a gentle form in discussions of the deferential treatment to be offered to guests and aged members of households. A small, inexpensive advice book published in 1857 by the New York City firm of Dick and Fitzgerald described the honorifics of seating:

> When any one enters, whether announced or not, the master or mistress should rise immediately, advance toward him, and request him to take a seat. If it is a young man, offer him an arm-chair, or a stuffed one; if an elderly man, insist upon his accepting the arm-chair; if a lady, beg her to be seated upon the sofa. If several ladies come in at once, we give the most honorable place to the one who, from age or other considerations, is most entitled to respect. In winter, the most honorable places are at the corners of the fireplace, if you have a fire in it.[21]

Seven-piece suites of the 1870s made a standardized and commercialized, but no less rhetorical, statement about formal social life. They represented the parlor as a gala apartment with French antecedents and the social life within its walls as orderly and hierarchical. The forms suggested not only appropriate use but also appropriate parlor deportment, which was controlled and dignified.[22] However, when the parlor suite became a codified unit in furniture manufacturing, its market was the expanding group of middle-class parlor makers, people whose houses probably included a single parlor and perhaps a sitting room or a dining room that could double as a second parlor. With its gentleman's armchair and lady's chair representing the master and mistress of a household, the seven-piece suite might also, for ordinary people, serve as a symbolic representation of the presence and natural hierarchy of a family in the parlor.

Given the large number of firms offering parlor suites, sales competition was probably intense by the late 1870s and encouraged constant innovation in upholstery, frames, and forms in order to attract and hold consumer attention. Thus, business necessity probably dictated that furniture manufacturers begin altering the seven-piece suite to attract new customers only a decade after its emergence as a standard unit of parlor furnishing (Fig. 50). Makers began to include new forms such as corner or window chairs, which also were available separately. With low backs and arms, window chairs were designed to sit beneath a window frame. Such chairs represented a departure from the older typology of parlor suites in that their design was based not on their place in the choreography of parlor sociability but on their surface appearance and the novelty of their specialized design and intended placement in rooms. This specialization in chair forms was one manifestation of the popular aesthetic of refinement.[23]

By the 1880s, the number of pieces in suites was commonly reduced to five, which may have reflected the smaller houses of less prosperous consumers. By that time too, the addition of rocking chairs, the most "domestic" and comfortable of all chairs, further blurred the eighteenth-century typology of gala sociability. In suites of the 1880s, platform rockers usually—and appropriately, because they were conventionally associated with women—replaced the lady's chair.

Some evidence suggests that the introduction of rocking chairs into matching parlor decor was an innovation "from the bottom." As ordinary folk had furnished parlors and sitting rooms for themselves throughout the nineteenth century, they had selected rocking chairs to accompany their simpler furnishings. Before incorporating rocking chairs into suites, upholsterers worked to make them acceptable for parlor furnishing by gussying up the frames of Boston or Grecian rockers with upholstery. For example, the price list for George J. Henkels City Cabinet Warerooms (in about 1855) included "Parlor Rocking Chairs"—with cane seats or spring seats with haircloth covers—only in its cheapest price line of "Plain Style Mahogany or Walnut Parlor Furniture."[24]

The incorporation of rocking chairs into parlor suites, even in disguise as platform rockers, may be the most decisive statement about middle-class efforts to embrace in one form both domestic comfort and the facade of culture. The platform rockers offered with suites of the 1880s were easier on parlor carpets, and their upper structures matched the rest of the set.[25] In the 1870s, parlor platform rocking chairs with fancy frames and covers had been sold in large numbers as single chairs, ornate enough to be the prize of the parlor in physically smaller or more economically modest households. They could also be purchased as a matching addition to a seven-piece suite: The August 7, 1880, price list of Gerrish and O'Brien of Boston offered seven-piece parlor suites and noted, "We furnish a 'Patent Rocker' to match each suite." Or the rocking chair could be used alone.[26]

**Figure 50.** Parlor suite No. 222, photograph in advertising mailer for H. H. Shrenkeisen and Co., New York, 1880–85. Along with the changing typology of forms in parlor suites, this example demonstrates the eclecticism of popular styles. The suite combines "renaissance revival" curves with such "Anglo-Japanese" details on the frame as the sunflowers on the triple back of the settee. Anglo-Japanese motifs were associated with the "aesthetic" design reforms of the 1870s and 1880s. The pleated tufting is like that found on French-style suites that would have been labeled "Pompadour" or "Napoleon" ten to twenty years earlier. Courtesy, Smithsonian Institution.

The reduced size of suites and the incorporation of rocking chairs may have reflected both the realities of furnishing in smaller parlors and the use of such spaces as both sitting and reception rooms, but the frontal and rigidly upright design of the chairs in modest parlor suites still suggested appropriate deportment and emphasized the ceremonial importance of the room. Suite design continued to suggest the desirability of controlled posture and of dignified ease rather than relaxation. It was certainly possible to lounge on a parlor tete or to fling oneself down in a sprawl in an armchair or even to sit with one or both legs off the floor in some larger pieces—and people probably did. But the forms taken by most parlor suites generally maintained the "feet on the floor" suggestion; the user was meant to comport himself or herself in the "easy manner" of gentility. And we have seen that even though parlor suites were padded and their upholstery visually softened parlor suites, until the late 1880s the upholstery was almost always stuffed to be tight and hard. Even the fabrics, particularly stiff horsehair and hot, scratchy mohair plush, did not invite repose. The popular introduction of Turkish furniture in the 1880s helped to break down these old messages about correct deportment (Fig. 51).[27] However, until well into the 1910s, parlor suites remained as metaphors of long-standing ideas about parlor etiquette. Their elements were proper seats for the controlled body postures and feelings of parlor people.

Still, the number of pieces in a parlor suite continued to shrink. In its 1895 catalog Montgomery Ward offered a few three-piece suites for small parlors and allowed customers to select a smaller number of pieces from larger sets; the 1908 Sears, Roebuck and Company catalog followed this practice as well. Three-piece sets eventually supplanted larger groupings and became the standard for catalog offerings of overstuffed living-room furniture in the 1910s. Mixed in with various kinds of other seating, the parlor suite at the turn of the century survived as a residual expression of the old vision of parlor sociability and probably as a reflection of the conservatism of older consumers, for whom the Victorian social conventions of their youths were still meaningful.

## THE AESTHETICS OF PARLOR SUITES

Suites not only signaled the nature of appropriate parlor social life but also allowed ordinary consumers to attain the prized ideal of matched room decor. According to Peter Thornton, unity in interior decoration "became the convention when the concept of *régularité* . . . came to be accepted as

**Figure 51.** Armchair and side chair from "Parlor Suit No. 20," engraving in *Supplement to Bub and Kipp's Illustrated Catalogue of 1885* (Milwaukee, Wisconsin, June 1885). Although Bub and Kipp offered seven-piece parlor suites in American mohair plush for as little as $50 wholesale, No. 20, an overstuffed "Turkish" suite with spring edges, cost $110 with the same cover. The higher cost reflected both the additional upholstery materials and the additional labor involved. Courtesy, The Strong Museum, Rochester, New York.

the basis of good taste in architecture. . . . by the 1640s, it must have been a commonplace in grand circles to have the textile furnishings of important rooms matching." *Régularité*, the sense of order and harmony created in rooms by their architecture and decoration, "seems to have been contrived by applying to the interior . . . the standard precepts of Renaissance architecture" and originally reflected a new sense of the proper qualities of intellectual and social life.[28]

In addition to introducing a standard formula for parlor furnishing, commercial parlors probably played a large role in popularizing the ideal of *régularité*, and by midcentury, middle-class consumers clearly wanted rooms that reflected their ability to plan and execute a comprehensive scheme of decoration, no matter how modest. Most had probably made do with carefully accumulated odds and ends of furniture, and the most dramatic antidote to past scarcity and the best signal of present prosperity was a room that matched from top to bottom. Popular admiration of the decor of public parlors suggests why matching remained an important criterion for parlor seating furniture even though suites were criticized as "stiff, and unhomelike" almost from the moment of their commercial introduction.[29] Unified decor was formal and gala; it resonated with gentility. It did not matter whether consumers understood the ideal of gentility and its beau monde imperfectly or whether the public's ideals of unified decor were derived from the commercialized gentility of hotel parlors, steamboats, and exposition displays. Matching parlor suites made manifest their own-ers' connections with the parlor of culture, even when the suite was embed-ded in a room setting containing many other kinds of furniture.

Beginning in the mid-1870s many advice writers, influenced by the tenets of a self-conscious and elite aestheticism, advocated "harmonious" rather than matching decor, but popular preferences in room decoration clearly still relied heavily on color matching and the domination of sets in a furnishing scheme. Throughout the century, advice for homemade up-holstery, for example, continued to stress matching. In *The American Wom-an's Home* (1869), Catharine Beecher and Harriet Beecher Stowe had ad-vised their readers on how to make a "green room" with thirty yards of chintz. In the late 1880s, directions for decorating a room with homemade upholstery still discussed creating all the furnishings out of a number of yards of one fabric, an inexpensive cretonne (unpolished printed cotton).[30]

Thus the decision to purchase a parlor suite as the centerpiece and start-ing point of parlor (and, later, living room) furnishing never became unfashionable for ordinary consumers. And suites sometimes had very long life spans. Until Victorian furniture was finally displaced by over-stuffed living room sets, parlors were repeatedly redecorated around suites purchased years before. In 1882 Augusta Kohrs, the wife of a prosperous Montana rancher, purchased her seven-piece cut-plush parlor suite in Chi-cago for the goodly sum of $300, and the set (which still bears its original figured red-plush covers) served as a constant through her parlor redeco-rating schemes in 1882–83, 1889–90 (when the parlor was made into dou-ble parlors), 1900, and 1915.[31]

In the last quarter of the nineteenth century, some innovative manufac-turers did try to accommodate advanced tastes for harmonious unmatched furniture with the convenience and guaranteed good taste that parlor suites apparently connoted to ordinary buyers. McDonough, Wilsey, and Com-pany of Chicago offered in its 1878 trade catalog one seven-piece suite with upholstery in several different colors.[32] By the turn of the century even Sears Roebuck and Co. offered to select nonmatching, "harmonious" suites for its customers.[33] The urgings of furniture advice books aside, evi-dence from trade catalogs, artifact survivals, and historical photographs suggests that sets of matching furniture continued to be an ideal for many ordinary consumers.

Just as styles (formulas of proportion and ornament) in average furniture stores today present a somewhat compressed range of the furniture options available from custom producers, factory-made parlor suites generally excluded the most radical furniture designs available from small, elite decorating firms. This was partly due to the calculations of factory owners about what would sell and would therefore merit the production of new templates, jigs, and patterns for the woodworkers and upholsterers. One imagines that the fact that most families owned only one or two parlor suites throughout their life spans also encouraged relatively conservative choices.

Still, the range of decorative options available to consumers in factory-made suites was significant. Manufacturers could offer a number of choices in frames by relying on applied ornament or carving on obvious places, such as the crest rails of chairs, at the same time that they used standard legs and seat rails. And frames generally did not constitute the major expense in manufacturing middle-range parlor suites, thanks to sophisticated American woodworking machinery. Depending on the degree of elaboration in both frames and upholstery, the spring structures and show covers usually accounted for between 60 and 80 percent of the cost of a suite. The upholstered profile of the individual pieces and the color and contrast of their show covers and trims provided most of the visual impact.

The popular taste for elaboration and visual complexity in objects encouraged furniture men to display great ingenuity in the use of materials, including furnishing fabrics. The upholstery of even inexpensive parlor suites could be coded as "refined" through some combination of the following techniques: choice of fabric, including the use of several different fabrics on each piece of furniture; elaboration in the handling of the fabric (buttoning, pleated tufting, ruffling, and puffing); and the use of details such as multicolored trims or buttons in contrasting colors and materials. Suites with absolutely plain upholstery were available for less money, but they appear only rarely in trade catalogs and household photographs. They probably seemed distressingly bald to consumers.

The most popular upholstery fabrics used on factory-made parlor suites tended to have emphatic visual and tactile qualities. Most fell into a few basic types: satin finishes prized for their sheen, bristly and dimensional pile fabrics, and a few types of woven figured fabrics and printed look-alikes. Middle-class consumers wanted heavy upholstery fabrics both because these implied "richness" and because such fabrics were believed to wear better, which was not always the case. For example, early power-loomed "furniture tapestries," woven with unmercerized cotton yarns, absorbed dirt and grew dingy soon after they were purchased (see Fig. 50). The tightly ribbed wool "rep" popular between 1860 and the early 1880s was relatively inexpensive and sturdy, and it was commonly dyed deep colors, typically red or maroon, green, a sepia brown, and golden yellow. More-expensive versions were woven with silk designs imitating stripes of needlework.

With the exception of rep, most suite upholstery fabrics mimicked the aesthetic characteristics of more expensive fabrics. Cotton satine, for example, offered the colors and sheen of silk satin, which was used on very expensive furniture. "Satin-de-laine" (satin-weave wool) was sometimes printed to resemble brocaded silks, whereas printed raw silk, which enjoyed a brief span of popularity in the late 1870s and 1880s, resembled upholstery tapestry. Stiff mohair plush, which wore better than the wool plush in use through the 1870s, appeared on both midquality and better furniture into the twentieth century, but cotton velveteens and "furniture velours," as well as heavy corduroy, offered a cheaper alternative after 1890 and could be printed in vivid colors. Even the cheapest suites were upholstered with fabrics that paraphrased midrange upholstery: "lasting" (a shiny black wool-and-cotton blend more commonly used for coat linings and women's shoe tops) was used in the 1870s as a look-alike for plain, black, power-loomed horsehair.

Advances in weaving technology also made new types of furnishing fabric available to makers of cheap parlor furniture. Imitation tapestry, woven with the jacquard mechanism on the loom, was apparently developed in England as early as the 1830s, becoming inexpensive in America in the 1890s, when the large upholstery weaving industry of Philadelphia made a specialty out of this textile as well as drapery chenilles and curtain lace.[34] In the mid-1880s, rapid growth occurred in the production and introduction of new mixed-fiber upholstery fabrics, which combined high percentages of sturdy, inexpensive cotton with more valuable fibers such as silk. "Silk-faced tapestry," for example, was mostly made of cotton. Little of this fabric survives, probably because the silk surface wore away and left a very shabby-looking cover in its wake. The construction of velvets and plushes also changed, so that only the extra set of warp or weft fibers that produced the pile was made of expensive fibers; the rest was made of cotton, which could withstand the tension of power looms. Velveteens or "velours," popular upholstery fabrics after 1890, were 100 percent cotton.

Along with this coded selection of fabrics, parlor suites also were elaborated through a variety of fabric and stuffing innovations that were new to the nineteenth century: pleated tufting, ruffling and puffing, and the use of contrasting bands of fabric on the same piece of furniture. Although evidence is fragmentary, these innovations were apparently transmitted directly to America by emigrating German and French upholsterers.[35] Sewed, pleated tufting on the backs and arms of chairs and sofas formed dimensional surfaces in a variety of geometric patterns—diamonds, squares, and rectangles. Pleated tufting was freely applied to printed or figured woven fabrics, producing a kaleidoscopic effect (see fig. 50). Such tufting was an elaboration on buttoning layers of stuffing together to prevent its movement on vertical surfaces. Simple buttoning was still in use as a decorative element on seat tops and backs throughout the second half of the nineteenth century, but by the mid-1870s, trade catalogs offered factory-made suites with "piped, plain, star, tufted or pleated backs." Another technique for increasing the visual impact of tufting was to use contrasting buttons in the tufts. These were typically covered with the fabric used on the seat front; brown or black enameled buttons were a second, cheaper choice.[36]

Applying contrasting bands of fabrics was another way of elaborating the upholstered surfaces of suites. Ruffling or puffing, accomplished by applying loosely pleated bands of fabric to the fronts of seats or along the sides or the top of the seat back, was a particularly popular decorative option in the 1870s (see Fig. 21 for both contrasting buttons and ruffling). This option always cost a few dollars extra. "Reform" or Eastlake furniture tended to have upholstery with flat surfaces of fabric, considered in keeping with its more rectangular lines, but to make such surfaces more decoratively complex, manufacturers resorted to a variation on ruffling, offering simple contrasting bands of fabric on seat fronts and backs. These were frequently made of a pile fabric such as mohair plush, which absorbed and reflected light in a pleasing manner.

Finally, the trims of even inexpensive suites offered pleasing visual detail in the cords that covered seams, the gimps that finished raw fabric edges tacked to frames, and the tassels and fringes that became increasingly important with the introduction of factory-made overstuffed "Turkish" furniture (a partial view of a settee that uses many of the techniques discussed above may be found in Fig. 1). Multicolored trims visually tied together and mediated the boundaries between different-colored fabrics and also provided a visual transition between upholstery and wooden frames.

Thus, in their typology of forms, seven-piece suites located in private middle-class parlors originally embodied the concept of gentility, the eighteenth-century ideal of personal cultivation and self-presentation. The formula for the number and types of pieces in parlor suites was subject to the ongoing tension between the parlor of culture and the parlor of comfort. Including rocking chairs in suites was an accommodation to domesticity and the comfortable parlor. Yet if the connection between the seating types in suites and the ideal of gentility became less clear, the elaborated upholstery of parlor suites continued to embody the peculiarly Victorian conception of refinement discussed in chapter 5, resulting in increasing complexity in the appearance of domestic artifacts. Here, "refinement" was characterized by proliferation, elaboration, and complexity. This conception of refinement lay behind consumer preferences for both the ornamentation of wood frames and the suite upholstery, with the skeletal traces of the ideal of gentility embodied in the forms of suite furniture.

### THE LOUNGE

In the mid-nineteenth century, families sometimes purchased a sofa to serve as their only piece of upholstered parlor furniture. By the 1870s, this choice was just as likely to be a lounge, a furniture type that could be made cheaply. It offered an important avenue of access to spring-seat upholstery and packed a remarkable amount of aesthetic information into its frame and cover (Fig. 52). The implications of its name notwithstanding, the parlor lounge was usually a formal-looking, physically stiff piece of furniture whose form and decoration manifested the tensions between parlor makers' aspirations toward appropriate parlor formality and their desire for domestic comfort.

Even when householders could gradually afford a few other pieces of factory-made upholstery, the lounge was often the most eye-catching and stylish piece of furniture. Lounges were always upholstered with springs, but intact examples seem typically to have been stuffed to be rigid and sturdy. Imposing and formal, they exemplified the tension between culture and comfort, seeming to suggest that sitting up straight was most appropriate even as they invited reclining and offered a certain amount of spring-seat resilience. Folding-bed lounges, a popular variation on the form, were used to provide extra sleeping space and were literally both throne and bed. In small houses the vocabulary of parlor furnishing was necessarily paraphrased, compressed to fewer emblematic objects. With their decorative upholstery, set in embellished wooden frames, lounges could serve the aesthetic functions that entire parlor suites served in larger, more affluent settings (Fig. 53). At their cheapest, lounges cost less than the cheapest

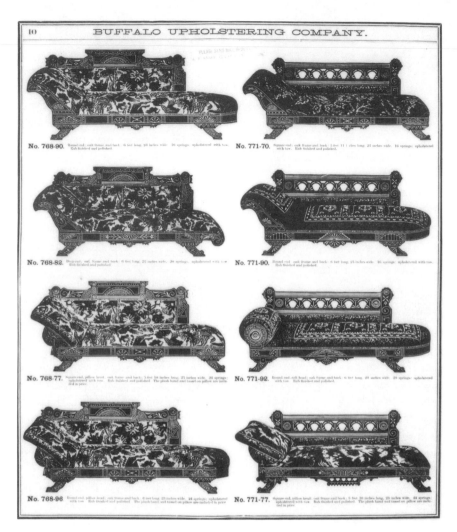

**Figure 52.** "Lounges," illustration in *1890 Catalogue for the Buffalo Upholstering Co.* (Buffalo, N.Y.). The raised backs in the No. 768 and No. 771 lines offered by this firm were identical; the aprons and legs of the lounges in each line could easily be varied with different incised patterns and applied ornament. The variation in each lounge frame appeared in the shape of the raised end and the rounded, squared, or "gondola" or dropped end. Courtesy, The Strong Museum, Rochester, New York.

**Figure 53.** Parlor in house of John Jay Niles and Hattie Hickok Niles, German, Chenango County, New York, about 1885. A lounge upholstered in carpet and further embellished with homemade patchwork pillows was the colorful center-piece of this parlor, which also used other cheap ready-made upholstery (the center table cover and portiere) to attain a refined appearance. Courtesy, Rochester Public Library, Local History Division.

sofa; in 1878 the Boston firm of Samuel Graves and Son wholesaled "Common Lounges with (12 Springs)" for as little as $3.50 in "enamel cloth" (oilcloth that was used as a substitute for horsehair or leather).[37]

Victorian lounges were descendants of seventeenth-century daybeds and late eighteenth-century and early nineteenth-century neoclassical couches or daybeds, which had asymmetrical backs, or no backs, and one raised end. Such couches were often sold in pairs for expensive and fashionable drawing rooms. Between 1850 and 1870, large sets of parlor furniture still sometimes incorporated a lounge. The Richard Tucker family's parlor suite of 1857 included one as part of the set at the time of purchase, and the double parlors of Southmayd, a Massachusetts summer house that contained furniture by Alexander Roux, also contained a walnut-framed lounge, upholstered with striped rep, en suite with the rest of the furniture (Fig. 54). By 1870, however, lounges were no longer offered as part of the formulaic factory-made parlor suite.

**Figure 54.** Lounge, attributed to Alexander Roux, walnut, original upholstery of striped wool rep, about 1870. This lounge was used in a pair of parlors containing labeled furniture by Roux at Southmayd, a Stockbridge, Massachusetts, summer home. Unlike later factory-made lounges, it has a spring structure resting on webbing. The back also is stuffed from a webbing foundation. Courtesy, Smithsonian Institution.

Lounges were not confined to parlors but also appeared in the dining rooms that doubled as family sitting rooms. The Yearick family of Konnarock, Virginia, furnished its dining and sitting room with a lounge and a rocking chair as well as a table and a sideboard.[38] Furnishing advice books directed to more prosperous consumers even suggested that leather-covered lounges should always be made a part of dining room furniture. Such use was associated with upper-class dinner-party etiquette, where men used the dining room as a place to smoke and talk after the meal. Lounges also appeared in libraries and bedrooms; Ella Rodman Church, author of *How to Furnish a Home* (1881), considered lounges "quite a necessary piece of furniture in a bedroom, in order that the bed may be kept in the immaculate condition which is its principal charm, as 'throwing' one's self down on it for an afternoon nap is no improvement to snowy covers, and gives a generally untidy appearance."[39]

Backless couches were also found in modest parlors as well as in more private rooms such as sitting rooms, bedrooms, and libraries. The unidentified Rockland County, New York, family in their parlor (see Fig. 19) sat across a backless couch as though it were a sofa. One particularly popular type of "Turkish" couch, which could be quite expensive in its best quality, was typically advertised as library furniture for larger houses.[40] Covered with dark brown or black leather or leather cloth, it was produced until at least 1915. Because backless couches gave sitters nothing to lean against, parlor makers sometimes piled the surface with cushions that could be arranged as needed.

A carpet-covered lounge made by Martyn Brothers of Jamestown, New York, in the mid-1880s demonstrates where most of the visual information of "style" was typically located on lounges (Fig. 55). The raised back is framed with decorative wood like the back of a parlor suite sofa or tete. The woodworkers created a complex composition of shapes, inscribed lines, and contrasts of dark and gilt using the simple, rapidly executed techniques of cutting out with a jigsaw, inscribing lines with a router, and using paint rather than inlay. This particular upholstery fabric, a brightly colored floral-pattern carpet, did not require additional ruffling to give the appearance of elaboration. The large-headed gimp nails, which were spaced widely to reduce their number, held the cheap cotton trim in place and provided another decorative detail. As Figure 52 suggests, lounges of the last quarter of the nineteenth century all used the same visual formula to express style. Backless couches, which became more popular after 1890, contained most of their visual information across the front, particularly on the raised end.

In modest households the lounge continued to be a centerpiece of parlor furnishing through 1910, at least partly because it did encapsulate so many of the structural and aesthetic characteristics of parlor suites. However, it was in time replaced by the overstuffed sprung sofa, which had a symmetrical raised back and two arms (see Fig. 63). (After 1910, such sofas often had complex structures with sprung decks and backs and loose seat cushions that also contained springs.) In about 1900, enterprising manufacturers of inexpensive upholstered furniture introduced a hybrid adjustable lounge dubbed the "Roman divan." The Roman divan was many times cheaper than its contemporary, the upholstered davenport, which it resembled when both ends were raised (Fig. 56). Roman divans offered "refined" visual qualities—ornamental frames, fancy fabrics, and tufted surfaces—along with spring-seat structures. They could be adjusted to conventionally formal positions with both arms upright; with one or both

**Figure 55.** Lounge, painted oak, tapestry, carpet, Martyn Brothers, Jamestown, New York, about 1885. This lounge exemplifies the design, structure, and material compromises that made the form a popular type of furniture for consumers with modest furnishing budgets. Its heavy springs rest on a board bottom, and the stuffing layer is excelsior (wood shavings). Courtesy, The Strong Museum, Rochester, New York.

ends down, they could accommodate reclining postures. Roman divans also served as a transitional form in the move toward the cheap overstuffed davenport sofas that became popular in the 1920s.

### LOUNGES AND FACTORY-ORGANIZED UPHOLSTERED FURNITURE

Lounges occupied an interesting and complicated niche in the burgeoning factory production of upholstered furniture in the second half of the nineteenth century. Through the 1890s, lounge manufacture was related to mattress manufacture. This was partly due to the established popularity of bed lounges, the forerunner of convertible sofas.[41] In the 1870s the Philadelphia factory of Samuel Cooper produced mattresses as the largest part of its business, which by the mid-1870s occupied a four-story building and employed more than one hundred people. Its annual output was fifteen to twenty thousand mattresses and beds and sixteen thousand lounges.[42]

**Figure 56.** Adjustable couch (called "Roman divan"), oak, pine, printed voided cotton velveteen, stamped-metal beaded trim, United States, 1900–1915. The *Sears, Roebuck and Co. Catalogue No. 111, 1902* (Chicago) introduced the "Roman Divan Couch" as the "Latest Invention" in upholstery, "one of the most attractive, and at the same time serviceable pieces of furniture ever manufactured. . . . It answers as a divan, sofa, Davenport and adjustable bed couch, and is equally comfortable in any position." Courtesy, The Strong Museum, Rochester, New York.

Lounges also were an important part of factory-organized upholstery production among companies that specialized in cheaper furniture lines. In the mid-1870s J. P. Reifsneider of Philadelphia produced both lounges and parlor furniture in a building that he shared with three other firms. The firms also shared the use of a collection of steam-powered woodworking equipment, including both band saws and jigsaws, a planer, and a molding machine. Reifsneider produced "about 100 (lounges) every working day," with the upholstering taking place in the "finishing department" over his downtown warerooms.[43] In 1872 the Baltimore firm Rand and McSherry was wholesaling "common lounges," "bed lounges," and "fancy" or "small French" lounges, most of which cost ten to fifteen dollars. The cheapest, the $6.50 common lounge "plain front and back," had no buttoning or other upholstery ornamentation but had a "lasting or fancy cover." Rand and McSherry's most expensive bed lounge, with a cover of lasting, Brussels carpet, or haircloth, cost twenty-three dollars.[44] The

Mueller and Slack Co. of Grand Rapids, Michigan, which billed itself as "Manufacturers of Upholstered Furniture," offered a similar range of goods in the 1890s.[45]

Such a large piece of furniture could be offered for so little money because lounges were subject to a number of ingenious compromises in production. Cost-saving strategies were applied to the frames, the spring structures, the materials used for decorative covers, and the ways those covers were handled, yet the finished product still expressed the aesthetics of refinement. To reach less affluent markets, businessmen whose firms produced and marketed modestly priced upholstery placed limits on their choice of materials, used technology where it was available, and compressed the number and kinds of steps involved in fabricating lounges.

To understand how this process worked, we can use modern-day women's "designer" purses and their knockoffs as an easily recognizable case study. Designer purses are often canvas bags printed with the initials of a designer and coated to make them waterproof. The monogram is recognizable to other women who know about fashion. Such bags are also well made. The pieces are carefully cut out and assembled so that the pattern made by the monogram is oriented squarely. The pieces are finished with leather welting; the leather bag handles are carefully rolled and stitched to be comfortable to grip; and the hardware is heavy cast brass. Inexpensive versions of the same bag are made from patterns and materials that, seen in passing or at some distance, resemble those of the prototype closely. However, seen at close range, the knockoff purse has fabric printed with an unknown monogram designed to look like the expensive one. The binding around the bag edges and handles is synthetic, and the stitching and finishes are much less carefully executed. The hardware is a soft "white metal" of unknown composition, plated with a thin brass finish.

The owner of the knockoff purse knows well that hers is not an "original." What her cheap purse provides is style, or what fashion magazines would call a "status look." Its appearance signals the owner's awareness of and participation in current fashion; she would have the expensive bag if she could. Although it could be argued that she is buying a "sham" and should settle for an inexpensive bag that is "honest"—that is, one that looks like an inexpensive canvas purse—it could also be argued that she is communicating her up-to-dateness and interest in the fashionable world through this detail. The bag is a rhetorical statement designed to persuade others about her taste and aspirations; it skirts the issue of her means.

Analyzing the economics of furniture design similarly requires comparing and interpreting the processes of production for both expensive and cheap objects rather than rendering judgments about quality.[46] Like manufacturers today, nineteenth-century furniture factories tended to specialize in a price level. One of the major differences between shops that produced cheap furniture and those that made expensive items was the amount of handcraftsmanship involved. Reducing handwork, which could never be completely eliminated, decreased costs.

The cost of lounges could first be cut by using power band saws and jigsaws to rough out frames and cut out decorative shapes; power planers made smooth surfaces and decorative moldings; power lathes turned legs and decorative spindles; routers made simple incised designs, sometimes on more than one piece at a time with the aid of a pantograph; and machines bored dowel holes to fit frame parts together. Finishing and decorating lounge frames always required some handwork, but as the Martyn Brothers lounge shows, the light and dark areas made by inlay in expensive furniture could be mimicked with paint, and carving could be implied in cut-out shapes or in incised-line decoration. In the cheapest lounges the cover fabric was simply pulled over the rough wooden frame, so the piece required no decorative finishing except on the legs, which could be easily turned with a foot- or steam-powered lathe.

Lounges of the 1850s through the early 1870s had featured curvilinear shapes made with curved moldings (see Fig. 55). They were sometimes made more ornamental through the application of a bunch of carved fruit or flowers at the highest point of the crest rail. When "reform" ("Queen Anne," "Anglo-Japanese") styles of furniture were introduced to American consumers in the late 1870s (see Figs. 50 and 52), lounge makers were able to take advantage of the rectilinear design of such furniture. They could easily assemble a variety of wooden parts to make the backs of lounges into complex compositions, the focus of design interest. Combining various back designs, seat-frame shapes, carved seat rails, and cover fabrics, manufacturers such as the Buffalo Upholstering Company were able to offer customers many choices in lounge design with a set of standard parts.

During the 1890s, the backless couch became increasingly popular. Having lost the raised back as a site for elaboration, manufacturers used carving to focus attention on the wooden rail around the couch frame, or they covered the entire frame with fabric, embellished it with "Turkish" fringe, and made the raised pillow head especially decorative. (The raised end sometimes took the guise of a movable pillow even though it was part of the lounge frame.) Eliminating carving and finishing altogether also saved money. One unidentified maker even used "hairy paw" feet and trim of cast metal (nailed over plain oak stubs), an alternative that allowed more

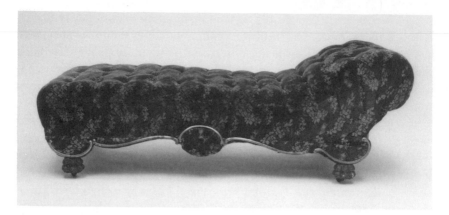

**Figure 57.** Couch, oak, cotton velvet, cast and stamped brass, United States, 1895–1905. The tufting on this couch, which features even rows of buttoning and horizontal pleats in the fabric, may be the product of a tufting board, which enabled upholsterers to avoid measuring the spaces for buttons. The round medallion of tufts appears to have been made separately from the rest of the upholstery and then applied to the frame. The couch is trimmed with cast strips of metal rather than textile gimp. Courtesy, Collections of the Public Museum of Grand Rapids.

attention to be paid to the upholstery within the allowed production budget for the piece and that also represented an effort to attract consumer attention with novelty (Fig. 57).

Along with reducing the costs of making the frame, lounge makers experimented with a second economics of design, dedicated mostly to reducing the cost of the upholstering itself. Cost cutting in the upholstering process required decreasing the costs of creating the multilayered upholstery sandwich and providing an appropriately decorative show cover while still offering customers a certain amount of style. By the 1880s, when cheap upholstered furniture proliferated, manufacturers had developed strategies to partially resolve both difficulties.

Because of its popularity in the furnishing of modest households and because of the size of the finished product, lounge making is a particularly useful demonstration of the search for shortcuts to reduce the amount of time and skilled labor involved in constructing the internal sandwich of spring-seat upholstery discussed in chapter 4: webbing, springs and twines, fabric, stuffing material, undercover, and show cover. (Cheap parlor suites display some but not all of these shortcuts because of the smaller size of the pieces.)

Resilient spring structures could fail in a number of ways—poor spring tying, rotted webbing and broken twines, improperly tempered springs—and were difficult to repair. However, the public clearly associated the simple presence of resilient seat structures with high-quality upholstery. The most expensive springs were the best tempered and most resilient; the heavier, less-expensive springs used by makers of cheap furniture seem to have been stiffer, but because they still gave and returned to shape, they were good enough. Coiled horsehair was the most resilient stuffing material, but it was also the most expensive. Plant materials—tow (linen waste), moss, and excelsior (wood shavings)—provided cheaper, although less springy and long-lived, alternatives, and it was to these materials that lounge makers turned.

The 1890 price list and trade catalog for the Buffalo Upholstering Company, which billed itself as "the Largest Lounge Manufactory in the World," demonstrates how differences in frames and seat structures affected price. The cheapest lounge wholesaled for five dollars in tapestry carpet or "Moquette Plush" (a similar carpet with cut pile); it had an "imitation walnut" frame, was upholstered with tow, and contained fifteen springs, probably stapled to a board bottom. The top-of-the-line lounge, with the same fabric cover, wholesaled for nineteen dollars; its frame was oak, and it featured thirty-three springs and a "web bottom," the traditional base for fine spring structures.[47]

Although they could save money by choosing materials carefully, upholstery factories faced other cost-cutting problems unfamiliar to companies producing tables or case furniture made only of wood. Upholstering was a process involving skilled hand labor. Traditionally, one upholsterer worked on a single piece of furniture from beginning to end. Upholstering could be performed in a large factory setting, but little work could be done with the help of machines other than the use of a sewing machine for seaming. Upholsterer's tools, which changed little in the eighteenth and nineteenth centuries, usually included an assortment of large straight and curved needles, hammers for tacking, "strainers" for pulling welding taut, and "regulators," long, pointed metal tools that permitted the upholsterer to rearrange stuffing materials inside the chair upholstery as it was built up.

Cost cutting in the production of spring structures developed along several lines over the nineteenth century. Producing separately framed, sprung, stuffed, and covered boxes, which sat on blocks in the seat frame like a large slip seat, had been a common strategy for producing upholstered chairs by the 1840s, evolving from the boxes with springs used around 1830 on chairs with board seats (see Figs. 35 and 36). Eventually, factory-scale production of box seats appeared in the railroad car industry as a way to make car seating that was sturdy and easy to remove, replace, repair, and refurbish. The upholsterer did not even touch the chair frame but simply followed a set of dimensional specifications. The production of spring-filled cushions for chairs and automobiles in the early twentieth century continued this line of problem-solving. Ironically, the heavy, recti-linear frames of Arts and Crafts chairs, chairs that were intended to recall the days of the artisan-craftsman, were particularly amenable to this kind of upholstery solution.

A second method for getting around the problem of constructing web seat bottoms was to close in the bottom of the seat frame itself with a solid board or a series of slats. At least one chair maker experimented with board chair bottoms by using metal clasps and hinges in the late 1860s and 1870s.[48] More commonly, furniture makers used a solid wooden bottom or slats rather than webbing, allowing them to anchor the springs with staples instead of sewing; the structure then was built up in the traditional manner. This method seems to have been applied first to beds. On August 25, 1831, Josiah French of Ware, Massachusetts, received Patent 6728 for a bed bot-tom consisting of a box. The end of each spring was seated in a groove in the box bottom and secured with a metal staple hammered in place. A grid of wood was set in place halfway between the box bottom and the top of its frame, with its wooden members running through the springs to hold them in position. By this method, Ware apparently sought to avoid any spring tying at all, as well as attempting to guarantee uniform elasticity in the mattress.[49]

Solid or slatted wooden bottoms, to which springs could be fastened with staples, became an important design compromise in the seat structure of cheap lounges, as did solid board backs that were often upholstered sepa-rately, then attached to the seat frame after the piece was delivered to the furniture wareroom. Such heavy, large frames gave upholsterers a lot of solid material for anchoring upholstery and required less skill than was needed to build structures over minimal frames hung with tightly stretched webbing. The finished product—the Martyn Brothers lounge again pro-vides an example—was a much heavier and less resilient piece of furniture (Figs. 58 and 59).

In the 1890s, inventors also experimented with the use of metal wires or strips and with wire grids, another development originating in bed produc-tion and commonly used for railroad and, later, automobile seating. Wire or mesh could be used as a means of anchoring springs instead of sewing them to a webbing base, or it could replace spring tying altogether. Wire

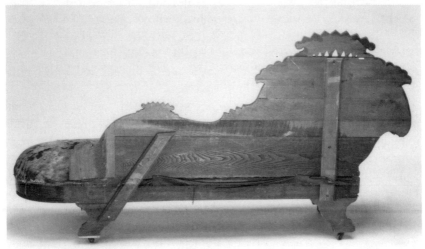

**Figure 58.** Underside of Martyn Brothers lounge (Figure 55), showing board. Compare this bottom with the diagram in Figure 34. Trade catalogs dating between 1880 and 1890 issued by the Buffalo Upholstering Company of Buffalo, New York, offered frames with similar board bottoms and solid board backs wholesale to upholsterers. Courtesy, The Strong Museum, Rochester, New York.

**Figure 59.** Back of Figure 55. Board backs made cheap lounges much heavier than lounges with backs made from webbing, but because board backs provided a sturdier base, these lounges required less skill of upholsterers and took less time to make. This lounge was probably shipped knocked down, with the back as a separate piece. Courtesy, The Strong Museum, Rochester, New York.

did not rot, as jute webbing was apt to, and it was more resilient than a wooden bottom. In 1908, Sears, Roebuck and Co. advertised that all its couches and suites with spring seats were sold with "all steel construction," including "corrugated steel wire bottoms," which, the company asserted, were sturdier than webbing. Wire bottoms on furniture also found favor because they were open, available for inspection, and therefore perceived as more "sanitary" than traditional structures at a time when health was a particular domestic concern.

As they experimented with methods of producing economical, if rather stiff, spring structures in lounges, manufacturers also tried to attain desirable visual qualities in their upholstery. Upholstery fabrics always had to be cut by hand from patterns, but the relatively simple shapes of lounges required neither much sewing of covers nor fabrication of separate cushions. The covers of lounges were typically showy, but the fabrics often were relatively inexpensive. Simple decorative buttoning all over the surface or one row of pleated tufts on a raised back made the upholstery more complex in appearance, but lounges were generally covered with fabrics that, upholstered "plain," still imparted visual detail and tactile richness through their pattern and texture, thus saving labor and yardage. Small labor and materials savings also could be realized in the process of trimming lounges by using gimps with adhesive backs or by using metal stripping as trim.

The use of carpet as upholstery fabric is the best example of this trend. Furniture manufacturers began experimenting with the cheaper grades of carpet as chair upholstery in the 1850s.[50] Tapestry carpet (an innovation of the 1830s), in which the warp of the carpet was printed with a stretched-out version of the desired pattern and then woven so that it was looped into a pile and the design was made visible, was the cheapest and most popular form of carpet upholstery. Patent folding chairs such as those manufactured by the New Haven Folding Chair Company and the Worcester, Massachusetts, firm of Edward W. Vaill frequently had custom-woven carpet with patented designs on their unpadded seats and backs. Carpet upholstery sometimes was offered in all of the popular kinds of looped or cut-pile carpet. Vaill's catalog for 1882–83 offered carpet-seat folding chairs with a rosewood or walnut finish in "Pattern Tapestry" carpet for forty-two dollars a dozen, "Pattern Brussels" or "Pattern Velvet" (cut-pile tapestry) for forty-eight dollars, and "Pattern Wilton" for sixty dollars a dozen.[51]

The apotheosis of carpet upholstery could be found in the factory-made lounge, however. As we have seen, consumers valued fabrics that looked "rich"—heavy, colorful, and often with pile surfaces. In addition, pattern-

woven detail was frequently labeled "rich" because of the historical connotations of work that it bore. Carpet upholstery had all these qualities. Because it was so heavy and stiff, carpet upholstery could not be tufted; therefore, less skill was required to apply it to the lounge frame. Sturdier than
many other inexpensive upholstery fabrics offered in the 1880s and 1890s,
it also was considerably more visually pleasing than the common inexpensive machine-woven black or gray plain horsehair, a middle-class staple,
which disappeared from catalog offerings in the 1880s. Consumers who
had limited budgets seem to have loved carpet upholstery, and it was not
replaced as the fabric of choice until after 1895, when cotton corduroy and
velveteen printed in bright patterns became popular.

To ordinary consumers shopping for factory-made upholstery, tufting
represented both the additional labor of high-quality production and the
aesthetics of refinement, just as it did to the clientele of custom upholstery
shops. However, pleated tufting added to the cost of furniture because it
required both skilled labor and 20 to 30 percent more show-cover material.[52] Companies making cheap lounges and mattresses, which also required buttoning to hold the stuffing in place, could reduce the amount of
skill and labor involved in tufting by availing themselves of several devices
invented after 1893. These "tufting forms" and "tufting machines" produced a mat of backing fabric, stuffing, and cover fastened together by
decorative buttons with shafts that clinched like paper fasteners. This mat
was then wrapped around a couch form like a large quilt, was cut to size,
and was fastened down with tacks.

The tufting machine was responsible for the introduction of "section
work" in large-scale upholstery shops. Before then, even in factory settings, the upholstery of a single piece was the product of one upholsterer,
a situation that still exists in better workrooms today. Craftsmen used a
price book to determine payment on a piecework basis. In New York, for
example, the 1870 labor rate for a parlor suite (probably of seven pieces)
was five dollars. (In a craft that relied so much on handwork, allowing one
upholsterer to complete a related grouping of furniture guaranteed that
the details would be handled identically.) As late as the 1890s, custom
upholstery work paid relatively well, and skilled upholsterers in some
cities were protected by unions. When work was steady, the members of
the New York Custom Upholstery Local earned between sixteen and
twenty-one dollars a week, wages on a par with those of other skilled
workmen.[53]

At the lower end of the upholstered furniture price spectrum, competition was keen; upholsterers were a skilled labor cost for which manufacturers were eager to find a partial substitute in tufting machines. Upholsterers

were equally anxious to resist such attempts. In one instance, on May 28, 1898, the craftsmen in the upholstering room of the Paine Bedding Company of Grand Rapids walked out because the company introduced a tufting machine and section work on backless couches. An article on the strike, which lasted at least until July 3, when Charles Paine was able to obtain an injunction against twenty-one members of the upholsterers' local, described the conflict and the nature of the work:

> Last Saturday the Paine company served notice on its upholsterers that thereafter they would require their work to be done in "section." "Section" means that a part of the work is done in one room by cheap labor and finished by skilled labor in another room. The workmen objected to this division of their work and a meeting of the Upholsterers' union was called Sunday morning. At that time, it was voted to agree to cut off from 25 to 35 cents per couch, but not to accept the divided labor. Monday morning they submitted their proposal, it was not accepted and eight of them walked out.[54]

Paine tried to hire boys as tufting machine operators, but harassment by the striking upholsterers led management to resort to hiring seven girls to operate the machines. At least one other strike was called as a result of the introduction of tufting machines: an unsuccessful walkout in 1899 by unionized upholsterers in New York City against the National Parlor Suite Company.[55] Cheap couches continued to be produced by less skilled labor, such as young boys, and manufacturers gradually introduced other refinements to section work, such as using prestuffed edge rolls rather than sewing the edges on the seat.

The "tufting machine" that led to the Grand Rapids strike was probably a power press that used a presser plate and a flat panel or form with either indentations or a set of raised pins to mark the positions of buttons. The first such device was patented in 1895.[56] The tufting machine produced a mat of fabric, stuffing, and backing material, punctuated and held together with buttons at regular intervals. Sometimes the buttons were fastened with string, but a number of patents were taken out after 1898 for buttons with metal clinchers that could be bent apart with pressure from the presser plate after insertion into the pad of fabric. Because the tufts themselves were not pleated and sewn into place, machine tufting required less fabric than pleated tufts, and the process could be applied to any plain upholstered surface. Workers soon gave this type of tufting power press the nickname "hay baler."[57] This type of continuous-action power press

Tufting Machine Power Press in Actual Operation.

Photographic reproduction of our up-to-date Power Press, showing class of labor employed and results obtained. Let us show it to you. We extend a cordial invitation for you to pay us a visit and we will guarantee to make it a profitable one for you.

# Novelty Tufting Machine Co.

A. FRESCHL, Manager

263 Dearborn Street,        CHICAGO, U. S. A.

**Figure 60.** Advertisement for Novelty Tufting Machine Company, illustration in *Directory of Wholesale Furniture Manufacturers of the United States 1903–4* (New York). Courtesy, The Strong Museum, Rochester, New York.

**Figure 61.** Detail of Figure 56. Viewed from the underside, the Roman divan reveals the complete range of shortcuts taken by manufacturers of cheap upholstered furniture by the turn of the century. The springs are stapled to pine boards (which are themselves braced with blocks) and are not tied; they are instead braced at the top by thick wire bands. The regular pattern of buttons clenched with metal shanks through round anchors (visible as black circles here) indicates that a tufting machine was used. The board back was upholstered separately, then fastened to the divan with two wooden braces after the piece had been shipped to a retail store or its new owner. Courtesy, The Strong Museum, Rochester, New York.

became the typical tufting machine, such as the one illustrated in a 1903 advertisement for the Novelty Tufting Machine Company (Fig. 60).

Machine-tufted upholstery seems to have provided new consumers with a satisfactory paraphrase of hand-tufted upholstery, although the appearance of the machinework was much different from that of the handwork. The cover of the Roman divan in Figure 56 was almost certainly tufted by machine (Fig. 61). The tufting machine led to a new method of upholstery construction, one in which the solid wooden sides of a lounge, a couch, or somewhat later, a davenport sofa disguise a hollow interior arrangement with a thin spring structure mounted across the top. This was one of the important shortcuts that made cheap "overstuffed" furniture available to the average consumer in the 1910s and 1920s.

# CHAPTER SEVEN

# Victorianism in the Modern Era

## At Home in the Living Room, 1910–1930

The old custom of setting apart a "best room" or parlor to be used only on special occasions, as for weddings, funerals, or the entertainment of company, is happily passing away. Only very wealthy people now have drawing-rooms reserved for state occasions. The present tendency is to call all the lower rooms of the house "living rooms," and to have all the members of the family use them freely. A room set apart from ordinary use, and hence shut up much of the time from sun and air, is not good for the physical or moral health of the household. Hygiene demands that sun and air should be admitted freely to all parts of the house. The furnishings themselves, if good care is given them, will be improved rather than injured by ordinary wear, and guests will receive a far pleasanter impression from the easy and graceful atmosphere imparted to a room by daily use, than from the stiff and formal restraints imposed by the old-fashioned parlor.

> Sidney Morse, *Household Discoveries: An Encyclopedia of Practical Recipes and Processes* (1909)

The "modern" parlor was the target of criticism virtually from the moment that making one became a real possibility for middle-class families in the mid-nineteenth century. In fiction, essays, and books of advice, authors argued that the parlor was "sacrificial" because it wasted family resources, confined family life to fewer rooms, and expressed the middle-class ideal of comfort inappropriately. This was the case not only because parlors were the rooms most subject to the whims of fashion but also because they were unbecoming and artificial—"the apotheosis of all refined discomfort," one writer called them, challenging in one phrase an entire set of cultural assumptions.[1]

Clearly, such public criticism did not stop many families from creating and furnishing parlors for themselves; in fact, as lower price lines of furniture and furnishing textiles appeared on the market and consumer credit became available, more families became parlor makers. These new consumers almost always furnished their rooms according to a set of conventions that communicated information about middle-class identity, favoring decorative objects that adhered to popular standards of refinement. Whether by necessity or by preference, they created rooms with a decor that occupied some middle ground, simultaneously gala and homey.

How ideas about culture and comfort were themselves understood also changed by the end of the nineteenth century. By then, "comfort" seems to have included more than the long-standing middle-class ideal of the domestic haven and a harmony between economic means and values. As parlor makers gradually opted for large-scale, overstuffed furniture that was less posture-specific than earlier parlor suites, the term *comfort* increasingly implied some relaxation in the traditional requirements for self-presentation in the parlor, standards that had seemed meaningful for a very long time. Particularly after 1915, advice authors began to regard these standards as "old-fashioned pomposity."[2] Mary Chambers, author of *Table Etiquette, Menus, and Much Besides* (1929) announced that a "revolution" in etiquette had occurred, a "happy tendency to naturalness and simplicity in social intercourse." Even the formal call, the raison d'être of so many parlor rituals, was replaced by visits without cards, "sometimes announced previously by telephone, sometimes unpremeditated, and on the spur of the moment."[3]

By the early twentieth century, most authors of furnishing advice, with the exception of those whose readership was well-to-do and able to continue what was once again an elite practice of having both a drawing room and a sitting room, chose the idea of the "living room" in preference to the parlor. The term once had signified a multipurpose room in small, very modest households, a room for a family on its way to economic success and future parlor making. Now the "living room" began to be defined as the space that served both as the principal family room and as the public room in middle-class houses and apartments.

The new middle-class living room evolved in part from the fact that the amount of living space, both in the proliferating new apartment buildings of the early twentieth century and in newly built single-family houses, tended to shrink in the 1910s and 1920s. People now opted to use their purchasing power on expensive domestic systems—heating, full plumbing including heated hot water, and electricity and cooking gas—instead of enclosing more space in larger living areas. In their study of the modernization of Muncie, Indiana, in the 1920s, sociologists Robert S. and Helen Merrell Lynd discovered that simply digging a basement for a furnace and plumbing added seven hundred dollars to the cost of a house. This was as much as the cost of an entire small house—a house without anything more than a cold-water tap in the kitchen—some years earlier.[4] The twentieth-century change in priorities away from domestic ceremony and toward systems that were part of large new networks of municipal service itself suggests a larger shift in family ideals away from the symbolically self-contained Victorian household.

Not only were middle-class houses often smaller than their counterparts of the 1890s; some, such as bungalows, also featured open floor plans in which the public spaces of houses flowed together (Fig. 62). These plans were not embraced by all new home builders, but where they were, they made the segregation of visitors from the hurly-burly of family life more difficult and the preservation of a sanctuary for visitors' entertainment unrealistic.[5]

Changing priorities for the use of discretionary income also influenced the creation of parlors. By the 1910s, thousands of ordinary families redirected a large part of the spending money that once might have gone to furnishings toward the purchase of an automobile. Autos were the largest single domestic expenditure for many families, exceeded only by the cost of a house itself. In 1913 the Ford Model T dropped in price from $950 to $600, but even the lower figure was equivalent to the average annual earnings of most employees in American businesses.[6] Until the advent of the General Motors Acceptance Corporation in the mid-1920s, consumer credit for auto purchases was limited. Still, despite the prohibitive cost, the Lynds found that by 1923 there were two passenger cars for every three Muncie, Indiana, families. It has been estimated that as many as half of the thirty million households in the United States owned or had access to a car by 1930.[7]

By the 1920s, the automobile clearly served as a portable social facade, so much so that the family car became the target of criticism because of the resources it diverted from furniture purchases. "So long as our judgment of others revolves largely around what makes of cars they drive, rather than the sorts of homes they live in," *The Modern Priscilla Home Furnishing Book* warned in 1925, "good furniture will wait until the car in the garage is paid

**Figure 62.** "A Bungalow Living-Room and Dining-Room with Buff Walls and Floors of Brown Jaspe Linoleum," illustration in Edward Stratton Holloway, *The Practical Book of Furnishing the Small House and Apartment* (1922). In bungalow floor plans, living rooms and dining rooms flowed together through wide doorways, just as pairs of parlors did in larger houses. Although these doorways have no drapery, portieres—often plain velours—were still common in bungalows in the 1910s and the 1920s. Holloway encouraged bungalow owners to use the same fabrics and color schemes "where rooms communicate with a wide opening," which further blurred the social distinctions that furnishings suggested. These rooms also reflect the new interest in simplified housekeeping routines and sanitation. All upholstery fabrics here are washable cottons, and the linoleum floor and small area rugs could be kept cleaner than wall-to-wall carpet or larger rugs. The living room curtains, however, still use both a fabric valance and side curtains. Author's collection.

for. And then, likely enough, we shall have our eye on a better car and continue to complain because good furniture is not to be had on the bargain counter."[8] By the 1920s, automobiles, a masculine purchase—not parlor furnishings, components of the feminized realm of the house—were the dangerously fashionable consumer goods that threatened to upset the middle-class symmetry of means and ends.

The decor of modern living rooms described and illustrated in advice books of the 1910s and 1920s contained many fewer things than the properly refined parlor had at the turn of the century. Deliberate simplification was another harbinger of change in priorities, at least among the authors of such advice and, presumably, among self-consciously up-to-date house-keepers. Changing ideas about domestic sanitation increasingly made some kinds of upholstery seem dirty; one home economist urged students to avoid "fringes and tassels . . . as they serve only to catch dust."[9]

In those decades the lives of women became more public as they entered the world of modern shopping and, aided by the automobile, participated in new forms of commercialized leisure. Because fewer servants were available, women who had once been able to rely on the help of at least a part-time laundress now took over all housework.[10] Parlors—even the rarely used "sacrificial parlors"—required more maintenance than some women were willing to supply. The authors of *The Modern Priscilla Home Furnishing Book* announced to readers, "We have discovered that the world is full of a number of things beside[s] the routine of housekeeping."[11]

Smaller living spaces, changes in housewives' work patterns and priorities, and new, compelling outlets for spending discretionary income were accompanied by the decreasing power of the idea of the parlor as a world within a room, as the emblem of family living, and as the memory palace of culture. Parlors that were deliberately simplified appeared as early as the 1890s, but these still contained some objects that functioned to support the earlier notions about the cultural role of the room. Displays of mementos on the desk or mantel and the "art group" of ceramics and glass atop the center table remained common enough. However, in decorating advice books of the 1910s and 1920s, the living room was discussed and illustrated as a room carefully stripped of many of the objects that Victorian culture enjoyed displaying and contemplating: emblems of personal cultivation, from fancy needlework to appropriately didactic books, and the eclectic mix of furnishings that carried historical or exotic associations. Hazel Adler, the author of *The New Interior: Modern Decorations for the Modern Home* (1916), instructed her readers, "Objects of sentimental associations, of affected culture, together with certain heirlooms and souvenirs which the scheme of decoration refuses to assimilate, should find a happy end in a memory chest where the viewing of them at intervals provides a source of interest and amusement."[12]

Like advice authors describing successful parlor decor fifty years earlier, these authors offering guides to living room furnishings suggested that such rooms were successful when they reflected the attributes and aspirations of their owners. However, the nature of those reflections had changed. Helen Koues, the author of a number of decorating books and articles for the magazine *Good Housekeeping*, instructed her readers that expressing "individuality" was one of the most important principles that could guide the furnishing of living rooms. Desirable rooms were "sympathetic," as were desirable personalities.[13] Their furnishings had "charm," another attribute of the modern personality.[14] One of the most influential volumes promoting the cult of "personality" in interiors was Emily Post's *The Personality of a House;* first published in 1930, it was reprinted a number of times through the 1940s.[15]

The argument that living rooms properly revealed the personality of a family used a twentieth-century understanding of the nature of the individual to recast the earlier argument about comfort: that a parlor should reveal a family's true character rather than its social facade. Occasionally the old rhetoric of "sincere" furnishing even appeared again, such as when Adler wrote, "Homes which cannot free themselves from the clutter of trivial and futile objects are mute declarations of the insincerity of their creator's pretensions to good taste and refinement in other directions."[16] But this argument now attacked the Victorian aesthetic of refinement, using the same key word with a very different meaning.

The early twentieth-century design reformers who attacked the parlor were often progressives with ties to the Arts and Crafts movement, manual arts training, and social work. Their critique of the parlor and its contents was based on a narrow, protomodernist definition of the term *function.* When *function* was defined as "physical use," it excluded the Victorian conception that parlor furnishings could be used symbolically to make statements about the personal domestic world of family and friends and the world of culture outside the parlor walls. Charlotte Calkins's *A Course in House Planning and Furnishing* (1916), a book intended as a guide to high school teachers, analyzed common household furnishings in categories related to their appearance and appropriate function. Her notes on selecting furniture urged students to ask the following questions: "Will this article be consistent with its surroundings? For what purpose is it to be used? Will it serve this purpose in a simple, honest, straightforward manner?"[17] Calkins too demanded sincerity in furnishing, a state that by then could be attained only by rigorously editing both the design and the quantity of personal possessions. It seems that middle-class people—and middle-class furnishings—were supposed to be functional rather than showy or aspiring.

Calkins was one of many reformers who attacked ordinary consumers' continuing preferences for the old aesthetic of refinement, with its emphasis on rich pattern, visually complex design, naturalistic ornament, and room compositions whose multiple layers had equivalent levels of visual detail. A series of compare-and-contrast exercises with lecture notes composed this critique. A plate comparing "good" and "bad" sofa pillows was accompanied by the statement:

> Pictures on sofa pillows and all other objects are out of place. No one should want to rest his head on anything that resembles real rose thorns, tennis rackets, pipes, flags, Indian heads and the like. Any of these ideas may be taken as a motif and treated in a flat conventional way, which will be appropriate for a flat surface and will conform to the shape and purpose of a pillow, but the designs will then be far from realistic. Avoid sofa pillows with elaborate ruffles, tassels, or other disconcerting details.[18]

Edward Stratton Holloway, the author of the popular book *The Practical Book of Furnishing the Small House and Apartment* (1922), also argued that the taste for naturalism was "vulgar" because of the poor quality of products expressing it; he singled out for criticism the "rose-bedecked carpet" and "mats containing lifelike portraits of huge dogs," exactly the sort of naturalistic designs whose realism Victorian Americans had found so thrilling.[19] The author of *Household Discoveries* (1909), a book directed to rural and small-town audiences, also described the "modern tendency" for simplicity, pointing out that the most beloved items of parlor upholstery—"flounces, valances, and other superfluous articles," as well as "stuffed plush and other upholstered articles of furniture in bright colors"—were "much less fashionable than formerly."[20]

The specificity of Calkins's plates—page after page of overstuffed and tufted Turkish rockers, doorstops shaped like dogs, lamps with ruffled shades, and lace curtains woven to give the illusion of festoons and tassles—along with Holloway's examples of unsuitable furnishings suggests that both critics still found much to react against in the typical front room of the ordinary, early twentieth-century household. Indeed, the upholstery of living rooms between 1910 and 1930 was an intriguing blend of old and new. The ideal of matching furnishings survived, but the prized parlor suite became the living room suite in the 1910s and 1920s. It was a bulky, overstuffed three-piece group that still sometimes included a rocking chair. Ideas about the three-piece living room "set" demonstrated continuity with ideas about the hierarchy of forms in Victorian parlor suites. Illustrating a living room in "good taste," for example, *The Modern Priscilla Home*

*Furnishing Book* noted that the "big easy chair" was intended for a father, the medium-size "women's chair" for a mother, and the "davenport" for the children.[21]

The economics of factory-organized upholstery, perfected by the 1890s, were put to good use in such furniture, especially when no wood that required careful finishing was exposed to view. In the three pieces of a set from the 1920s, the large form is not full of stuffing but consists of a shallow deck of springs and stuffing constructed over a deep hollow well, like the turn-of-the-century backless couch and the later Roman divan. The sofa and chairs could have had long, finished wooden legs, but instead the empty wooden boxes with fabric covers, implying the presence of luxurious, expensive layers of upholstery that did not actually exist (Fig. 63), were finished with low feet. Such sets even continued to meet popular requirements for richness and detail through their fabric covers. Popular preferences for upholstery that had rich, deep colors and texture and displayed a certain amount of elaboration and detail survived into the 1920s.

Concerns about sanitation did not spell the end of inviting piles of elaborately stitched sofa pillows, lace curtains, and other now-traditional kinds of upholstery seen in the photographs of rooms throughout this volume. Consumers probably heeded these concerns selectively, consigning the worst offenders to the attic as they continued to use other types of upholstery, but the simplified living rooms no longer had much to say about the softening, polishing effects of culture.

The very gradual decline of the American parlor reflects the uneven decline of American Victorianism itself. Not having experienced the direct shock of World War I's destruction of lives and land, Victorian culture in the United States faded more slowly than it did in Europe. On the Continent, the lingering effects of the four-year slaughter provided a fertile field for the apparently radical breaks with the designed past—of Corbusier, the Futurists, and the Machine Age—as well as one final decorative reinterpretation of French eighteenth-century furniture in the Style Moderne (Art Deco), popularly introduced in the Paris Exposition International des Arts Decoratifs et Industriels Modernes of 1925.

Among manufacturers and consumers with no particular ax to grind, the term *living room* replaced *parlor* gradually. In furniture advertising, the former term was common by around 1910. By 1919 it had completely replaced *parlor* in articles in the *Grand Rapids Furniture Record*, a trade magazine for the furniture business. However, through the first thirty years of the twentieth century, houses continued to have parlors, even if they were called "living rooms" (or sometimes "front rooms," a designation that was

# verstuffed Sets

TRUE luxury is to be found in this fine quality overstuffed set and the low price emphasizes the value. The frame is strongly made of hard wood and the exposed parts are hand rubbed in a Brown Mahogany finish. Removable cushion seats are supremely comfortable, and permit easy cleaning underneath.

**Davenport.**—In the seat, thirty coil springs are attached to a steel slat foundation, the tops firmly tied with steel wires and covered with burlap. The removable cushion seats have 30 springs each, softly padded with cotton. The deep padded three paneled back has 27 pillow springs. Size of seat, 63 by 21 inches. Height of back from seat, 17 inches. Entire height, 34 inches. Entire length, 50 inches.

**SHOWING CONSTRUCTION OF SPRING SEATS**

**Chair and Rocker.**—Nine coil springs in the seat of each. The deep removable cushions are made with 30 cushion springs, padded with fine flaxtow and a thick layer of soft cotton. Nine pillow springs in the deeply padded back. Size of seat, 21 by 19 inches. Height of back, from seat, 17 inches. Entire height, 34 inches.

**Choice of Upholstery.**—The upholstery is in two highly favored materials—a fine quality velour or a rich floral tapestry. The blue mulberry or colored velour is velvet like in its soft pile and is attractively flowered. The floral tapestry is in a pleasing harmony of colors—artistically blended. State color wanted.

Complete Set In Velour **$139.75**

| | Chair | Rocker | Davenport | 3-piece Set |
|---|---|---|---|---|
| 266 C 1005—Velour | $39.45 | $40.75 | $70.75 | $139.75 |
| 266 C 1006—Tapestry | 39.35 | 40.65 | 70.65 | 139.65 |
| Shipping weight, about | 100 lbs. | 100 lbs. | 200 lbs. | 400 lbs. |
| Shipped from Factory near Chicago or Central N. Y.; allow about one week for shipment. | | | | |

**Figure 63.** "Big Values in Overstuffed Sets," illustration in *Montgomery Ward and Co. Catalogue No. 97, Fall and Winter, 1922–1923.* Courtesy, The Strong Museum, Rochester, New York.

especially apt in urban apartments in which the parlor was the only room facing the street). Furnished with the best pieces in the house, these rooms continued to be reserved for the modest domestic occasions of state that punctuated everyday life.

The age of a family sometimes accounted for such continuity in habits of use. The Ruth family of Lebanon, Pennsylvania, occupied a Georgian revival house built in the early 1890s that featured the traditional pair of parlors connected by a wide doorway. The room facing the street served as a formal parlor (and the term *parlor* was always used) until around 1956. It was furnished with a colonial-revival sofa covered in horsehair, several small chairs, a chandelier, a baby grand piano, and a pier glass with a table that held a lamp whose crystal drops reflected light. The back parlor had been decorated with mission furniture before 1910, and the Ruths called it the "library" or "study." As the Neupert family of Buffalo, New York, and the Yearick family of Konnarock, Virginia, also had done, the Ruths customarily sat in this back room every day. The parlor, enframed by the wide doorway, became a vignetted view, an emblem of their most formal social selves.[22]

The desire to maintain community traditions may also have contributed to decisions to keep formal parlors. In rural places, such rites of passage as funerals (including laying out the dead) were not delegated to new settings such as funeral parlors but continued to take place at home well into the twentieth century. John Arnold, who was born and raised in the north-central Pennsylvania community of Warren, recalls the laying out of his grandfather in the parlor in 1930. So that the old man's last night at home would not be spent alone, fourteen-year-old John was required to spend the night in the parlor with the coffin, sleeping on a fully reclined Morris chair. Arnold recalls that the same room also was the site for courtship and holiday celebrations in the house.[23]

Even when the room was called a living room and furnished in an informal fashion, it was sometimes treated as a formal parlor. The house in which Robert Vance Stewart grew up in the 1910s and 1920s had been constructed by his grandfather in 1887 and contained three generations of the family. The first floor contained a living room, a dining room, a kitchen, a pantry, and a small bedroom. The kitchen saw the most daily use and contained a couch, two sewing machines, and a rocking chair as well as the usual appliances and kitchen furniture. The living room, on the other hand, "wasn't used very much on a day to day basis. Saturdays, Sundays, and holidays, when we had company. When Eleanor [his sister] was taking piano lessons she went in there every day to practice." The room contained a sofa, chairs, the piano, a gramophone, a desk, a bookcase, and a center table, which still was used as the locus for reading and other activities.[24]

Thus, patterns of room use, the requirements of changing domestic architecture and housekeeping routines, and the forms and aesthetic qualities of upholstery associated with the living room changed gradually and unevenly between 1910 and 1930. Some families continued to have parlors in spirit, if not in name. This tradition still survives; in South Philadelphia, for example, Italian-American families continue to keep parlors with wall-to-wall carpeting, overstuffed furniture draped with antimacassars, and elaborate window draperies. Modern suburban house plans that distinguish a "den" or "family room" from the "living room" follow, in essence, the Victorian distinction between the everyday "sitting room" and the formal "parlor."

Even so, these modern-day parlors differ from their Victorian predecessors in the ways their owners think about them. Something more fundamental than the chair types and the appearance of window drapery has changed. The power of the parlor as a central location for symbols lessened as families turned outward and linked themselves to urban and suburban communities that could provide new services and entertainments. The Victorian cast of mind, embellishing and commercializing the eighteenth-century concept of gentility and finding meaning in the progressive refinement of the world, did not disappear by 1930, but it probably had a generational boundary. It was a dying worldview.

If anything, belief in the desirability of owning things was even more widespread in the 1930s, and the skillful use of objects for the purposes of self-presentation counted just as much in 1925 as it had in 1875. Being middle class—having that state of mind both compelled and repelled by consumption as a form of cultural rhetoric, seeking a balance between culture and comfort—may be a fundamental component in a dynamic consumer society. The constant tension between purchasing and saving, restraint and desire must always be present, even if the cultural framework that shapes questions about what is valuable and worthy evolves over time. In the context of a developing consumer society, both ends of the Victorian polarity—cultured self-display and sincere domestic comfort—were articulated through forms of consumption, through furnishing as well as through the rhetoric of popular literature. In the post-Victorian era, the era of the living room, a different dynamic tension, between the dwelling and the world beyond, framed questions about domestic consumption and self-presentation.

# ✐otes

PREFACE

1. For an overview and discussion of the growing literature on gentility and consumption, see Cary Carson, "The Consumer Revolution in Colonial British America: Why Demand?" in Cary Carson, Ronald Hoffman, and Peter J. Albert, eds., *Of Consuming Interests: The Style of Life in the Eighteenth Century* (Washington, D.C.: U.S. Capitol Historical Society; Charlottesville: University Press of Virginia, 1994), 483–700.

2. See chapter 6: "Table Manners and the Control of Appetites," in John F. Kasson, *Rudeness and Civility: Manners in Nineteenth-Century Urban America* (New York: Hill and Wang, 1990), 182–214; Kathryn Grover, ed. *Dining in America, 1850–1900* (Amherst: University of Massachusetts Press for the Margaret Woodbury Strong Museum, 1987).

3. In this abridgement, I have confined myself to a close analysis of parlor seating furniture. However, readers interested in pursuing my argument in more detail may want to refer to the discussion of drapery forms and homemade furnishings in the original edition of *Culture and Comfort.*

## INTRODUCTION

1. Janet E. Ruutz-Rees, *Home Decoration: Art Needlework, and Embroidery; Painting on Silk, Satin and Velvet; Panel Painting; and Wood-Carving* (New York: D. Appleton and Company, 1881), 57, 42.

2. Walter R. Houghton et al., *American Etiquette and Rules of Politeness* (New York: Powers and LeCraw, 1886), 13, 20.

3. Daniel Walker Howe, "Victorian Culture in America," in Daniel Walker Howe, ed., *Victorian America* (Philadelphia: University of Pennsylvania Press, 1976), 3–26. Although the Anglo-American link is indeed important, an examination of continental bourgeois culture in the same period suggests that the definition should perhaps be broadened, at least in relation to material culture. See, for example, the extraordinary collection of American, English, and continental middle-class interiors in Peter Thornton, *Authentic Decor: The Domestic Interior, 1620–1920* (New York: Viking Penguin, 1984), especially those chapters covering the years between 1820 and 1920.

4. Richard A. Wells, *Manners, Culture, and Dress* (Springfield, Mass.: King, Richardson and Company, 1891), 11.

5. "Home" seems to have been one of at least three "symbol sets" that had distinct identities in nineteenth- and early twentieth-century America and that mark the boundaries of Victorian culture in America. Although much remains to be done before the dimensions and character of each set are fully outlined, the scholarship of John Kasson, Leo Marx, Richard Hofstadter, Henry Nash Smith, and others suggests that one symbol set revolves around the concepts of technology and the image of the machine as the vehicle for civilization's progress. Another set is the bundle of popular thinking and associations that may be designated by the image of the wilderness and what Leo Marx has termed the "middle landscape" of the cultivated garden. The classic texts that began charting the dimensions and meanings of these symbols include John F. Kasson, *Civilizing the Machine: Technology and Republican Values in America, 1776–1900* (New York: Grossman Publishers, 1976), Leo Marx, *The Machine in the Garden* (New York: Oxford University Press, 1964), and Henry Nash Smith, *Virgin Land: The American West as Symbol and Myth* (1950; reprint, New York: Vintage Books, 1961).

6. Julia McNair Wright, *The Complete Home: An Encyclopedia of Domestic Life and Affairs* (Philadelphia: Badley, Barretson and Company, 1879), 3.

7. Rev. W. K. Tweedie, *Home; or, The Parents' Assistant and Children's Friend* (Norwich, Conn.: Henry Bill Publishing Company, 1873), 34–41.

8. Catharine E. Beecher and Harriet Beecher Stowe, *The American Woman's Home* (New York: J. B. Ford and Company, 1869), 18–19, 24.

9. As anthropologist Victor Turner has noted, such a relocation of symbols should be expected to occur in societies that have become complex and in which religion is pluralistic and a matter of choice: "Symbols once central to the mobilization of ritual action, have tended to migrate directly or in disguise, through the cultural division of labor, into other domains, esthetics, politics, law, popular culture, and the like." Turner, "Variations on a Theme of Liminality," in Sally F. Moore and Barbara Myerhoff, eds., *Secular Ritual* (Amsterdam: Van Gorcum, Assen, 1977), 36.

10. Richard L. Bushman, "Family Security in the Transition from Farm to City, 1750–1850," *Journal of Family History*, fall 1981, 250–51.

11. Ibid.; see also Stephan Thernstrom, *Poverty and Progress: Social Mobility in a Nineteenth Century City* (Cambridge, Mass.: Harvard University Press, 1964).

12. Mrs. Lydia H. Sigourney, *Letters to Mothers* (Hartford, Conn.: by the author, 1838), 15.

13. Harriet Beecher Stowe [Christopher Crowfield, pseud.], "Woman's Sphere," *The Chimney Corner* (Boston: Ticknor and Fields, 1868), vol. 8 of *The Writings of Harriet Beecher Stowe* (Cambridge, Mass.: Riverside Press, 1896), 252. Tweedie also discussed what he termed "The Republic of Home" in *Home,* 38.

14. Almira Seymour, *Home: The Basis of the State* (Boston: A. Williams and Company, 1869), 7.

15. Books of architectural advice from the middle decades of the nineteenth century made much of the connection between domestic architecture and character. In a representative statement, Lewis F. Allen, author of *Rural Architecture* (1852), argued: "As the man himself—no matter what his occupation—be lodged and fed, so influenced, in a degree, will be his practice in the daily duties of his life. A squalid, miserable tenement, with which they who inhabit it are content, can lead to no elevation of character, no improvement in condition, either social or moral, of its occupants." Allen, *Rural Architecture* (New York: C. M. Saxton, 1852), xii.

16. Beecher and Stowe, *American Woman's Home,* 84.

17. "The Domestic Use of Design," *Furniture Gazette* 1, 1 (April 12, 1873): 4.

18. Harriet Beecher Stowe, *We and Our Neighbors* (New York: J. B. Ford and Company, 1875), 152.

19. Ibid.

20. Clarence Cook, *The House Beautiful* (New York: Scribner, Armstrong and Company, 1878), 49.

21. Gwendolyn Wright, *Moralism and the Modern Home* (Chicago: University of Chicago Press, 1980). American utopian communities, which mirrored the larger interests and concerns of the society for which they proposed themselves as alternatives, were often as compelled by the symbol of "home" as were ordinary people. Architectural historian Dolores Hayden has argued, "When communities issued tracts or posters to recruit new members, they often illustrated them with sketches of their dwellings as tangible proof of their achievements." The motto on the masthead of Oneida's *American Socialist* was, "Devoted to the enlargement and protection of home." Hayden, *Seven American Utopias: The Architecture of Communitarian Socialism, 1790–1975* (Cambridge, Mass.: MIT Press, 1976), 9, 24.

22. Siegfried Giedion discusses the "mechanization of adornment," for example, as a process that devalued symbolic ornament (as in the application of the classical symbols of power to many kinds of furnishings). In his argument, the meaning of objects themselves deteriorated, since the meaning of ornament and the connection among craftsmanship, rarity, and value were broken through mechanized production. Giedion, *Mechanization Takes Command: A Contribution to Anonymous History* (New York: Oxford University Press, 1948), 338–46.

23. According to Clifford Geertz, a symbol is "any object, act, event, quality, or relation which serves as a vehicle for a conception—the conception is the symbol's meaning." Geertz, "Religion as a Cultural System," *The Interpretation of Cultures* (New York: Basic Books, 1973), 91.

24. Lawrence J. Taylor, "Death in Godey's: Women and Death in Nineteenth-

Century America" (paper presented at the Henry Francis du Pont Winterthur Museum, Winterthur, Del., April 1982), 16. Taylor has noted that the theory of associations was first formulated as part of an eighteenth-century epistemology, but evoking the chain of associations was at that time viewed as an act of cognition and reason alone. In later forms, including the popular verse published in *Godey's*, associations were more intuitive and emotional, and the ability to feel them was "a natural inclination, and like 'influence,' a feminine characteristic." Although men could, and did, perceive chains of associations, women especially were empowered.

25. "Miss Cook," "The Old Arm-Chair," *Godey's Lady's Book*, March 1855, 273.

26. Ibid.

27. Victor Turner, "Symbols in Ndembu Ritual," *The Forest of Symbols* (Ithaca, N.Y.: Cornell University Press, 1970), 19.

28. A brief discussion of Geertz's understanding of "sensibility" may be found in his essay "Art as a Cultural System," *Local Knowledge* (Berkeley: University of California Press, 1983), 96, 99.

29. Historians of science and technology interested in innovation recognize this boundary, and how it is sometimes consciously used, when they discuss problem-solving through the "mind's eye," where problems are analyzed and solved without translation into a verbal form. See Eugene S. Ferguson, "The Mind's Eye: Nonverbal Thought in Technology," *Science*, August 26, 1977, 827–36.

30. In an essay on the phenomenon of the "miniature," Susan Stewart has also perceived and described the limits of such description: "We find that when language attempts to describe the concrete, it is caught in an infinitely self-effacing gesture of inadequacy, a gesture which speaks to the gaps between our modes of cognition—those gaps between the sensual, the visual, and the linguistic." She notes further that attempts at such description "threaten an infinity of detail that becomes translated into an infinity of verbality" without describing the experience of perceiving miniatures. Stewart, *On Longing* (Baltimore: Johns Hopkins University Press, 1984), 52.

31. Daniel Biebuyck has defined this term in "Symbolism of the Lega Stool," in *Working Papers in the Traditional Arts 2 & 3* (Philadelphia: Institute for the Study of Human Issues, 1977), 7–37. He analyzes the way objects used in ceremonies, in this instance the stool, are described and classified in relation to Lega aesthetic and cultural values.

32. Wells, *Manners, Culture, and Dress*, 441–50.

33. Mrs. H. O. Ward, *Sensible Etiquette of the Best Society, Customs, Manners, Morals, and Home Culture*, 16th ed. (Philadelphia: Porter and Coates, 1878), xv.

34. *Social Culture; A Treatise on Etiquette, Self Culture, Dress, Physical Beauty and Domestic Relations . . .* (Springfield, Mass.: King-Richardson Company, 1903), 7.

35. Communications-based approaches to the study of artifacts that also have had recourse to analogies with language may be found in the cultural anthropology literature that discusses the visual arts; for a survey that includes communications-based approaches, see Robert S. Layton, *The Anthropology of Art* (New York: Columbia University Press, 1981). The work of Mary Douglas and Baron Isherwood in *The World of*

*Goods* is particularly apropos. They argue that the abstract concepts used by a culture are "difficult to remember, unless they take on a physical appearance." Hence, "Goods assembled together in ownership make physical, rational statements about the hierarchy of values to which their chooser subscribes." Douglas and Isherwood, *The World of Goods: Towards an Anthropology of Consumption* (New York: W. W. Norton and Company, 1979), 5.

36. According to the *Oxford English Dictionary*, "rhetoric," the art of using language to persuade or influence other people, consists of "a body of rules to be observed by a speaker or writer in order that he may express himself with eloquence." When a person makes a rhetorical statement, he or she may be understood by the receiver of the message even if the receiver does not believe or accept the content of that statement. Family portraits make a clearly rhetorical statement about that family's happiness and health, even when an observer of that portrait knows the "truth" about the family's personal problems. *Oxford English Dictionary*, s.v. *rhetoric*.

37. Neil Harris, *The Artist in American Society: The Formative Years, 1790–1860* (New York: Clarion Books, Simon and Schuster, 1970), 43.

38. Walter J. Ong, a scholar of rhetoric and the structure of knowledge and thought in literate and oral cultures, has argued that critical differences exist between the interpretation of images and texts: "Although we look both at pictures and at texts, we don't read pictures as we read texts. A text encodes specific words for you to say. Pictures do not do this. . . . We are so locked into literacy, and literacy is so tremendously helpful, enabling us to do all kinds of things, that we use the term 'text' to characterize everything that contains information or calls for interpretation." "Syntax is simply our English version of the Greek term for putting together in order," Ong has argued, although he considers visual syntax as relating to "conventions rather than grammars in any verbal sense." "Interview with Walter J. Ong," *Exposure*, winter 1985, 20. See also Ong, *Orality and Literacy: The Technologizing of the Word* (New York: Methuen, 1982).

39. On the hunting symbolism associated with dining in nineteenth-century America, see Kenneth L. Ames, "Murderous Propensities: Notes on Dining Iconography of the Mid-Nineteenth Century," in Nancy H. Schless and Kenneth L. Ames, eds., *Three Centuries, Two Continents* (Watkins Glen, N.Y.: American Life Foundation, 1983). An updated version of this essay appears in Kenneth L. Ames, *Death in the Dining Room and Other Tales of Victorian Culture* (Philadelphia: Temple University Press, 1993).

40. For a study of popular iconography that uses the idea of "paraphrasing," see Hedvig Branden Johnson et al., *Visual Paraphrases: Studies in Mass Media Imagery*, Acts Universitatis Upsaliensis *Figura*, n. s., 27 (Stockholm, Sweden: Almquist and Wiksell International, Uppsala, 1984)].

41. *Oxford English Dictionary*, s. v. *emulation*.

42. Thorstein Veblen, *The Theory of the Leisure Class* (New York: Vanguard Press, 1922), 34.

43. Johnson et al., *Visual Paraphrases*.

44. "A Visit to Henkels' Warerooms in Chestnut Street above Fifth," *Godey's Lady's Book*, August 1850, 126.

45. Francis Salet, introduction to Genevieve Souchal, *Chefs-d'oeuvre de la tapisserie du XIVe au XVIᵉ siecle* (Masterpieces of Tapestry From the Fourteenth to the Sixteenth Century), trans. Richard A. H. Oxby (New York: Metropolitan Museum of Art, 1973), 17–18; see also Penelope Eames, "Furniture in England, France, and the Netherlands from the Twelfth to the Fifteenth Century," *Furniture History* 13 (1977).

46. Rolla Tryon, "The Transition from Family-to-Shop and Factory-made Goods," and "The Passing of the Family Factory," *Household Manufactures in the United States, 1640–1860* (Chicago: University of Chicago Press, 1917), 242–376.

47. Daniel Webster, "Lecture before the Society for the Diffusion of Useful Knowledge" in Michael Brewster Folsom and Steven D. Lubar, eds., *The Philosophy of Manufactures: Early Debates over Industrialization in the United States* (Cambridge, Mass.: MIT Press and Merrimack Valley Textile Museum, 1982), 395; *Eighty Years' Progress of the United States*, 2 vols. (Hartford, Conn.: L. Stebbins, 1867), 1:286.

48. *Niles Weekly Register* 21 (1821): 35, cited in Tryon, *Household Manufactures*, 284.

49. Tryon, *Household Manufactures*, 276.

50. *Eighty Years' Progress*, 1:291.

51. Gladys Palmer, "Labor Relations in the Lace and Lace-Curtain Industries in the United States," *Bulletin of the U.S. Bureau of Labor Statistics* 380 (November 1925); A. F. Barker, *Textiles* (New York: D. Van Nostrand Company, 1910), 257–58.

## CHAPTER I. IMAGINING THE PARLOR

1. *Humphrey's Journal of Photography* 5, 1 (April 15, 1853): 10–11.

2. Neil McKendrick, John Brewer, and J. H. Plumb, *The Birth of a Consumer Society: The Commercialization of Eighteenth-Century England* (Bloomington: Indiana University Press, 1982), xx. Students of Anglo-American and French culture of the eighteenth and nineteenth centuries have begun the process of reconstructing the economic aspects of the growth of consumer culture and have focused particularly on the department store and on international exhibitions, beginning with the Crystal Palace of 1851. Since 1980, excellent books have been published on the Bon Marché, a Parisian dry goods establishment that evolved into perhaps the first department store in the world in the 1850s; on the French expositions and the response of French intellectuals to consumer culture; and on consumer culture in the fiction of Honoré de Balzac and Émile Zola. See Michael B. Miller, *The Bon Marché* (Princeton, N.J.: Princeton University Press, 1980); Rosalind B. Williams, *Dream Worlds: Mass Consumption in Late Nineteenth-Century France* (Berkeley: University of California Press, 1983); and Rachel Bowlby, *Just Looking: Consumer Culture in Dreiser, Gissing, and Zola* (New York: Methuen, 1985). Similar studies of American department stores include John Hower, *History of Macy's of New York, 1858–1919* (Cambridge, Mass.: Harvard University Press, 1943); Neil Harris, "Museums, Merchandising, and Popular Taste: The Struggle for Influence," in Ian M. D. Quimby, ed., *Material Culture and the Study of American Life* (New York: W. W. Norton, 1977), 140–74; and Daniel J. Boorstin, *The Americans: The Democratic Experience*

(New York: Random House, 1973). A number of dissertations-in-progress are reported to be examining similar topics in American consumer culture. Still, some of the oldest monographs on single businesses, such as John Hower's on Macy's, stand as seminal works. Harris's important essay linked department stores, expositions, and museums as nineteenth-century tastemakers, but no research since has expanded on his initial observations. Boorstin's work, one of the pioneering attempts at interpreting the first monographic studies of department stores, advertising, mass media, and other elements of American consumer culture, is also correct in citing the department store and the exposition as key nineteenth-century expressions of consumer culture.

3. See, for example, McKendrick, Brewer, and Plumb, *Birth of a Consumer Society*, for a discussion of the spread of habits of consumption beginning with the adoption of items of fashionable clothing by working people.

4. McKendrick, Brewer, and Plumb, "The Consumer Revolution," in ibid., 20–21.

5. Penelope Eames, "Furniture in England, France, and the Netherlands from the Twelfth to the Fifteenth Century," *Furniture History* 13 (1977): xvii.

6. Ibid., 57–58.

7. For an analysis of this changing concept of unified decor and architecture, which included more complicated furnishings, see Peter Thornton, *Authentic Decor: The Domestic Interior, 1620–1920* (New York: Viking Penguin, 1984).

8. Williams, *Dream Worlds*, 8–9.

9. *American Cabinet Maker, Upholsterer, and Carpet Reporter* contained in virtually every issue a statement like this one in the November 25, 1876, issue: "The demand for novelties in cabinet-work require a manufacturer to be constantly on the look-out for something fresh and new." Vol. 14, 2 (November 25, 1876): 4.

10. Richard Donald Jurzhals, "Initial Advantage and Technological Change in Industrial Location: The Furniture Industry of Grand Rapids, Michigan" (Ph.D. diss., Michigan State University, 1973), 95–98; James Stanford Bradshaw, "Grand Rapids, 1870–1880: Furniture City Emerges," *Michigan History* 45, 4 (winter 1971): 332.

11. Martha Craybill McClaugherty, "Household Art: Creating the Artistic Home, 1868–1893," *Winterthur Portfolio* 18 (1983): 1–26.

12. Fanny Kemble, *The Journal of Frances Anne Butler, Better Known as Fanny Kemble*, 2 vols. in 1 (1835; reprint, New York: Benjamin Blom, 1970), 1:74.

13. See Richard Sennett, "The Fullness of Life . . ." and "Little Islands of Propriety . . .," *Families against the City: Middle Class Homes of Industrial Chicago, 1872–1890* (Cambridge, Mass.: Harvard University Press, 1970); Sam Bass Warner, *Private City: Philadelphia in Three Periods of Its Growth* (Philadelphia: University of Pennsylvania Press, 1968).

14. "A Bargain: Is a Penny Saved, Twopence Got?" *Gleason's Pictorial Drawing-Room Companion*, September 2, 1854, 150 (hereafter cited as *Gleason's*).

15. Ibid., 151.

16. *Catalogue of Handsome Household Furniture, to be sold by Bleeker and Van Dyke on Thursday, April 22, 1841, at No. 2 Albion Place* (New York, 1841); *Catalogue of Genteel Household Furniture, for Sale at Auction, by Henry H. Leeds and Co., on Friday, April 29, 1853, at Half-past Ten O'Clock, at No. 231 East 10th Street* (New York, 1853).

17. Ann Sophia Stephens, *High Life in New York, by Jonathan Slick, Esq. of Weathersfield, Conn.* . . . (New York: Bunce and Brother, 1854), 269.

18. Winston Weisman, "Commercial Palaces of New York, 1845–1875," *Art Bulletin* 34 (December 1954): 285–302.

19. "Charleston Hotel," *Gleason's*, April 24, 1852, 265; "The Girard House, Philadelphia," *Gleason's*, February 21, 1852, 113.

20. Reuben Vose, *Reuben Vose's Wealth of the World Displayed* (New York: by the author, 1859), 5, 40.

21. Ibid., 181–82 (emphasis in original).

22. "Boarding Out," *Harper's Weekly*, March 7, 1857, 146.

23. *Humphrey's Journal of Photography*, April 15, 1853, 11.

24. "The Girard House," 113. Other descriptions of commercial parlors later in this chapter are additional examples.

25. Nicholas B. Wainwright, ed., *A Philadelphia Perspective: The Diary of Sidney George Fisher Covering the Years 1834–1871* (Philadelphia: Historical Society of Pennsylvania, 1967), 116.

26. See Costard Sly [pseud.], *Sayings and Doings at the Tremont House in the Year 1832, Extracted from the Notebook of Costard Sly, Solicitor and Short-Hand Writer, of London. And Edited by Dr. Zachary Vangrifter,* 2 vols. (Boston: Allen and Ticknor, 1833), for a "factual account" of social life in the hotel setting.

27. Francis J. Grund, *The Americans in Their Moral, Social, and Political Relations*, vol. 2 (1837; reprint, New York: Augustus M. Kelley, 1971), 234.

28. Ibid.

29. Anthony Trollope, *North America*, vol. 2 (1862; reprint, London: Dawson's of Pall Mall, 1968), 328.

30. Jefferson Williamson, *The American Hotel: An Anecdotal History* (New York: Alfred A. Knopf, 1930), 12.

31. Russell Lynes was the first social historian to call attention to the enthusiasm of the American public for these hotels and the power of their image as "palaces of the people," in *The Tastemakers* (1954; reprint, New York: Grosset and Dunlap, 1972), 81–96. See also Williamson, *American Hotel*, 301.

32. "American House, Boston," *Gleason's*, July 10, 1852, 24.

33. Trollope, *North America*, 314.

34. *A Description of Tremont House* (Boston: Gray and Bowen, 1830), 41.

35. Ibid., 12.

36. *Boston Legal Advertiser* (1829), unpaginated.

37. E. Page Talbot, "The Furniture Industry in Boston, 1810–1835" (master's thesis, University of Delaware, 1974), 73.

38. "La Pierre House," *Gleason's*, October 8, 1853, 225, 239.

39. "New Furniture," *Godey's Lady's Book*, February 1850, 152–53, and "A Visit to Henkels' Warerooms in Chestnut Street above Fifth," *Godey's Lady's Book*, August 1850, 123–24.

40. *Catalogue of Furniture, George J. Henkels, City Cabinet Warerooms, 173 Chestnut St.* (Philadelphia, [1855?]), Winterthur Museum.

41. For a discussion of Henkels's "Antique" furniture, an analysis of a group of surviving examples, and a brief business history, see Kenneth Ames, "George Henkels, Nineteenth-Century Philadelphia Cabinetmaker," *Antiques*, October 1973, 641–50.

42. "Fashion Plates for Decorating Parlor Windows: The Latest Styles," *Godey's Lady's Book*, February 1854, 97, 166.

43. Nicholas Dean, "An Exquisite Victorian Puzzle," *Historic Preservation*, October 1985, 40–45; correspondence with Arlene Palmer Schwind, Victoria Society of Maine, February 6, 1986.

44. Sly, *Sayings and Doings at the Tremont House*, 220.

45. Ibid.

46. "C. M." [Charles Mackey], "Transatlantic Sketches: The Mississippi River," *Illustrated London News*, April 10, 1858, 378.

47. Trollope, *North America*, 328–29.

48. "The Waverly Hotel," *Rochester (N.Y.) Daily Advertiser*, May 6, 1848, 2.

49. Grund, *The Americans*, 236.

50. *Eighty Years' Progress of the United States*, 2 vols. (Hartford, Conn.: L. Stebbins, 1867), 2:261.

51. Eliza Leslie, *The Ladies' Guide to True Politeness and Perfect Manners; or, Miss Leslie's Behavior Book* (Philadelphia: T. B. Peterson and Brothers, 1864), 108, 116.

52. "William Brown," "American Homes in New York Hotels," *Harper's Weekly*, December 26, 1857, 824–25.

53. "Boarding Out," 146.

54. Ibid.

55. Carl D. Lane, *American Paddle Steamboats* (New York: Coward-McCann, 1943), 11.

56. David Lear Buckman, *Old Steamboat Days on the Hudson River* (New York: Grafton Press, 1907), 34–55.

57. Donald C. Ringwald, *Hudson River Day Line: The Story of a Great American Steamboat Company* (Berkeley: Howell-North Books, 1965), 12.

58. The French traveler Michael Chevalier commented on the appearance of such vessels: "The Western steamboats look very much like the Vigier baths on the Seine; they are huge houses of two stories. . . . In the interior they have that coquettish air that characterizes American vessels in general; the cabins are showily furnished, and make a very pretty appearance. The little green blinds and the snugly fitted windows, pleasingly contrasting with the white walls, would have made Jean-Jacques sigh with envy." See Chevalier, *Society Manners and Politics in the United States* (1839; reprint, New York: A. P. Kelley, 1966), letter XX, 17.

59. Marianne Finch, an 1853 traveler, quoted in Lane, *American Paddle Steamboats*, 82.

60. Mrs. Caroline M. Kirkland, "Mrs. Pell's Pilgrimage," *A Book for the Home Circle* (New York: Charles Scribner, 1853), 144–61; Kemble, *Journal*, 2:97–98.

61. J. Howland Gardner, "The Development of Steam Navigation on Long Island Sound," *Historical Transactions, 1893–1943: The Society of Naval Architects and Marine Engineers* (New York: by the Society, 1945), 104, 107.

62. Wainwright, *Philadelphia Perspective*, 198 (diary entry for September 24, 1847). For information on the operation of palace steamers on the East Coast, see George W. Hilton, *The Night Boat* (Berkeley: Howell-North Books, 1968).

63. Erik Heyl, "The 'City of Buffalo': Last of the Great Lakes' Palace Steamers," *Niagara Frontier* 4, 1 (spring 1957): 10–11.

64. Mark Twain, *Life on the Mississippi* (1883; reprint, New York: Library of America, 1982), 457, 461.

65. Thomas Curtis Clarke, John Bogart, et al., *The American Railway: Its Construction, Development, Management, and Appliances* (New York: Charles Scribner's Sons, 1889), 240.

66. John White, author of an exhaustive history of the American railroad car, has documented the development of comfortably equipped, elegantly decorated passenger cars so thoroughly that a lengthy chronological recapitulation is unnecessary. White, *The American Railroad Passenger Car* (Baltimore: Johns Hopkins University Press, 1978).

67. *Rochester (N.Y.) Evening Post* quoted in *American Railroad Journal* (June 15, 1842), as cited in August Mencken, *The Railroad Passenger Car: An Illustrated History of the First Hundred Years, with Accounts by Contemporary Passengers* (Baltimore: Johns Hopkins University Press, 1957), 16–17.

68. White, *The American Railroad Passenger Car*, 208.

69. *Buffalo City Directory* (1880), unpaginated.

70. White, *The American Railroad Passenger Car*, 209.

71. Ibid., 378, 381; Alfred Spitzli, *A Manual for Managers, Designers, Weavers, and All Others Connected with the Manufacture of Textile Fabrics* . . . (Troy, N.Y.: A. and A. F. Spitzli, Publishers, 1881), 126.

72. "Princely Parlor Furniture," *Sears, Roebuck and Co. Catalogue No. 104, 1897* (1897; reprint, New York: Chelsea House, 1976), unpaginated.

73. Benjamin Franklin Taylor, *The World on Wheels and Other Sketches* (Chicago: S. C. Griggs and Company, 1873), 157–58.

74. "Centennial Passenger Coaches," *National Car-Builder* 7, 6 (June 1876): 86.

75. *The Modern Priscilla Home Furnishing Book: A Practical Book for the Woman Who Loves Her Home* (Boston: Priscilla Publishing Company, 1925), 2.

76. *Gleason's*, April 1, 1854, 208.

77. *Rochester (N.Y.) Daily Advertiser*, March 3, 1848, 1. In the same issue, the Emporium Daguerreotype Gallery, a competitor, advertised the addition of "a new and magnificent SERAPHINE [a type of reed organ], of fine tone, for the amusement of visitors," to its receiving gallery.

78. Advertisement for T. Mercer, Branch Daguerreotype Gallery, *Rochester (N.Y.) Daily Advertiser*, March 3, 1848, 1.

79. Advertisement for "Powelson's Photographic Rooms," *Rochester Directory* (1864).

80. H. J. Rodgers, *Twenty-Three Years under a Sky-Light* (1872; reprint, New York: Arno, 1973), 150.

81. Robert Taft, *Photography and the American Scene* (1938; reprint, New York: Dover Publications, 1964), 76.

82. *Daguerreian Journal* 1, 4 (January 1, 1851): 58; advertisement for the Emporium Daguerreotype Gallery, *Rochester (N.Y.) Daily Advertiser*, March 3, 1848, 1.

83. Richard Rudisill, *Mirror Image* (Albuquerque: University of New Mexico Press, 1971), 203.

84. M. A. Root, *The Camera and the Pencil* (Philadelphia: by the author, 1864), 45.

85. E. K. Hough, "Expressing Character in Photographic Pictures," *American Journal of Photography* 1, 14 (December 15, 1858): 211.

86. Neil Harris, "Museums, Merchandising, and Popular Taste," in Quimby, *Material Culture*, 145.

87. Williams, *Dream Worlds*, 58.

88. Ibid., 59.

89. See, for example, the "panoramic" wood engraving of the New York Crystal Palace of 1853 published in *Gleason's*, February 4, 1854, 73–80; fabrics are clearly displayed as "waterfalls" of color and texture.

90. James D. McCabe, *The Illustrated History of the Centennial Exhibition . . .* (Philadelphia: National Publishing Company, 1876), 376.

91. This account of the New England Kitchen and possible sources of influence is condensed from Rodris Roth, "The New England, or 'Olde Tyme,' Kitchen Exhibit at Nineteenth-Century Fairs," in Allen Axelrod, ed., *The Colonial Revival in America* (New York: W. W. Norton, 1985), 159–83.

92. Walter Smith, *Industrial Art*, vol. 2 of *The Masterpieces of the Centennial Exhibition, Illustrated* (Philadelphia: Gebbie and Barrie, [1876]), 123.

93. McCabe, *Illustrated History of the Centennial Exhibition*, 375–77. See also *Gems of the Centennial Exhibition: Consisting of Illustrated Descriptions of Objects of an Artistic Character . . .* (New York: D. Appleton and Company, 1877), 139–40. An engraving of the exhibited room appears on page 138.

94. See Thornton, *Authentic Decor*, 188, 194, 195.

95. Smith, *Industrial Art*, 121; Frank H. Norton, *Illustrated Historical Register of the Centennial Exhibition, Philadelphia, 1876, and of the Exposition Universelle, Paris, 1878* (New York: American News Company, 1879), 384–85.

96. *Artistic Houses* (1883; reprint, New York: Benjamin Blom, 1971).

97. Smith, *Industrial Art*, 122.

98. "Union Hall," *Ballou's Pictorial Drawing-Room Companion*, January 3, 1852, 73.

99. "New York Atheneum," *Daguerreian Journal* 1, 2 (November 15, 1850): 59.

100. "C. M." [Charles Mackey], "Transatlantic Sketches: American Firemen," *Illustrated London News*, January 23, 1858, 92.

101. Ibid., 92.

102. See, for example, the photograph of the parlors of the Active Hose Company, Rochester, New York, ca. 1873, in Katherine C. Grier, *Culture and Comfort: People, Parlors, and Upholstery, 1850–1930* (Rochester, N.Y.: Strong Museum, 1988), 54.

103. Thomas L. McKenney cited in Ringwald, *Hudson River Day Line*, 96.

104. Kemble, *Journal*, 2:97–98.

105. Ibid., 172. See also Charles Dickens, *American Notes for General Circulation* (1842; reprint, Boston: Ticknor and Fields, 1867).

106. Taylor, *World on Wheels*, 156–57.

107. This statement has been attributed to Pullman by Mrs. Duane Doty, as quoted in *The Town of Pullman Illustrated: Its Growth with Brief Accounts of Its Industries* (1893; reprint, Pullman, Ill.: Pullman Civic Organization, 1974), 23.

108. David Lear Buckman, *Old Steamboat Days on the Hudson River* (New York: Grafton Press, 1907), 55; Lynes, *The Tastemakers*, 126.

109. Buckman, *Old Steamboat Days*, 84–87.

110. Russell Lynes, *The Tastemakers: The Shaping of American Popular Taste* (1954; reprint, New York: Dover Publications, 1980), 93–94, 96. Lynes was the first to recognize the importance of hotels, steamboats, and railroad cars as shapers of the popular sensibility, but he did not acknowledge them as sources of furnishing information and influences on household taste.

## CHAPTER TWO. THE COMFORTABLE THEATER

1. Clarence Cook, *The House Beautiful* (New York: Scribner, Armstrong and Company, 1878), 47. Basing his definition on the work of Erik Erikson, sociologist Richard Sennett provides a concise definition of the term *social identity:* "the meeting point between who a person wants to be and what the world allows him to be . . . one's place in a landscape formed by the intersections of circumstance and desire." This definition seems particularly appropriate to the study of consumer culture and consumer aspirations involved in creating parlors. Richard Sennett, *The Fall of Public Man* (New York: Vintage Books, 1978), 107.

2. Ethel Spencer, *The Spencers of Amberson Avenue: A Turn-of-the-Century Memoir* (Pittsburgh: University of Pittsburgh Press, 1983), 16.

3. Cook, *House Beautiful*, 98–99.

4. Correspondence of Mrs. George Ware Fulton, George Ware Fulton Papers, Barker History Archive, University of Texas, Austin.

5. Spencer, *Spencers of Amberson Avenue*, 17.

6. Edith Wharton and Ogden Codman Jr., *The Decoration of Houses* (New York: Charles Scribner's Sons, 1897), 124.

7. This information relies on Peter Thornton, *Authentic Decor: The Domestic Interior, 1620–1920* (New York: Viking Penguin, 1984), "1670–1720" and "1720–1770." Mark Girouard describes the elaborate plans of the largest Victorian country houses in England as the most exaggerated form of the impulse to segregate varieties of activity. In his words, they were "enormous, complicated and highly articulated machines."

> Victorian country houses were complicated partly because they had to contain so many people, to a lesser extent because of the new mechanical devices that were incorporated in them, but mainly because the activities and interrelationships of their occupants were so minutely organized and subdivided. In an age when government was organized into departments, the middle classes into pro-

fessions, science into different disciplines and convicts into separate cells, country house life was divided up into separate parcels.

See Girouard, *The Victorian Country House*, rev. ed. (New Haven, Conn.: Yale University Press, 1979), 27–28.

8. Thornton, *Authentic Decor,* 50, 93.

9. Adam quoted in ibid., 145.

10. As Richard L. Bushman has argued, "In those marvelously adorned public rooms we can picture them displaying their clothing, their wit and worldly knowledge, their fine manners and physical grace—all within a beautiful space suitable for a civil and refined society." Bushman, "American High-Style and Vernacular Cultures," in Jack P. Greene and J. R. Pole, eds., *Colonial British America* (Baltimore: Johns Hopkins University Press, 1984), 351–52.

11. *The Century Dictionary,* vol. 4 (New York: Century Company, 1890), 4295.

12. Catharine E. Beecher and Harriet Beecher Stowe, *The American Woman's Home* (New York: J. B. Ford and Company, 1869), 86.

13. Henry T. Williams and Mrs. C. S. Jones, *Beautiful Homes; or, Hints in House Furnishing* (New York: Henry T. Williams, 1878), 110.

14. Ibid., 110.

15. Noah Webster, *American Dictionary of the English Language,* rev. ed. (Springfield, Mass.: G. and C. Merriam, 1882), 950.

16. Calvert Vaux, *Villas and Cottages* (New York: Harper Brothers, 1864).

17. Frank Luther Mott, *A History of American Magazines, 1865–1885,* vol. 3 (Cambridge, Mass.: Belknap Press, 1970), 7.

18. *Montgomery Ward and Co. Catalogue No. 57, Spring and Summer, 1895* (1895; reprint, New York: Dover Publications, 1969), 45. In the author's private library is a copy of the unnumbered 1900 edition of Reed's book, bearing a small bookplate that identifies the source of purchase as Sears, Roebuck and Co.

19. Samuel B. Reed, *House-Plans for Everybody* (New York: Orange Judd and Company, 1878), 63–64.

20. Ibid., 51–55.

21. Ibid., 54, 65–66.

22. "New Furniture," *Godey's Lady's Book,* February 1850, 152–53; see also Fanny N. Copeland, "Draperies, Blinds, and Curtains," *Peterson's Magazine,* April 1860, 269–72.

23. "New Furniture," 153.

24. Ibid., 152.

25. Mrs. Caroline M. Kirkland, *A Book for the Home Circle* (New York: Charles Scribner, 1853), 110.

26. Rodd L. Wheaton, "High Style in Montana: The Kohrs Parlor," in Kenneth L. Ames, ed., *Victorian Furniture,* published in *Nineteenth Century* 8, 3–4 (1982): 245.

27. "Daisy Fields," "How We Furnished the Parlor," *The Household,* June 1882, 180–81.

28. *The Household:* December 1881, 265; September 1881, 193; December 1881, 279.

29. Nicholas B. Wainwright, ed., *A Philadelphia Perspective: The Diary of Sidney George Fisher Covering the Years 1834–1871* (Philadelphia: Historical Society of Pennsylvania, 1967), 76.

30. See *Social Culture; A Treatise on Etiquette, Self Culture, Dress, Physical Beauty and Domestic Relations* . . . (Springfield, Mass.: King-Richardson Company, 1903); Emily Thornwell, *The Lady's Guide to Perfect Gentility* (New York: Derby and Jackson, 1856); *Etiquette for Ladies; with Hints on the Preservation, Improvement, and Display of Female Beauty* (Philadelphia: Lea and Blanchard, "successors to Carey and Co.," 1838; appendix dated 1856).

31. The author remembers being astonished at the enormous number of calling cards in the collection of a state historic site—cards used by the citizens of several small southeastern Texas towns, people who obviously knew each other, given the size of the communities.

32. *Etiquette for Ladies*, 23, 25.

33. Walter R. Houghton et al., *American Etiquette and Rules of Politeness* (New York: Powers and LeCraw, 1886), 127.

34. Karen Halttunen has made extended use of the metaphor of the theater in her discussion of the "genteel performance" in manners and dress in what she has termed "sentimental culture" between 1830 and 1870. Her thesis centers on the discomfort that middle-class people felt in the new urban world of strangers and on their efforts to define an ideal of "sincere" manners between 1830 and 1850. Karen Halttunen, *Confidence Men and Painted Women: A Study of Middle-Class Culture in America, 1830–1870* (New Haven, Conn.: Yale University Press, 1982), 186.

35. Catharine Harbeson Esling, *The Book of Parlour Games* (Philadelphia: Peck and Bliss, 1854), 20–23, 110–11, 248; Frank Bellew, *The Art of Amusing* (New York: Carleton, 1866; London: S. Low, Son and Company, 1866). Halttunen also has taken the craze for parlor pastimes as evidence of the decline of sentimental culture and of a corresponding acceptance and enjoyment of the theatricality of parlor social life by middle-class people who once were preoccupied with its possible "hypocrisy." See Halttunen, "Disguises, Masks, and Parlor Theatricals: The Decline of Sentimental Culture in the 1850s," *Confidence Men and Painted Women*, 153–90.

36. Bellew, *Art of Amusing*, 10–11.

37. M. E. Dodge, *A Few Friends and How They Amused Themselves* (Philadelphia: J. B. Lippincott and Company, 1869), 11.

38. Caroline L. Smith (Aunt Carrie), *The American Book of In-Door Games, Amusements, and Occupations* (Boston: Lee and Shepard, 1873), 89.

39. Esling, *Book of Parlour Games*; Smith, *American Book of In-Door Games*, 112.

40. See Smith, *American Book of In-Door Games*, and Bellew, *Art of Amusing*.

41. See, for example, Mary D. Robertson, ed., *Lucy Breckenridge of Grove Hill: The Journal of a Virginia Girl, 1862–1864* (Kent, Ohio: Kent State University Press, 1979), 117.

42. See ibid.

43. Although manners books usually devoted much attention to mourning dress

and customs, the display of the body in the parlor and the execution of the actual funeral ceremony were rarely discussed. A few manners books do document the role of parlors in death preparations: "If guests are invited to go from the house to the church, the corpse is usually exposed in the drawing-room, while the family are assembled in another apartment," Richard Wells noted in his 1891 *Manners, Culture, and Dress.* "No one should call upon a bereaved family while the dead remains in the house." Wells explained at length the differences in behavior associated with funerals held at home in the parlor and those held at churches, which suggests that recent changes in traditional practices required such specific advice. See Richard A. Wells, *Manners, Culture, and Dress* (Springfield, Mass.: King, Richardson and Company, 1891), 314–15.

44. See Harriet Beecher Stowe, *We and Our Neighbors* (New York: J. B. Ford and Company, 1875).

45. Alice Hughes Neupert, "In Those Days: Buffalo in the 1870's," *Niagara Frontier* 24, 4 (winter 1977): 77–78. The author of this memoir died in 1953 at the age of seventy-three. The manuscript, which seems to have been produced for the entertainment of her family, was submitted to the journal by her daughter-in-law.

46. Ibid., 77–79.

47. This kind of careful preservation also is recorded in other family histories, such as Ethel Spencer's memoir of growing up in Pittsburgh. See Spencer, *Spencers of Amberson Avenue*, 17.

48. A. C. Steele, *Aunt Teeks in Memory Land*, vol. 1 (Windsor, Mass.: Progressive Club, 1959), 9.

49. Katherine Yearick Foster Cavano, interview with the author, Pennington, N.J., March and December 1986.

50. Spencer, *Spencers of Amberson Avenue*, 17.

51. Margaret Frances Byington, *Homestead: The Households of a Mill Town* (1910; reprint, New York: Arno Press, 1969).

52. Louise Bolard More, *Wage-Earners' Budgets: A Study of Standards and Cost of Living in New York City* (New York: Henry Holt and Company, 1907), 133–34.

CHAPTER THREE. "ORTHODOX AS THE HYMN BOOK"

1. Invoice of Meader Furniture Co., Cincinnati, Ohio, December 27, 1876, George Ware Fulton Papers, Barker History Archive, University of Texas, Austin.

2. [George A. Martin], *Our Homes: How to Beautify Them* (New York: O. Judd and Company, 1887), 43.

3. Mary Gay Humphreys, "The Parlor," *Decorator and Furnisher* 11, 5 (May 1888): 52.

4. Ada Cone, "Aesthetic Mistakes in Furnishing: The Parlor Centre Table," *Decorator and Furnisher* 17, 4 (January 1891): 132.

5. Henry T. Williams and Mrs. C. S. Jones, *Beautiful Homes; or, Hints in House Furnishing* (New York: Henry T. Williams, 1878), 56. Who the intended audience was

for such advice books is a vexing question but an important one to try to answer. Careful reading can often divulge to whom an author chose to write, as can observation of the quality of the book itself, its cost when new (if known), and the kinds of other titles the publisher advertised in the book front and back matter. The survival of numerous copies of a book in research libraries can suggest its widespread distribution, if not its specific readership. Furnishing advice books that seem to have been directed to audiences in rural areas, audiences with small disposable incomes, or new consumers include the following: Williams and Jones, *Beautiful Homes;* [Martin], *Our Homes;* Louis H. Gibson, *Convenient Houses, with Fifty Plans for the Housekeeper, Architect and Housewife* . . . (New York: T. Y. Crowell and Company, 1889); and *Household Conveniences; Being the Experience of Many Practical Writers* (New York: Orange Judd Company, 1884). Their advice seems to express many of the most conventional ideas about furnishing houses and the meanings of those furnishings, because they introduced ideas about interior decoration to consumers with limited budgets, living away from the centers of fashion.

6. See *Sears, Roebuck and Co. Catalogue No. 104, 1897* (1897; reprint, New York: Chelsea House, 1976), unpaginated.

7. Alice Hughes Neupert, "In Those Days: Buffalo in the 1870's," *Niagara Frontier* 24, 4 (winter 1977): 77–79.

8. Williams and Jones, *Beautiful Homes,* 50.

9. See Victor Turner, "Symbols in Ndembu Ritual," *The Forest of Symbols* (Ithaca, N.Y.: Cornell University Press, 1970), 30:

> Ritual, scholars are coming to see, is precisely a mechanism that periodically converts the obligatory into the desirable. The basic unit of ritual, the dominant symbol, encapsulates the major properties of the total ritual process which brings about this transmutation. Within its framework of meanings, the dominant symbol brings the ethical and jural norms of society into close contact with strong emotional stimuli. . . . Norms and values, on the one hand, become saturated with emotion, while the gross and basic emotions become ennoble through contact with social values. The irksomeness of moral constraint is transformed into the "love of virtue."

10. Following the lead of Arthur M. Schlesinger's *Learning How to Behave: A Historical Study of American Etiquette Books* (1946), Karen Halttunen has suggested this change in American understandings of gentility in her analysis of etiquette books dating between 1830 and 1870. See Karen Halttunen, *Confidence Men and Painted Women: A Study of Middle-Class Culture in America, 1830–1870* (New Haven, Conn.: Yale University Press, 1982), 84–85.

11. Arthur Martine, *Martine's Handbook of Etiquette, and Guide to True Politeness* (New York: Dick and Fitzgerald, 1852, 1866), title page; John A. Ruth, *Decorum: A Practical Treatise on Etiquette and Dress of the Best American Society* (New York: Union Publishing House, 1881; Chicago: Chas. L. Snyder and Company, 1881), 1.

12. Florence Hartley, *The Ladies' Book of Etiquette, and Manual of Politeness* (Boston: G. W. Cottrell, 1860), 151–52, 149.

13. *Etiquette for Ladies; with Hints on the Preservation, Improvement, and Display of Female Beauty* (Philadelphia: Lea and Blanchard, "successors to Carey and Co.," 1838; appendix dated 1856), 19.

14. This account of "sincere" etiquette in sentimental culture draws on Halttunen, "Sentimental Culture and the Problem of Etiquette," in *Confidence Men and Painted Women*.

15. Ibid., 93.

16. Hartley, *Ladies' Book of Etiquette*, 149.

17. *Chesterfield's Art of Letter-Writing Simplified, to which is appended the Complete Rules of Etiquette, and the Usages of Society* (New York: Dick and Fitzgerald, Publishers, 1857, 1860), 41.

18. Norbert Elias, *The History of Manners*, vol. 1 of *The Civilizing Process* (New York: Pantheon Books, 1978), 35–50. Originally published as *Uber den Prozess der Zivilisation* (Switzerland: Haus zum Falken, 1939).

19. Jonathan Swift, "Good Manners," *The Tatler No. 298* (London: William Harrison, 1711), reprinted in Diarmuid Russell, ed., *The Portable Irish Reader* (New York: Viking Press, 1946), 10.

20. Edwin Harrison Cady, "The Gentleman: Traditions and Meanings," *The Gentleman in America: A Literary Study in American Culture* (Syracuse, N.Y.: Syracuse University Press, 1949), 9–14.

21. John F. Kasson discussed the ambivalence of American thinkers toward technology in *Civilizing the Machine: Technology and Republican Values in America, 1776–1900* (New York: Grossman Publishers, 1976).

22. Neil Harris has discussed the dimensions of this debate over virtue, fashion, and luxury as it affected the arts and architecture in Harris, *The Artist in American Society: The Formative Years, 1790–1860* (New York: Simon and Schuster, 1966), although I would not agree with his position that the argument had been resolved by the 1830s.

23. Halttunen, *Confidence Men and Painted Women*, 89.

24. Mrs. Lydia H. Sigourney, *Letters to Mothers* (Hartford, Conn.: by the author, 1838), 157.

25. "Boarding Out," *Harper's Weekly*, March 7, 1857, 146.

26. Mrs. Parkes, *Domestic Duties; or, Instructions to Young Married Ladies . . .* , 3d ed. (New York: J. and J. Harper, 1829), 59.

27. "A Parlor View," *Gleason's*, November 11, 1854, 300.

28. For a discussion of the "French renaissance" styles with further illustrations of the type, see Kenneth Ames, "George Henkels, Nineteenth-Century Philadelphia Cabinetmaker," *Antiques*, October 1973. Just as French etiquette and culture were considered the most refined in the world, so too French fashion and taste in furnishing, since the eighteenth century, represented to members of American elites the most cultivated vision of parlor life.

29. Rosalind B. Williams, *Dream Worlds: Mass Consumption in Late Nineteenth-Century France* (Berkeley: University of California Press, 1983), 38.

30. John Cornforth, *English Interiors, 1790–1848: The Quest for Comfort* (London:

Barrie and Jenkins Ltd., 1978), 13. In a letter written in 1799, Lady Louisa Stuart discussed Archerfield, a country house in which she then was a guest, by comparing it unfavorably with Dalkeith, another English country house. "It wants nothing but more furniture for the middle of rooms. I mean all is set out in order, no comfortable tables to write or read at; it looks a fine London house prepared for company; quite a contrast to the delightful gallery at Dalkeith, where you can settle yourself in any corner."

31. See ibid.; see also the illustrations of middle-class rooms in Scandinavia, Austria, Germany, and Holland in Peter Thornton, *Authentic Decor: The Domestic Interior, 1620–1920* (New York: Viking Penguin, 1984).

32. Mrs. Caroline M. Kirkland, *A Book for the Home Circle* (New York: Charles Scribner, 1853), 197.

33. This concern seems to have had a regional character, for it is clear that the gentry of the South were not worried about these issues. Rather, many seem to have been aligned firmly with the "aristocratic" taste.

34. Harriet Beecher Stowe [Christopher Crowfield, pseud.], *House and Home Papers* (Boston: Fields, Osgood, and Company, 1869), 21.

35. Alice B. Neal, "Furnishing; or, Two Ways of Commencing Life," *Godey's Lady's Book*, November 1850, 299–305.

36. Stowe, *House and Home Papers*, 40, 34.

37. Catharine Beecher, *Miss Beecher's Domestic Receipt Book*, 3d ed. (New York: Harper and Bros., 1858), 274.

38. Ibid., 275.

39. Henry William Cleaveland, William Backus, and Samuel D. Backus, *Village and Farm Cottages: The Requirements of American Village Homes Considered and Suggested . . .* (New York: D. Appleton and Company, 1856), 132.

40. Almira Seymour, *Home: The Basis of the State* (Boston: A. Williams and Company, 1869), 57.

41. Emma Wellmont, *Uncle Sam's Palace; or, The Reigning King*, 2d ed. (Boston: Sanborn, Carter, Bazin and Company, 1853), 180.

42. Cleaveland, Backus, and Backus, *Village and Farm Cottages*, 131.

43. Between 1836 and 1853, about 10,000 patents were issued in the United States; by 1876, more than 200,000 had been granted. By 1873, more than 2,000 patents had been issued for improved clothes washers alone. William and Marlys Ray, *The Art of Invention: Patent Models and Their Makers* (Princeton, N.J.: Pyne Press, 1974), 35.

44. Kirkland, *Book for the Home Circle*, 208. This recognition of the dual physical and psychological nature of "comfort" actually accords with its history as a concept. The lexicography of the word *comfort* reveals that using the term to designate a physical condition or state is almost unknown before the eighteenth century. Rather, *comfort* relates to succoring, moral or spiritual strengthening, heartening, and supporting in trouble or grief. The *Oxford English Dictionary*'s eighth definition of the verb *to comfort*—"to bring into a comfortable state (of body and feelings), allay physical discomfort, make comfortable"—notes that this understanding is "App. only of modern use." Its sixth definition of the noun *comfort*—"a state of physical and material well-being, with free-

dom from pain and trouble, and satisfaction of bodily needs"—is supported by examples of use no earlier than 1818, although the use of the word in this sense can be found several decades earlier. Although psychological state is still factored into such definitions, it is now a secular state ("a tranquil enjoyment") rather than a condition of moral or spiritual solace.

45. Seymour, *Home*, 57.

46. Kirkland, *Book for the Home Circle*, 198–99.

47. Cleaveland, Backus, and Backus, *Village and Farm Cottages*, 129.

48. Ibid., 133.

49. Harriet Beecher Stowe, *Uncle Tom's Cabin; or, Life among the Lowly in Three Novels* (1852; reprint, New York: Library of America, 1982), 162.

50. "Boarding Out," 146.

51. See the introduction to [Miriam Berry Whicher], *The Widow Bedott Papers* (New York: J. C. Derby, 1856), 2, for the use of this term. The genre also includes more famous examples, such as in Richard Haliburton's "Sam Slick" stories and Ann Sophia Stephens's *High Life in New York, by Jonathan Slick, Esq. of Weathersfield, Conn. . . .* (New York: Bunce and Brother, 1854).

52. [Whicher], *Widow Bedott*, 223.


CHAPTER FOUR. BODILY COMFORT AND
SPRING-SEAT UPHOLSTERY

1. Lewis F. Allen, *Rural Architecture* (New York: C. M. Saxton, 1852), 59.

2. John Bullock, *The American Cottage Builder* (New York: Stringer and Townsend, 1854), 122.

3. Henry William Cleaveland, William Backus, and Samuel D. Backus, *Village and Farm Cottages: The Requirements of American Village Homes Considered and Suggested . . .* (New York: D. Appleton and Company, 1856), 132; Allen, *Rural Architecture*, 238, 239.

4. William C. Richards, *A Day in the New York Crystal Palace, and How to Make the Most of It* (New York: G. P. Putnam and Company, 1853), 44.

5. Penelope Eames, "Furniture in England, France, and the Netherlands from the Twelfth to the Fifteenth Century," *Furniture History* 13 (1977): 181–214; Peter Thornton, *Seventeenth-Century Interior Decoration in England, France, and Holland* (1978; reprint, New Haven, Conn.: published for the Paul Mellon Centre for Studies in British Art by Yale University Press, 1983), 198.

6. Eames, "Furniture in England, France, and the Netherlands," 192–96.

7. *Oxford English Dictionary*, s. v. *ease*. In this definition, *transf.*, or "transferred sense," refers to a broadening of meaning.

8. A *conversation piece* is defined as "a portrait group in a domestic or architectural setting in which the sitters are engaged in conversation or social activity of a not very vigorous character. Conversation pieces are usually, though not always, small in scale. They were produced in large numbers in Britain during the eighteenth century, but the

use of the term is not confined to British painting or to this period." Harold Osborne, ed., *The Oxford Companion to Art* (Oxford: Oxford University Press, 1971), 278.

9. See, for example, the illustrations in Gervase Jackson-Stops, "Johan Zoffany and the Eighteenth-Century Interior," *Antiques*, June 1987, 1264–79.

10. See, for example, Georges Duby, *William Marshall: The Flower of Chivalry*, trans. Richard Howard (New York: Pantheon Books, 1986). William Marshall, a knight and baron who served three English kings including Richard the Lionhearted, was described in ballad as tall and straight, part of a code of conventional description applied to people of quality. His posture and bearing were considered an important signal of his honest and courageous nature.

11. Florence Hartley, *The Ladies' Book of Etiquette, and Manual of Politeness* (Boston: G. W. Cottrell, 1856), 152.

12. Silas Lapham experienced the torments of this perilous no-man's land between the easy manner of etiquette and the crude self when he, his wife, and his daughter were invited to a dinner party at the home of the Corey family, Boston Brahmins. After the agonies of escorting Mrs. Corey to the dining room, Lapham "fetched a long sigh of relief when he sank into his chair and felt himself safe from error if he kept a sharp lookout and did only what the others did." By doing so, however, Lapham took wine with each course (something he never did at home) and humiliated himself by becoming drunk at dinner. William Dean Howells, *The Rise of Silas Lapham*, in *William Dean Howells: Novels, 1875–1886* (1885; reprint, New York: Library of America, 1982), especially chapter 14, 1034–54.

13. Eliza Leslie, *The Housebook; or, A Manual of Domestic Economy* (Philadelphia: Carey and Hart, 1840), 198.

14. Ibid., 194. Recall British actress Fanny Kemble's comment that the "vibratory motion" of rocking chairs in ladies' parlors on American steamboats of the 1830s contributed to an overall sense of tumult in these rooms.

15. *Chesterfield's Art of Letter-Writing Simplified, to which is appended the Complete Rules of Etiquette, and the Usages of Society* (New York: Dick and Fitzgerald, Publishers, 1857, 1860), 20–21.

16. Hartley, *Ladies' Book of Etiquette*, 152.

17. Ann Sophia Stephens, *High Life in New York, by Jonathan Slick, Esq. of Weathersfield, Conn. . . .* (New York: Bunce and Brother, 1854), 22.

18. "An Erect Position," *Gleason's*, August 28, 1852, 142.

19. "How to Sit on a Divan," *Decorator and Furnisher* 18, 5 (October 1891): 8.

20. For histories of nineteenth-century underwear, see Cecil Saint-Laurent, *The Great Book of Lingerie* (New York: Vendome Press, 1983); Nora Waugh, *Corsets and Crinolines* (New York: Theatre Arts Books, 1954); and C. Willett and Phyllis Cunnington, with revisions by A. D. Mayfield and Valerie Mayfield, *The History of Underclothes* (Boston: Faber and Faber, 1951, 1981).

21. The lessening constraints of parlor clothing for men suggest that the social roles of gentlemen lay somewhere other than parlor culture. In comparison, eighteenth-century gentlemen's tailored clothing constrained their movements at a time when they,

as members of the upper classes, were also considered conservators and expressors of civility.

22. Unattributed quotation cited in Willett and Cunnington, *History of Under-clothes,* 114.

23. Saint-Laurent, *The Great Book of Lingerie,* 119.

24. *Montgomery Ward and Co. Catalogue, Fall and Winter, 1894–1895* (1894; reprint, New York: Dover Editions, 1969), 85. The U.S. Patent Office also issued a number of patents addressing this problem, such as William A. Nettleton's 1882 patent for "corset stiffeners" made from short sections of horn or whalebone wrapped together with thread so that they could "break joints in the manner specified" and return to shape when the sitter rose or straightened. Patent No. 265,534 in *Official Gazette, U.S. Patent Office* 22 (1882): 1220.

25. Saint-Laurent, *The Great Book of Lingerie,* 120. Long corsets not only altered sitting and "lounging" but changed the nature of a fashionable woman's gait as well. An advertisement for Warner's '98 Model Corsets explained to readers: "For grace of figure when walking the form should bend slightly forward from the line of waist, and unless Nature has given this art it can only be produced by raising the bust, thereby tapering the waist and forcing the shoulders erect. The hips are next in importance. They should be well rounded to the centre, then sloping toward the back, which is accomplished by drawing in the abdomen with the aid of the corset." Advertisement for Warner's '98 Model Corset in *Ladies' Home Journal,* November 1897, 32.

26. Hartley, *Ladies' Book of Etiquette,* 77.

27. For more specific information on seat structures before the advent of the spring seat, see Lizanne Landis, "The Regulator's Art: Early American Upholstery, 1660–1930," *Antiques and the Arts Weekly,* April 15, 1883, 1–2, 40; Andrew Passeri and Robert F. Trent, "Two New England Queen Anne Easy Chairs with Original Upholstery," *Maine Antiques Digest,* April 1983, 26A–28A; Karin M. Walton, "The Golden Age of English Furniture Upholstery, 1660–1840" (catalog of an exhibition at Stable Court Exhibition Galleries, Temple-Newsam House, Leeds, England, August 15–September 15, 1973).

28. George Himmelheber, *Biedermeier Furniture,* trans. and ed. Simon Jervis (London: Faber and Faber Limited, n.d.), 89–90.

29. Dorothy Holley, "Furniture Springs," *Furniture History* 7 (1981): 64–67. There is also inconclusive evidence that French furniture makers, always on the cutting edge of their craft, experimented with the use of "elastic springs" inside seating furniture during the reign of Louis XV. See Roger de Felice, *French Furniture under Louis XV,* trans. Florence Simmonds (New York: Frederick A. Stokes, [1920]), 25–26.

30. Holley, "Furniture Springs," 65.

31. Rhoda and Agnes Garrett, *Suggestions for House Decoration in Painting, Woodwork, and Furniture* (Philadelphia: Porter and Coates, 1877), 64. Badly tempered springs apparently remained a problem worthy of particular note for decades after their common use in chairs. In its article "Easy-Chairs That Are Easy," *Cassell's Household Guide* praised the springs of chairs provided by C. and W. Trapnell, of Bristol, England: "Being made

of the best charcoal wire they retain their elasticity, and will not snap, which is frequently the case with springs made of ordinary hard-drawn wire." "Easy-Chairs That Are Easy," *Cassell's Household Guide*, vol. 3 (London: Cassell, Petter, and Galpin, [ca. 1870]), 308–9.

32. John Claudius Loudon, *Loudon Furniture Designs from the Encyclopedia of Cottage, Farmhouse, and Villa Architecture and Furniture, 1839* (East Ardsley, Yorkshire, and London: S. R. Publishers Ltd. and The Connoisseur, 1970), 336. This edition reprints sections of the *Encyclopedia* and retains the original pagination.

33. Fern Tuten, *American Domestic Patented Furniture, 1790–1850: A Compendium* (Ann Arbor, Mich.: University Microfilms, 1969), 74–75.

34. Ibid., 83. See also Siegfried Giedion, *Mechanization Takes Command: A Contribution to Anonymous History* (New York: Oxford University Press, 1948), 382–85, for a discussion of Samuel Pratt's 1827 and 1828 English patents for springs associated with shipboard furniture. These were intended to relieve seasickness.

35. Thornton, *Seventeenth-Century Interior Decoration in England, France, and Holland*, 196–97; Morrison H. Heckscher, *In Quest of Comfort: The Easy Chair in America* (New York: Metropolitan Museum of Art, 1971), 10–11; Shirley Glubok and Evelyn Hofer, "Glimpses of Holland's Golden Age: Two Seventeenth-Century Dollhouses Celebrate Daily Life in Old Amsterdam," *The Connoisseur*, December 1984, 112–18. One of the realistic dollhouses discussed in the Glubok and Hofer article contains a lying-in room furnished with a tilt-back chair designed for pregnant women.

36. Loudon, *Encyclopedia of Cottage, Farmhouse, and Villa Architecture and Furniture*, 322.

37. *The Marks Improved Adjustable Folding Chair* (New York: Marks Improved Adjustable Folding Chair Company, n.d.); Ethel Spencer, *The Spencers of Amberson Avenue: A Turn-of-the-Century Memoir* (Pittsburgh: University of Pittsburgh Press, 1983), 70, 73.

38. See the advertisement for Boston furniture dealer Sherlock Spooner in *The Boston Directory* (Boston: Charles Stimpson, Jr., 1829), unpaginated.

39. Advertisements for J. Hancock and Co. in *Desilver's Philadelphia Directory, and Stranger's Guide* (Philadelphia: Robert Desilver, 1831, 1833), unpaginated; advertisement for Davis and Scholes in *Matchett's Baltimore Director, 1833* (Baltimore: Richard J. Matchett, 1833), 7.

40. Jane Williams Insley, "Once Upon a Time" (typescript, memoir delivered at a "Fortnightly Literary Club" meeting, Indianapolis, Indiana, 1943), 12. A copy was obtained from the author's granddaughter, Elizabeth Insley Traverse.

41. See, for example, the advertisement for Joseph Crook, upholsterer and paper hanger, in *Matchett's Baltimore Director, 1831* (Baltimore: Richard J. Matchett, 1831), unpaginated. In this advertisement, "Spring Seat Sofas" and "Patent Spring Seat Rocking Chairs" are separated from the other upholstered furniture offered. Other upholsterers' ads in the same edition do not yet mention spring upholstery.

42. Edwin T. Freedley, *Philadelphia and Its Manufactures: A Hand-Book* (Philadelphia: Edward Young, 1858), 272.

43. Loudon, *Encyclopedia of Cottage, Farmhouse, and Villa Architecture and Furniture*, 322.

44. "New Wagon Springs," *Scientific American*, July 31, 1847, 355; *Scientific American*, October 27, 1849, 3.

45. "Elasticity of Bodies," *Scientific American*, April 9, 1846, n.p.; "Improved Blind-Fastenings," *Scientific American*, March 20, 1847, 204; "Sundry Improvements," *Scientific American*, April 10, 1847, 228.

46. Charles C. Quick, *Tufting Secrets* (Los Angeles: American Book Institute, 1954), 49. In a discussion of "Buttoning as Ornament," John W. Stephenson noted, "The buttoning of upholstering was not alone intended to assist in creating greater comfort in connection with curved and softly-filled surfaces but it was also to serve as a means of ornamentation, the placing of the buttons creating pipes and diamond or bisquit-shaped spaces which were stuffed up so that pleats were formed from button to button." John. W. Stephenson, "Furniture Upholstering," in William J. Etten, ed. *Manual of the Furniture Arts and Crafts* (Grand Rapids, Mich.: A. P. Johnson Company, 1928), 508.

47. John Phin, author of *The Practical Upholsterer*, noted: "There has been a decided revolution in upholstery work during the past few years. Artistic forms, combined with French luxuriousness, are much sought after. . . . This style of work is upholstered very soft, and can only be done with a good quantity of hair, otherwise it will lose its proper shape before it has been in use any length of time." [John Phin], *The Practical Upholsterer* (New York: Industrial Publications Company, 1891), 41.

48. *How to Build, Furnish, and Decorate* (New York: Cooperative Building Association, 1889), 6.

49. "How to Sit on a Divan," 8.

50. "Among the Stores," *Decorator and Furnisher* 3, 3 (December 1883): 102.


CHAPTER FIVE. THE QUEST FOR REFINEMENT

1. *The Oxford English Dictionary* defines *formal* used in this context as "pertaining to the outward form, shape, or appearance (of a material object); also, in immaterial sense, pertaining to the form, arrangement, external qualities (e.g. of a work of art, a composition, etc.)." *Oxford English Dictionary*, s. v. *formal*.

2. Mrs. Jane Weaver, "Ornamental Bracket," *Peterson's Magazine*, September 1877, 217. See also, by the same author, "Ornamental Bracket, Valence [*sic*], Chair-Back, etc.," *Peterson's Magazine*, January 1862, 77, and "Bracket," *Peterson's Magazine*, May 1852, 419.

3. The term *lambrequin* appears to be an Americanism adapted from a French nineteenth-century decorating term. The original French meaning of *lambrequin* was "a scarf or piece of stuff worn over the helmet as a covering. In heraldry represented with one end (which is cut or jagged) pendant or floating." *Oxford English Dictionary*, s. v. *lambrequin*.

4. "Fashion Plates for Decorating Parlor Windows: The Latest Styles," *Godey's Lady's Book*, February 1854, 166.

5. Henry T. Williams and Mrs. C. S. Jones, *Beautiful Homes; or, Hints in House Furnishing* (New York: Henry T. Williams, 1878), 57.

6. *Sears, Roebuck and Co., 1908, Catalogue No. 117: The Great Price Maker* (1908; reprint, Northfield, Ill.: Digest Books, 1971), 901.

7. J. R. Pugh, "The Best Room: Its Arrangement and Decoration at Moderate Cost," *Decorator and Furnisher* 13, 1 (October 1888): 19.

8. For discussion of design economics in the nineteenth-century furniture industry, see Michael J. Ettema, "Technological Innovation and Design Economics in Furniture Manufacture," *Winterthur Portfolio* 16, 2/3 (summer/autumn 1981): 197–223.

9. *Sears, Roebuck and Co. Catalogue No. 104, 1897* (1897; reprint, New York: Chelsea House, 1976), unpaginated.

10. *Sears, Roebuck and Co. Catalogue No. 111, 1902* (Chicago: Sears, Roebuck and Co., 1902), 787.

11. Ibid., 784, 785.

12. In his essay "Art as a Cultural System," Clifford Geertz argues that no culture's art forms can be studied and made intelligible by only "inter-aesthetic" (internal) analysis of its forms and rules. He wrote, "The means of an art and the feeling for life that animates it are inseparable." The problem, for Geertz, is how to place "aesthetic force," in whatever form it takes, "within the other modes of social activity"—to recognize that the aesthetic system of a culture "grows out of a distinctive sensibility the whole of life participates in forming." See Geertz, "Art as a Cultural System," *Local Knowledge* (Berkeley: University of California Press, 1983), 97–98. *Sensibility*, as Geertz uses the term, may be defined as the character of a particular culture's general awareness, or mental perception, of itself in the world. For Geertz, the most profitable analysis of any culture's art forms compares many forms of expression and leads inevitably to the broadest questions of how people make meaningful "the profusion of things that happen to them." Exploring an art form by analyzing the ways in which it is connected to other forms of cultural expression is ultimately an exploration of the "collective formulation" that is the sensibility of a culture. For Geertz, art objects express the meaning of collective life, they "materialize a way of experiencing, bringing a particular cast of mind out into the world of objects, where men can look at it" (ibid., 99).

13. Robert Farris Thompson quoted in ibid., 98.

14. See Daniel P. Biebuyck, *The Lega: Art, Initiation, and Moral Philosophy* (Berkeley: University of California Press, 1973), and Daniel P. Biebuyck, "Symbolism of the Lega Stool," *Working Papers in the Traditional Arts 2 & 3* (Philadelphia: Institute for the Study of Human Issues, 1977), 1–36.

15. Biebuyck, "Symbolism of the Lega Stool," 20. The association does this through levels of codified knowledge, each requiring tutoring and initiation ceremonies involving music and dance, proverbs and stories, and the manipulation of a variety of artifacts such as ivory carvings and stools and natural objects such as large snail shells.

16. Baxandall also discusses how some aspects of painting, particularly the formal geometry of pictures, could be meaningful to men who knew the complicated mathematics of "gauging" for commercial purposes, and how the colors used in paintings, particularly blue and gold, were legible signals of the wealth of the patron. Michael Baxandall, *Painting and Experience in Quattrocento Italy* (Oxford, England: Clarendon Press, 1972), 56–64.

17. Michael Baxandall is developing this work further, and some of the information above was presented in a lecture, "Renaissance Art Criticism," delivered on August 28, 1986, at the Institute for the Study of Critical Theory held at Hobart and William Smith Colleges, Geneva, New York.

18. Two other related genres of associations emphasized the ways in which the outside world of Western civilization, including commerce and technology, were brought into the service of the parlor. One consisted of a loosely understood set of historical and exotic meanings that encompassed ornament and historical style. The other emphasized the transformation of the world's material resources into parlor objects. In this way, the parlor became not only a site for domestic associations but also a memory palace of culture, history, and technology—a museum.

19. [George A. Martin], *Our Homes: How to Beautify Them* (New York: O. Judd and Company, 1887), iii.

20. See Karen Halttunen, "Sentimental Culture and the Problem of Etiquette," *Confidence Men and Painted Women: A Study of Middle-Class Culture in America, 1830–1870* (New Haven, Conn.: Yale University Press, 1982), 92–123, for a discussion of proper feeling in manners.

21. Richard A. Wells, *Manners, Culture, and Dress* (Springfield, Mass.: King, Richardson and Company, 1891), 297.

22. *Manual of Politeness, Comprising the Principles of Etiquette and Rules of Behavior in Genteel Society, for Persons of Both Sexes* (Philadelphia: W. Marshall and Company, 1837), 15.

23. Williams and Jones, *Beautiful Homes*, 179.

24. *Eighty Years' Progress of the United States*, 2 vols. (Hartford, Conn.: L. Stebbins, 1867), 2:245, 260.

25. "An Antiquarian," "Our Home: Its History and Progress, with Notices of the Introduction of Domestic Inventions," *Household Journal*, September 28, 1861, 407.

26. Benjamin Butterworth, comp., *The Growth of Industrial Art* (Washington, D.C.: G.P.O./U.S. Patent Office, 1892), 80.

27. Historically, many different social and economic factors have contributed to making certain furnishing fabrics especially desirable. Rarity and difficulty in obtaining large yardages sometimes made what now seem to be ordinary textiles intensely desirable; the printed cottons imported to Europe from India in the late sixteenth and the seventeenth centuries were expensive and appeared only in wealthy, fashionable households both in England and on the Continent. Peter Thornton, *Seventeenth-Century Interior Decoration in England, France, and Holland* (1978; reprint, New Haven, Conn.: published for the Paul Mellon Centre for Studies in British Art by Yale University Press, 1983), 116.

28. See Penelope Eames, "Furniture in England, France, and the Netherlands from the Twelfth to the Fifteenth Century," *Furniture History* 13 (1977).

29. Mrs. Caroline M. Kirkland, "Fashionable and Unfashionable," *A Book for the Home Circle* (New York: Charles Scribner, 1853), 102–29.

30. These do-it-yourself upholstery projects are described and analyzed in Katherine C. Grier, *Culture and Comfort: People, Parlors, and Upholstery, 1850–1930* (Rochester,

N.Y.: Strong Museum, 1988), chapter 9, "Making Do: Homemade and Recycled Upholstery," 262–85.

31. Yi-Fu Tuan, *Segmented Worlds and Self: Group Life and Individual Consciousness* (Minneapolis: University of Minnesota Press, 1982), 115. The term *proximate senses* is used by Tuan to designate the senses that require direct bodily contact in order to function.

32. *How to Build, Furnish, and Decorate* (New York: Cooperative Building Association, 1889), 8.

33. [John Phin], *The Practical Upholsterer* (New York: Industrial Publications Company, 1891), 41.

34. William Dean Howells, *The Rise of Silas Lapham*, in *William Dean Howells: Novels, 1875–1886* (1885; reprint, New York: Library of America, 1982), 968.

35. "Editor's Easy Chair," *Harper's New Monthly Magazine*, July 1854, 262; *Sears, Roebuck and Co., 1908*, 901.

36. [Martin], *Our Homes*, 43.

37. Fanny N. Copeland, "Draperies, Blinds, and Curtains," *Peterson's Magazine*, April 1860, 269–72.

38. *Victor Manufacturing Co. Special Up-to-Date Catalogue* (Chicago, 1899), unpaginated.

39. "A Visit to Henkels' Warerooms in Chestnut Street above Fifth," *Godey's Lady's Book*, August 1850, 123.

40. "Mosaic Hearth Rug," *Frank Leslie's Ladies' Gazette of Paris, London, and New York Fashions*, September 1854, 167.

41. Ann Sophia Stephens, *High Life in New York, by Jonathan Slick, Esq. of Weathersfield, Conn. . . .* (New York: Bunce and Brother, 1854), 20, 92.

42. Charles L. Eastlake, *Hints on Household Taste in Furniture, Upholstery, and Other Details* (London: Longmans, Green, and Company, 1872), 94–95.

43. James Carruthers, "Dry Goods Stores as Furnishing Emporiums," *Decorator and Furnisher*, 19, 2 (November 1891): 51.

44. Carroll L. V. Meeks, *The Victorian Railroad Station* (New Haven, Conn.: Yale University Press, 1956), 3–5.

45. "A Chapter on Book Illustrations," *Ladies' Repository and Home Magazine*, October 1869, 259.

46. C. T. Hinkley, "The Art of Engraving," *Godey's Lady's Book*, August 1859, 109, 110.

47. "A Chapter on Book Illustrations," 259.

48. Daguerreotyping was introduced to American inventors just weeks after Louis Jacques Mandé Daguerre's introduction of the process in Paris, and with no patent restrictions to prevent its widespread adoption, photography in America became an inexpensive, popular process of picture making by the 1850s. See Robert Taft, *Photography and the American Scene* (1938; reprint, New York: Dover Publications, 1964).

49. Oliver Wendell Holmes, "The Stereoscope and the Stereograph," in Vicki Goldberg, ed., *Photography in Print: Writings from 1816 to the Present* (New York: Simon and Schuster, 1981), 107–8.

50. *How to Build, Furnish, and Decorate*, 10.

51. Baxandall, *Painting and Experience*, 24.

52. *History of the Brooklyn and Long Island Fair, February 22, 1864* (Brooklyn: Executive Committee [of the Fair], 1864), 38. See also William C. Richards, *A Day in the New York Crystal Palace, and How to Make the Most of It* (New York: G. P. Putnam and Company, 1853), a small guidebook that gave readers a tour of the exhibits item by item in a text that also implies the pleasures of so much visual experience gathered together in one location.

53. *History of the Brooklyn and Long Island Fair*, 47.

54. Daniel Biebuyck, for example, suggests that symbolic objects may serve as "cosmic or historical archives" or as vehicles for expressing and elaborating moral philosophy. Objects bearing symbolic meaning in Victorian culture may serve these functions but also bear other kinds of meaning; they may also be repositories of sentiment, expressions of social ideals, or expressions of the nature of sex roles. Biebuyck, "Symbolism of the Lega Stool," 28; Biebuyck, *The Lega*, 234.

55. Commenting on Lega ascription of meaning to art objects, Biebuyck offers an observation that would seem to have broad application to the study of any form of material culture as a form of communication. He notes, in the case of the Lega use of ceremonial stools in ritual, that the manipulation of meaningful objects is part of a highly redundant communications process of stories, proverbs, dances, and objects. Important messages are never communicated only once. Biebuyck, "Symbolism of the Lega Stool," 28.

56. Facing a similar phenomenological problem in his observations on the "cognitive style" of Renaissance people looking at paintings, Baxandall qualifies his observations by offering a useful set of "boundaries." He argues that three "culturally relative" variables are employed in the interpretation of visual data: "a stock of patterns, categories and methods of inference, training in a range of representational conventions, and experience, drawn from the environment, in what are plausible ways of visualizing what we have incomplete information about." Because perception skills are both culturally relative and learned, not all Quattrocento viewers of pictures possessed all the skills that would enable them to enjoy a particular picture. Conversely, not all pictures contained all the elements such as body postures and paint handling that made up the repertoire of artistic aesthetic options. Instead, understanding and enjoying a picture was, in part, a question of matching two mental sets of the language of painted signs, one held by the painter and the other in the viewer's educational background. Baxandall wrote:

> To sum up: some of the mental equipment a man orders his visual experience with is variable, and much of this variable equipment is culturally relative, in the sense of being determined by the society which influenced his experience. Among these variables are categories with which he classifies his visual stimuli, the knowledge he will use to supplement what his immediate vision gives him, and the attitude he will adopt to the kind of artificial object seen. The beholder must use on the painting such visual skills as he has, very few of which are normally special to painting, and he is likely to use those skills his society esteems

highly. The painter responds to this; his public's visual capacity must be his medium. Whatever his own specialized professional skills, he is himself a member of the society he works for and shares its visual experience and habit.

Baxandall, *Painting and Experience*, 32, 34, 40.

57. An example of landscape painting on a window shade may be found in Grier, *Culture and Comfort*, 250.

58. At the Crystal Palace of 1851, for example, papier-mâché was the object of particular admiration, particularly when paper pulp was transformed into large pieces of furniture such as beds, sofa frames, and piano cases. See *The Great Exhibition of the World's Industry*, vol. 2 (London: John Tallis and Company, 1851), 209–19. A library table of glass made by Baccarat for the 1878 Paris Universal Exposition was another conceptually related tour-de-force. This table is in the collection of the Corning Museum of Glass, Corning, New York. In his important essay "High Victorian Design," Nikolaus Pevsner discussed this "pride in ingeniousness" with understanding, if not complete approbation. Nikolaus Pevsner, "High Victorian Design," *Victorian and After*, vol. 2 of *Studies in Art, Architecture, and Design* (New Yorok: Walker and Company, 1968), 47.

59. Copeland, "Draperies, Blinds, and Curtains," 269–72. The same article, with no author named, was published a second time as a three-part series in *Godey's Lady's Book*: March 1860, 78; April 1860, 325; and June 1860, 506–9.

60. "Hints and Notions," *Decorator and Furnisher* 12, 1 (March 1888): 198.

61. Marcel Duchamp quoted in Calvin Tomkins, *The Bride and the Bachelors: Five Masters of the Avant Garde* (New York: Penguin Books, 1976), 19.

## CHAPTER SIX. PARLOR SUITES AND LOUNGES

1. See, for example, a stereograph titled "2122. Parlor, Twin Mountain House, Carroll, N.H.," photographed and published by Kilburn Brothers, Littleton, New Hampshire, between 1866 and 1877, in Katherine C. Grier, *Culture and Comfort: People, Parlors, and Upholstery, 1850–1930* (Rochester, N.Y.: Strong Museum, 1988), 203.

2. Philip M. Johnston, "Dialogues between Designer and Client: Furnishings Proposed by Leon Marcotte to Samuel Colt in the 1850s," *Winterthur Portfolio* 19, 4 (winter 1984): 268.

3. *Catalogue of Genteel Household Furniture, for Sale at Auction, by Henry H. Leeds and Co., on Friday, April 29, 1853, at Half-past Ten O'Clock, at No. 231 East 10th Street* (New York, 1853).

4. Household inventory of George Clinton Latta, Charlotte, N. Y., 1856, in Rare Books Collection, University of Rochester. Thanks to Joan Sullivan, who transcribed the inventory, and to William Siles, who called it to my attention.

5. Gail Dennis, "Factory-Made Parlor Suites, 1870–1901" (master's thesis, Winterthur Program in Early American Culture, University of Delaware, 1982), 9–11. Dennis did a statistical analysis of sixty furniture trade catalogs and price lists for the years

1871–1901. The sample was slightly biased toward the first fifteen years of her scope (thirty-seven examples). In her analysis of the 924 parlor suites offered for sale, 687 consisted of seven pieces: a sofa and a selection of chair types. She identified and discussed nine "salient characteristics" of parlor suites: (1) inclusion of a sofa; (2) two or more pieces of furniture; (3) seating furniture only; (4) associated with the parlor; (5) visually related pieces of furniture; (6) spring upholstered; (7) range of prices (fifteen to four hundred dollars, with most from forty to two hundred dollars); (8) choices of style; and (9) options available in decoration rather than in types of forms.

6. Richard Holbrook Tucker Family Papers, Castle Tucker, Wiscasset, Maine, Society for the Preservation of New England Antiquities.

7. *Catalogue of Furniture, George J. Henkels City Cabinet Warerooms, 173 Chestnut St.* (Philadelphia, [1855?]), Henry Francis du Pont Winterthur Museum, Winterthur, Del. The range of prices for sets is based on calculating the prices presented for each piece offered in the catalog. Henkels's business and the styles of furniture he offered have been discussed by Kenneth L. Ames in "Designed in France: Notes on the Transmission of French Style in America," *Winterthur Portfolio* 12 (1977): 103–14. Henkels's store was described several times in fiction and articles published by *Godey's Lady's Book* during the 1850s. See "A Visit to Henkels' Warerooms in Chestnut Street above Fifth," *Godey's Lady's Book*, August 1850, and Alice B. Neal, "Furnishing; or, Two Ways of Commencing Life," *Godey's Lady's Book*, November 1850."

8. An 1870 supplement to the trade catalog put out by the Boston furniture concern F. M. Holmes and Co. depicted one such suite, consisting of a "Tete," two "Easy Chairs," and four armless "Parlor Chairs." The suite's number "45" suggests that it was an addition to a larger line; at $185 wholesale, it probably retailed for about twice the price of the Tucker family's eight-piece set. An unillustrated 1872 price list from the large New York City furniture concern of M. and H. Schrenkeisen offered fifty such suites for sale. These suites ranged in wholesale price from forty-eight dollars for the "No. 0 Suit, Plain or Carved Top" to two hundred dollars for the "Grand Duchess," which had carvings of women's faces on the chair and sofa arms, extra-fancy piping, and extra hair stuffing. See *Catalogue Supplement, F. M. Holmes and Co.* (Boston, October 15, 1870); price list of M. and H. Schrenkeisen Co. (New York, March 22, 1871).

9. Price list of Baxter C. Swan (Philadelphia, May 1, 1880), in National Museum of American History, Smithsonian Institution, Washington, D.C.

10. Catalog of furniture and carpets of Jordan and Moriarty (New York, 1883).

11. *Montgomery Ward and Co. Catalogue No. 57, Spring and Summer, 1895* (1895; reprint, New York: Dover Publications, 1969).

12. Boris Emmet and John E. Jeuck, *Catalogues and Counters: A History of Sears, Roebuck and Company* (Chicago: University of Chicago Press, 1950), 187–95. For an influential article on working-class material culture at the turn of the century, see Lizabeth A. Cohen, "Embellishing a Life of Labor: An Interpretation of the Material Culture of American Working-Class Homes, 1885–1915," *Journal of American Culture* 3, 4 (winter 1980): 752–75. Cohen's interpretation of some aspects of working-class material culture, particularly parlors, differs from my own.

13. See Louise Bolard More, "The Standard of Living: General" and "The Stan-

dard of Living: Typical Families," *Wage-Earners' Budgets: A Study of Standards and Cost of Living in New York City* (New York: Henry Holt and Company, 1907).

14. Ibid., 145–46.

15. F. J. B. Watson, *Louis XVI Furniture* (1960; reprint, New York: Saint Martin's Press, 1973), 37. Summarizing the French seating types throughout the eighteenth century, Watson noted, "The evolution of furniture and particularly of the seat in all its forms was dictated to a remarkable extent by these two factors: comfort and the facilities of conversation."

16. For a discussion of set-back arms, see ibid., 34. See also Roger de Felice, *French Furniture under Louis XIV*, trans. F. M. Atkinson (New York: Frederick A. Stokes Company, n.d.), 135–36. For images of women's informal accommodations undertaken in order to sit in armed chairs with voluminous skirts, see Peter Thornton, *Authentic Decor: The Domestic Interior, 1620–1920* (New York: Viking Penguin, 1984), figures 110, 139, and 141, all of which date from the 1720s and 1730s.

17. *Price List of Parlor Furniture, Lounges, Mattresses, &c., Mackie and Hilton* (Philadelphia, 1883).

18. Frank R. Stockton and Marian Stockton, *The Home: Where It Should Be and What to Put in It* (New York: G. P. Putnam and Sons, 1872), 47.

19. The only exception known to the author is one suite offered by the Chicago firm of McDonough, Wilsey and Co. in 1878. This firm was also one of the first to offer rocking chairs and other chair novelties as part of suites. A surviving taboret or ottoman, attributed to Herter Brothers, New York, is walnut, with silk velvet and silk embroidered needlepoint top, knotted fringe, made in about 1875 (courtesy Wadsworth Atheneum, Hartford, Conn.; gift from estate of Mrs. James J. Godwin).

20. de Felice, "Seats," *French Furniture under Louis XIV*, 88. For a lucid explanation of the concept of precedence, see Penelope Eames, "Furniture in England, France, and the Netherlands from the Twelfth to the Fifteenth Century," *Furniture History* 13 (1977).

21. *Chesterfield's Art of Letter-Writing Simplified, to which is appended the Complete Rules of Etiquette, and the Usages of Society* (New York: Dick and Fitzgerald, Publishers, 1857, 1860), 15–16.

22. Deportment suggested by parlor furniture is discussed in more detail in chapter 3.

23. The appearance of such novelties in suite chair forms was analogous to the novelties in silver flatware that appeared at about the same time. This urge to create objects with specialized uses, however spurious, is one of the underlying cultural characteristics of Victorian popular thought; it is discussed in further detail in chapter 5.

24. *Catalogue of Furniture, George J. Henkels City Cabinet Warerooms, 173 Chestnut St.*, 12.

25. For a detailed history of the rocking chair, including parlor rockers in various forms, see Ellen Paul Denker and Bert Denker, *The Rocking Chair Book* (New York: Mayflower Books, 1979).

26. Price list of Gerrish and O'Brian (Boston, August 7, 1880).

27. For a more detailed discussion of Turkish-style furniture, see Grier, *Culture and*

*Comfort,* chapter 6: "Comfort and Glitter: Popular Taste for French and Turkish Upholstery, 1875–1910," 163–99.

28. Peter Thornton, *Seventeenth-Century Interior Decoration in England, France, and Holland* (1978; reprint, New Haven, Conn.: published for the Paul Mellon Centre for Studies in British Art by Yale University Press, 1983), 103–4.

29. Stockton and Stockton, *The Home,* 47.

30. Catharine E. Beecher and Harriet Beecher Stowe, *The American Woman's Home* (New York: J. B. Ford and Company, 1869), 87–90; [George A. Martin], *Our Homes: How to Beautify Them* (New York: O. Judd and Company, 1887), 146–48.

31. Rodd L. Wheaton, "High Style in Montana: The Kohrs Parlor," in Kenneth L. Ames, ed., *Victorian Furniture,* published in *Nineteenth Century* 8, 3–4 (1982): 243–54.

32. *Catalog of McDonough, Wilsey, and Company* (Chicago, 1878), 12, Collection, Historical Society of Wisconsin, Madison.

33. *Sears, Roebuck and Co. Catalogue No. 111, 1902* (Chicago: Sears, Roebuck and Co., 1902), 780–81.

34. In 1910 A. F. Barker, author of the technical manual *Textiles,* noted: "So little was the success of the Jacquard power-loom known outside the Bradford district, however, that the writer well remembers in the year 1884 or 1885 a supposed authority on the trade questioning whether it ever could be a success as a power loom, i.e. twenty or thirty years after it was running by the hundred, or perhaps the thousand, in the Bradford district. Today the tapestry loom . . . is employed upon the simplest kinds of tapestries, consisting of little more than reversed warp and weft sateens, up to imitations of the Gobelin tapestries." See A. F. Barker, *Textiles* (New York: D. Van Nostrand Company, 1910), 257–58. George S. Cole's *Dictionary of Dry Goods* for 1894 describes Jacquard loom tapestry as "Neuilly tapestry" or "Jacquard tapestry," woven in imitation of Gobelins. Its description of production suggests that weaving was only partly mechanized by that date, still requiring the presence of the weaver to pass the weft shuttles through the warp. "Carpet tapestry," also called "moquette," was commonly used on lounges and hassocks in the last quarter of the nineteenth century. It is discussed in chapter 6, along with lounge production. George S. Cole, *A Complete Dictionary of Dry Goods . . . ,* rev. ed. (Chicago: J. B. Herring Publishing Company, 1894), 348.

35. See, for example, Sharon Darling, "Upholstered Parlor Furniture, 1873–1917," *Chicago Furniture, 1830–1980* (Chicago and New York: Chicago Historical Society and W. W. Norton and Company, 1984), and Thornton, *Authentic Decor,* 359, 373–75, 405.

36. See plate 25 in Grier, *Culture and Comfort,* for another example of contrasting buttoning.

37. Wholesale price list of Samuel Graves and Son (Boston, 1878), National Museum of American History, Smithsonian Institution, Washington, D.C.

38. Katherine Yearick Cavano was able to recall the appearance of the lounge and its location in the dining-sitting room because she fell across it as a small child, breaking her nose against the raised end. Cavano, interview with the author, Pennington, N.J., March and December 1986.

39. Ella Rodman Church, *How to Furnish a Home* (New York: D. Appleton and

Company, 1881), 86. Every bedroom of the Grange, the Codman family house in Lincoln, Massachusetts, today operated by the Society for the Preservation of New England Antiquities, was equipped with a lounge for daytime resting.

40.  *Christmas Gifts* (Grand Rapids, Mich.: Fred Macey Company, [ca. 1910]). The Fred Macey Company advertised itself as "Makers of Office and Library Furniture." The three leather Turkish lounges advertised in this catalog retailed at prices from fifty-nine dollars to eighty dollars, making them too expensive for most consumers.

41.  Bed lounges are even more rare than common lounges today, either because they wore out and were discarded or because they were too eccentric a form of furniture to be retained in the twentieth century. Fern Tuten has noted that sofa-bedsteads were "the most frequently patented single item" among all forms of convertible furniture (reclining chairs, table-chairs, and so on) before 1850. Fern Tuten, *American Domestic Patented Furniture, 1790–1850: A Compendium* (Ann Arbor, Mich.: University Microfilms, 1969), 78.

42.  E. Page Talbot, "The Furniture Industry in Boston, 1810–1835" (master's thesis, University of Delaware, 1974), 107, 109.

43.  Ibid., 82, 115.

44.  Price list and catalog of Rand and McSherry (Baltimore, May 14, 1872). Sofa prices in *Price List and Illustrated Catalogue of J. W. Hamburger* (New York, 1874), 4.

45.  Advertisement for Mueller and Slack Co. in *Michigan Artisan* 14, 12 (June 1894): 31.

46.  See Michael J. Ettema, "Technological Innovation and Design Economics in Furniture Manufacture," *Winterthur Portfolio* 16, 2/3 (summer/autumn 1981): 199. In this article on the economics of design for furniture woodworking, Ettema proposed a broader understanding of the appearance of inexpensive furniture, setting aside the question of "quality" in favor of another that applied Thorstein Veblen's understanding of "emulation" and "ostentation" to "high-style" objects, those whose materials and craftsmanship are not constrained by the necessity to keep production costs and retail prices low: "A desire to emulate makes high-style artifacts models for the entire scale. The less expensive objects are not naive imitations of inferior quality, they are less labor and material intensive, and therefore are simplified objects designed in the same style. . . . Since costs are, in part, dependent upon labor intensity of their technologies, manufacturers must design pieces with the capabilities of their tool in mind, constantly compromising between cost and style."

47.  *1890 Catalogue for the Buffalo Upholstering Co.* (Buffalo, New York, 1890), 1, 14; *1890 Price List for the Buffalo Upholstering Company* (Buffalo, New York, 1890).

48.  This reading chair, manufactured by P. J. Hardy, New York, between 1866 and 1878, is in the collection of The Strong Museum, Rochester, N. Y. See Grier, *Culture and Comfort*, 230, for two photographs of the chair.

49.  Tuten, *American Domestic Patented Furniture*, 116–19.

50.  A centripetal spring chair by the American Chair Company of Troy, New York, dated about 1855, is one of the earliest known examples of tapestry carpet used as uphol-

stery. It is in the collections of the National Museum of American History, Smithsonian Institution, Washington, D.C.

51. *Edward W. Vaill, Forty-First Semi-Annual Catalog of Fine Folding Chairs, Autumn and Winter 1882–1883* (Worcester, Mass., 1882), 3.

52. The author of *The Practical Upholsterer* provided estimates of the amount of fabric required for "an ordinary parlor suite with mouldings on the seat rails and plain seats" (probably with simple buttoning on the back) and "a similar suite with buttoned [button tufted] seats and backs":

| Velvet or plush | 18–20 yards | 20–26 yards |
|---|---|---|
| Rep | 8–9 " | 10–12 " |
| Tapestry | 8–9 " | 10–12 " |
| Cretonne | 14–16 " | 18–20 " |
| Cord | 22 " | 22 " |
| Gimp | 36 " | 36 " |
| Buttons | 1/2 gross | 2 gross |

[John Phin], *The Practical Upholsterer* (New York: Industrial Publications Company, 1891), 40.

53. Peter A. Stone and John Newton Thurber, "The Upholsterers' International Union: Story of the First Seventy-Five Years," vol. 1, "Early Beginnings: Craft and Trade Unionism, 'Voluntarism,' and Struggle for Legality, 1882–1932" (Philadelphia, "Proposed for Publication in Early 1956," typescript on deposit with the Library of Congress, Washington, D.C.), 16, 48.

54. "Came to Blows: Striking Employees of the Paine Bedding Company. A Strict Blockade Is Being Maintained by the Insurgents around the Factory," *Grand Rapids Evening Post*, May 25, 1898, 1. Factory upholsterers were once again able to command better salaries and more control over their working conditions, at least in Grand Rapids, when the burgeoning mass production of automobiles created new demand for their skills.

55. Stone and Thurber, "The Upholsterers' International Union," 56.

56. The first patent for a tufting machine, called an "Upholstering Device," appears to be one filed by Henry B. Pitner of Princeton, Illinois, on December 6, 1892. He received Patent No. 511,649 for what appears to be a board for mattress tufting, a way of placing a number of buttons at once; see *Official Gazette, U.S. Patent Office* (December 6, 1892), 2024. In 1895 several devices for tufting mattresses and cushions received patents, as in G. K. Bagby's Patent No. 549,840 for a machine that tufted mattresses using needles and clamps on a grooved table; see *Official Gazette, U.S. Patent Office* (November 12, 1895), 1095. Alfred Freschl, the eventual owner of the Novelty Tufting Machine Company of Chicago, first appears as a patent holder in 1895 for a cushion tufting device; see Patent No. 537,385 in *Official Gazette, U.S. Patent Office* (April 9, 1895), 271.

57. Stone and Thurber, "The Upholsterers' International Union," 56.

CHAPTER SEVEN. VICTORIANISM IN THE MODERN ERA

1. "The Sacrificial Parlor," in Susan Anne Brown, comp., *Home Topics: A Book of Practical Papers on House and Home Matters* (Troy, N.Y.: H. B. Nims and Company, 1881), 488, 490. This book contains articles from *Scribner's Monthly* and *St. Nicholas* magazine. At least three articles were devoted to attacking parlor making: "The Sacrificial Parlor," "Outdoor Parlors," and "Best Parlors."

2. *Vogue's Book of Etiquette: Present-Day Customs of Social Intercourse with the Rules for Their Correct Observance* (New York: Conde-Nast Publications, 1924), 173.

3. Mary D. Chambers, *Table Etiquette, Menus, and Much Besides* (Boston: Boston Cooking-School Magazine Company, 1929), unpaginated introduction, 177.

4. Robert S. Lynd and Helen Merrell Lynd, *Middletown: A Study in Modern American Culture* (New York: Harcourt, Brace and World, 1929, 1956), 98–99.

5. Alan Gowans has discussed the resistance of some middle-class families to bungalow floor plans in *The Comfortable House: North American Suburban Architecture, 1890–1930* (Cambridge, Mass.: MIT Press, 1986), 27.

6. "Series D722–727: Average Annual Earnings of Employees, 1900 to 1970," *Historical Statistics of the United States: Colonial Times to 1970*, vol. 1 (Washington, D.C.: Department of Commerce, Bureau of the Census, 1975), 168.

7. Ruth Schwartz Cowan, *More Work for Mother: The Ironies of Household Technology from the Open Hearth to the Microwave* (New York: Basic Books, 1983), 83.

8. *The Modern Priscilla Home Furnishing Book: A Practical Book for the Woman Who Loves Her Home* (Boston: Priscilla Publishing Company, 1925), 97.

9. Charlotte Wait Calkins, *A Course in House Planning and Furnishing* (Chicago: Scott, Foresman and Company, 1916), 46.

10. Cowan, *More Work for Mother*, 69–101.

11. *Modern Priscilla Home Furnishing Book*, 162.

12. Hazel H. Adler, *The New Interior: Modern Decorations for the Modern Home* (New York: Century Company, 1916), 38.

13. Helen Koues, *How to Be Your Own Decorator* (New York: Good Housekeeping, 1926), 24, 25.

14. Ekin Wallick, *Inexpensive Furnishings in Good Taste* (New York: Hearst's International Library Company, 1915), 39.

15. Emily Post, *The Personality of a House: The Blue Book of Home Design and Decoration* (New York: Funk and Wagnalls, 1930).

16. Adler, *The New Interior*, 38.

17. Calkins, *Course in House Planning*, 55.

18. Ibid., 63.

19. Edward Stratton Holloway, *The Practical Book of Furnishing the Small House and Apartment* (Philadelphia: J. B. Lippincott and Company, 1922), 79.

20. Sidney Morse, *Household Discoveries: An Encyclopedia of Practical Recipes and Processes* (New York: Success Company, 1908, 1909), 33–34.

21. *Modern Priscilla Home Furnishing Book*, 134.

22. Anna F. Grier, interview with the author, Pennington, N.J., November 1987.

23. John Arnold, interview with the author, Rochester, N. Y., January 21, 1988.

24. Robert Vance Stewart, "When Grandpa Was a Boy: Reminiscences of Robert Vance Stewart" (1982, typescript in the collections of the Genesee Charlotte Lighthouse Historical Society), 7.

# *Index*

Page numbers in italics indicate illustrations